COSTING, REPORTS' & RETURNS

tutorial

NVQ LEVEL 3
ACCOUNTING

David Cox
Michael Fardon

consultant:
Roger Petheram

OSBORNE
BOOKS

Published by Osborne Books Limited
Unit 1B Everoak Estate
Bromyard Road
Worcester
WR2 5HN
Tel 01905 748071
Email books@osbornebooks.co.uk
www.osbornebooks.co.uk

Printed by the Bath Press, Bath.

British Library Cataloguing in Publication Data
A catalogue record for this book is available from the British Library

ISBN 1 872962 48 3

CONTENTS

ACKNOWLEDGEMENTS

The authors wish to thank the following for their help with the production of the book: Jean Cox, Michael Gilbert, Jon Moore and Anita Sherwood. Thanks are also due to the Association of Accounting Technicians for their advice and to the Lead Body for Accounting for permission to reproduce extracts from the Standards of Competence for Accounting. The publisher is grateful to a number of organisations which have been helpful in providing information and in granting permission to reproduce material: Barclays Bank PLC, the Department of Trade and Industry, Hereford and Worcester Chamber of Commerce, and the Independent Publishers Guild. A special word of thanks is due to the Droitwich office of HM Customs & Excise and to McKnight Winwood & Co, a Worcestershire firm of Chartered Certified Accountants, who have provided expert guidance and practical advice on the intricacies of Value Added Tax. The VAT forms, Sales Lists and Intrastat Declarations reproduced in this book are Crown Copyright and are reproduced here with the kind permission of the Controller of Her Majesty's Stationery Office.

AUTHORS AND CONSULTANT

David Cox has had more than twenty years' experience teaching accountancy students over a wide range of levels. Formerly with the Management and Professional Studies Department at Worcester College of Technology, he now lectures on a freelance basis and carries out educational consultancy work in accountancy studies. He is author and joint author of a number of textbooks in the areas of accounting, finance and banking.

Michael Fardon has had extensive teaching experience on a wide range of banking, business and accountancy courses at Worcester College of Technology. He now specialises in writing business and financial texts and is General Editor at Osborne Books. He is also an educational consultant and has worked extensively in the areas of Key Skills and GNVQ development.

Roger Petheram, who is consultant for this text and an experienced accounting lecturer at Worcester College of Technology, has provided invaluable help in reading, checking and providing practical advice.

INTRODUCTION

Osborne tutorials

Costing, Reports & Returns Tutorial has been written to provide a study resource for students taking courses based on the NVQ Level 3 Accounting Unit 6 'Recording cost information' and Unit 7 'Preparing reports and returns'. The companion Osborne text *Financial Accounting Tutorial* covers Unit 5 'Maintaining financial records and preparing accounts'.

Costing, Reports & Returns Tutorial deals with the recording and analysis of direct and indirect costs, including the allocation, apportionment and absorption of overhead costs. An important costing method is the use of standard costing and the calculation of variances from the standard; the presentation of variances in the form of standard cost reports is important management information.

The completion by individuals and organisations of reports and returns is covered in the second part of this book. The text explains how data is recorded and presented for internal reporting and how a variety of returns is completed for external bodies. The concluding part of the book explains the principles of Value Added Tax and the completion of the VAT Return.

The chapters of *Costing, Reports & Returns Tutorial* contain:

- a clear text with worked examples and case studies
- a chapter summary and key terms to help with revision
- student activities – with answers at the end of the book

The tutorial text is therefore useful for classroom use and also for distance learning students. More extended student exercises and practice assessments, without answers in the text, are available in the *Costing, Reports & Returns Workbook* (see below).

Osborne workbooks

Costing, Reports & Returns Tutorial has been written to be used alongside the *Costing, Reports & Returns Workbook* which contains extended student activities and sample Central and Devolved Assessments.

The answers to these tasks are included in a separate Tutor Pack.

If you would like a workbook, please telephone Osborne Books Sales Office on 01905 748071 for details of how to order.

NVQ UNITS COVERED

UNIT 6: RECORDING COST INFORMATION

element 1

record and analyse information relating to direct costs

element 2

record and analyse information relating to the allocation, apportionment
and absorption of overhead costs

element 3

prepare and present standard cost reports

Details of coverage of performance criteria by chapter are to be found on page 2.

UNIT 7: PREPARING REPORTS AND RETURNS

element 1

prepare and present periodic performance reports

element 2

prepare reports and returns for outside agencies

element 3

prepare VAT returns

Details of coverage of performance criteria by chapter are to be found on page 180.

NOTE ON UNIT NUMBERING

In 2000 the Unit numbers of the two NVQ Units covered in this book were
changed. In effect the Unit numbers were each increased by one. These
changes are reflected in the introductory pages of this book. References
in subsequent pages should be adjusted accordingly.

recording cost information

NVQ competences covered

UNIT 5: RECORDING COST INFORMATION

element 1

record and analyse information relating to direct costs	chapter
❏ direct costs are identified in accordance with the organisation's costing procedures	2, 3, 4
❏ information relating to direct costs is clearly and correctly coded, analysed and recorded	2, 3, 4, 8
❏ direct costs are calculated in accordance with the organisation's policies and procedures	2, 3, 4, 6
❏ standard costs are compared against actual costs and any variances are analysed	7
❏ information is systematically checked against the overall usage and stock control practices	2
❏ queries are either resolved or referred to the appropriate person	2, 3, 4

element 2

record and analyse information relating to the allocation, apportionment and absorption of overhead costs	chapter
❏ data are correctly coded, analysed and recorded	5
❏ overhead costs are established in accordance with the organisation's procedures	5
❏ information relating to overhead costs is accurately and clearly recorded	5, 8
❏ overhead costs are correctly attributed to producing and service cost centres in accordance with agreed methods of allocation, apportionment and absorption	5, 6
❏ adjustments for under or over recovered overhead costs are made in accordance with established procedures	5, 8
❏ standard costs are compared against actual costs and any variances are analysed	7
❏ methods of allocation, apportionment and absorption are reviewed at regular intervals in discussions with senior staff, and agreed changes to methods are implemented	5
❏ staff working in operational departments are consulted to resolve any queries in the data	5

element 3

prepare and present standard cost reports	chapter
❏ standard cost reports with variances clearly identified are presented in an intelligible form	7
❏ unusual or unexpected results are identified and reported to managers	7
❏ any reasons for significant variances from standard are identified and the explanations presented to management	7
❏ the results of the analysis and explanations of specific variances are produced for management	7
❏ staff working in operational departments are consulted to resolve any queries in the data	7

1 AN INTRODUCTION TO COST ACCOUNTING

this chapter covers . . .

- the purpose of cost accounting and its role in providing information to the managers of a business
- cost units and cost centres
- identification and coding of costs
- the categories into which costs can be classified
  - by element
  - by function
  - by nature
- how the cost of goods and services is calculated
- the layout of a total cost statement

Set out below are the NVQ competences covered by this chapter. As you will see they involve the "Knowledge and Understanding" content of the course.

NVQ PERFORMANCE CRITERIA COVERED

unit 5: RECORDING COST INFORMATION

KNOWLEDGE AND UNDERSTANDING – ACCOUNTING PRINCIPLES AND THEORY

❑ the distinction between fixed, semi-fixed and variable costs

KNOWLEDGE AND UNDERSTANDING – THE ORGANISATION

❑ understanding of the ways the accounting systems of an organisation are affected by its organisational structure, its administrative systems and procedures and the nature of its business transactions

PURPOSE OF COST ACCOUNTING

Cost accounting, as its name implies, enables the managers of a business to know the cost of the firm's output – whether a product or a service. Once costing information is available, managers can use it to help with decision-making, planning and control. They can use it to assess performance and to make decisions which will affect what the business does in the future.

It is important to appreciate that cost accounting is widely used by all types of businesses – the cost of a hospital operation, the cost of tuition to a student, the cost of a swim at a sports centre, the cost of a passenger's bus journey are all just as important as the cost of making a product. Business – whether it provides a service or makes a product – needs to keep its costs under review; in order to do this it needs accurate cost information. Thus a cost accounting system will provide answers to questions such as:

What does it cost us to provide a student with a day's accountancy course?

What does it cost us to carry out a hip replacement operation?

What does it cost us to make a pair of trainers?

What does it cost us to serve a cheeseburger and fries?

What does it cost us to provide a week's holiday in the Canaries?

The Case Study that follows shows how cost accounting enables the managers of a business to have better information about its activities.

CASE STUDY

S & T MANUFACTURING COMPANY

situation

The following information is given for S & T Manufacturing Company, a two-product (S and T) company, for last year:

			£	£
Sales:	S			100,000
	T			200,000
				300,000
Less:	Cost of materials	S	50,000	
		T	95,000	
	Labour costs	S	40,000	
		T	50,000	
	*Cost of overheads	S	20,000	
		T	30,000	
				285,000
Profit				15,000

* Overheads include factory rent, depreciation of machinery, and other production costs.

How would you present this information in a way which will be of more use to the management of the business? What conclusions do you draw for this business?

solution

The information is best presented in a way which analyses the cost and profit of each product:

	S	T	Total
	£	£	£
Cost of materials	50,000	95,000	145,000
Labour costs	40,000	50,000	90,000
Cost of overheads	20,000	30,000	50,000
Total cost	110,000	175,000	285,000
Sales	100,000	200,000	300,000
Less Total cost	110,000	175,000	285,000
Profit/(loss)	(10,000)	25,000	15,000

On the basis of this information, product S should be discontinued because it is making a loss. However, there may be other factors which will have to be considered, eg sales of product T may be linked to sales of S; the overheads of T are likely to increase if S is discontinued.

This Case Study emphasises two important functions of cost accounting:

- to find out the costs (in this case for each product)
- to give responsibility to someone for those costs (here for the manager of product S to investigate the reasons for the loss of £10,000)

COST UNITS AND COST CENTRES

Before we begin our study of costing we need to understand the terms: cost units and cost centres.

Cost units are units of output to which costs can be charged.

A cost unit can be:

- a unit of production from a factory such as a car, a television, an item of furniture

- a unit of service, such as a passenger-mile on a bus, a transaction on a bank statement, an attendance at a swimming pool, a call unit on a telephone

Care should be taken in choosing the appropriate cost unit. Within a business – particularly in the service industry – there may well be several cost units that can be used. For example, in an hotel the cost units in the restaurant will be meals, and for the rooms, the cost units will be guest nights.

Cost centres are sections of a business to which costs can be charged.

A cost centre in a manufacturing business, for example, is a department of a factory, a particular stage in the production process, or even a whole factory. In a college, examples of cost centres are the teaching departments, or particular sections of departments such as the college's administrative office. In a hospital, examples of cost centres are the hospital wards, operating theatres, specialist sections such as the X-ray department, pathology department.

IDENTIFICATION AND CODING OF COSTS

Both cost units and cost centres have costs charged to them. This process is carried out in two steps:
- *identification* of the cost unit or cost centre to which the cost is to be charged
- *coding* the cost so that it is charged to the correct cost unit or cost centre

Code numbers are used in cost accounting because:
- they are easier to process than a description of a cost
- once coded there is no doubt as to which cost unit or cost centre the item relates
- they are easily input into a computer accounting system

Various systems are used to code costs. It is for a business to use the system that meets its needs – a smaller business will use a less sophisticated system than does a larger business. Most codes incorporate two sets of numbers that indicate:
- the nature of the cost, eg wages, materials
- where the cost has been used, eg the cost unit or cost centre

For example:

- code for salaries, 200
- code for administration office, 500
- code for sales department, 550

Thus the cost code for administration salaries is 200500; the cost code for sales department salaries is 200550. In this way the cost is charged to the correct cost centre.

CLASSIFICATION OF COSTS

Within any business, whether it manufactures a product or provides a service, there are certain costs involved at various stages to produce the units of output. The diagram below shows the costs of a manufacturing business which are incurred by the three main sections of the business, ie the factory, the warehouse, the office.

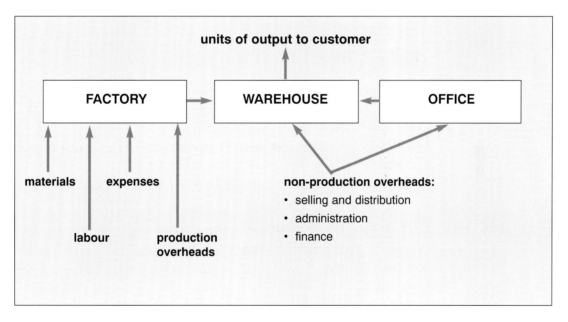

costs incurred in a manufacturing business

Note that while the above diagram shows the costs of a manufacturing business, it can be adapted easily to fit non-manufacturing organisations, such as a shop, a hospital, a school or college, a church, a club. While the units of output of these organisations differ from those of a manufacturer, nevertheless they still incur costs at various stages of the 'production' process.

Having identified costs for each main section of a business, we can now classify the costs. This can be done in three ways:

- by element
- by function
- by nature

classification of costs by element

We can see from the diagram that there are three elements of cost:

- materials, ie the cost of goods used
- labour, ie the cost of employees' wages and salaries
- expenses, ie other costs, including overheads

Each of the cost elements can be categorised between:

- direct costs – those costs that can be identified directly with each unit of output
- indirect costs – all other costs, ie those that cannot be identified directly with each unit of output

Thus the cost elements for a manufacturing business can be shown as:

MATERIALS	direct	materials from which the finished product is made
	indirect	other materials used in the factory, eg grease for machines, cleaning materials, etc
LABOUR	direct	wages paid to those who work the machinery on the production line or who are involved in assembly of the product
	indirect	wages and salaries paid to those who are not directly involved in production, eg supervisors, maintenance staff, etc
EXPENSES	direct	expenses which can be attributed to particular units of output, eg royalties payable to the designer of a product, special items bought in for a particular product
	indirect	other expenses, such as rent, rates, telephone, lighting, heating, which cannot be attributed directly to output

The direct costs of materials, labour and expenses form the *prime cost* of the business:

direct materials + direct labour + direct expenses = prime cost

The indirect costs of materials, labour and expenses form the *overheads* of the business:

indirect materials + indirect labour + indirect expenses = overheads

classification of costs by function

Each section of a business, eg factory, warehouse, office, retail outlet, performs a function. Thus, for example, the office provides an administrative function. In carrying out these functions, costs are incurred and can be classified by function. For a manufacturing business the main functions are:

* production
* selling and distribution
* administration
* finance

Other functions can be added to suit the needs of a particular business. For example, a company might spend large sums of money in researching and developing new products – the costs incurred by this function will be classified under the research and development heading.

Non-manufacturing organisations – such as a hospital or a college – will use some of the same functions listed above, and will add other, specialist, functions. Both direct and indirect costs can be classified by function. It is important to note that, when costs are classified by function, they are the same costs used in classifying by element, but are presented in a different way in order to show the cost of each function.

classification of costs by nature

It is important in cost accounting to appreciate the nature of costs – in particular to understand that not all costs increase or decrease directly in line with increases or decreases in output. By nature, costs are:

* fixed, or
* semi-fixed (also known as semi-variable), or
* variable

The diagram on the next page shows the differences between these.

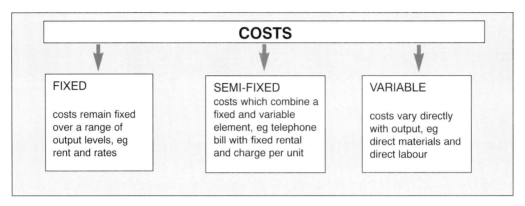

classifying costs by nature

It is important to know the nature of costs and how they are affected by changes in the level of output. For example, a business decides to increase its output by 25% – will all costs increase by 25%? Fixed costs, such as rent and rates, are likely to remain unchanged, provided that there is capacity for the increased output within the existing building. Variable costs, such as direct materials and direct labour, are likely to increase by 25% as they generally vary directly with output (unless any economies of scale can be achieved). Semi-fixed costs, such as the telephone bill, will increase as the extra business generates more 'phone calls; however, the increase should certainly be much less than 25%.

REASONS FOR CLASSIFYING COSTS

The question might be asked, "Why classify costs in three ways?" The answer is that we can see the same business from three different viewpoints – this will help management to run the business better:

- *by element*

  looking for the high cost elements in order to make savings, eg labour might be identified as being too high

- *by function*

  looking at the different departments to see which are the high-spending departments – perhaps savings can be made

- *by nature*

  identifying the costs as being fixed, semi-fixed, or variable – the business might be able to make savings by altering the balance between fixed and variable costs

Thus classifying costs helps management with:

- decision-making, when implementing changes
- planning, when preparing forecasts and budgets
- control, when checking actual results against what was planned

CALCULATING THE COST OF GOODS AND SERVICES

Using the principles of costing will help the owner of a business to calculate the cost of a product – whether goods or services. Only when the cost of producing each unit of output is known, can a business make decisions about the selling price.

The steps towards calculating the cost of goods and services are:

identify the unit of output

The cost units for a particular business must be identified. As we have seen earlier, these are the units of output to which costs can be charged. Only by recovering costs through the sales of output can a business make a profit.

calculate the number of units of output for a particular time period

Once the unit of output is identified, the business is then able to calculate how many units can be produced or provided in a given time period, such as a day, week, month, quarter or year. For example, a garage will work out how many hours of mechanics' time are available, or a car manufacturer will calculate how many cars it can produce in a year.

calculate the direct costs for a particular time period

Having established the number of units of output for a particular time period, the next task is to calculate the direct costs, or prime cost, for that time period. As we have seen earlier in this chapter, the direct costs comprise:

direct materials   identifiable with the product

direct labour   the wages paid to those who make the product

direct expenses   attributable to the product

The amounts of the direct costs are added together to give the total direct costs (prime cost) of the output for the time period.

calculate the indirect costs for a particular time period

The indirect costs, or overheads, of the production or service must be calculated for the particular time period. Indirect costs comprise:

indirect materials   materials used that are not attributed directly to production

indirect labour   wages and salaries paid to those who are not directly involved in production

indirect expenses   expenses of the business not attributed directly to production

Once the indirect costs have been calculated, we must then ensure that their total cost is charged to the cost units for a particular time period. Only by including indirect costs in the total cost of the output can a business recover their cost from the sales made.

The amounts of the indirect costs are added together to give the total indirect costs (overheads) for the time period.

calculate the total cost of a unit of output

Once the direct and indirect costs for a time period are known, the total cost of a unit of output can be calculated, as follows:

$$\frac{direct\ costs\ +\ indirect\ costs}{units\ of\ output}\ =\ total\ cost\ of\ a\ unit\ of\ output$$

The total cost is also known as the absorption cost – because it absorbs (includes) both the direct costs and the indirect costs. Once total cost is known, the business can use the information to help it make pricing and other decisions.

calculating the cost – a summary

The process of calculating the cost of output is illustrated in the diagram below.

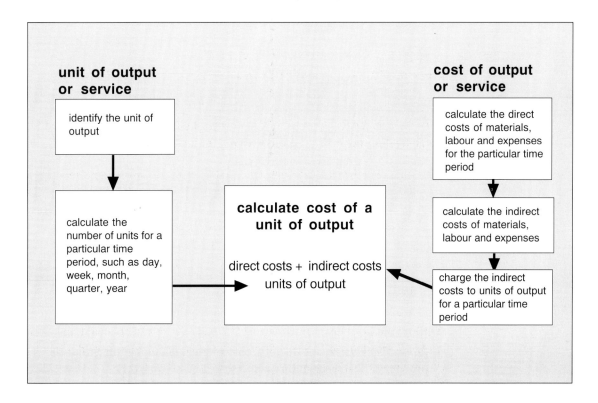

calculating the cost of a unit of output

TOTAL COST STATEMENT

The total cost statement brings together all the costs involved in producing the output of a business. It can be prepared on the basis of:

- a single cost unit, eg the cost of making one car in a car factory
- a batch, eg the cost of making 1,000 'special edition' cars
- the whole factory, eg the cost of all the car factory's output for a given time period

The total cost statement is prepared as follows:

```
┌─────────────────────────────────────────────────────────────────────┐
│                                                                       │
│            TOTAL COST STATEMENT                                       │
│                                                                 £     │
│                                                                       │
│            Direct materials                                     x     │
│                                                                       │
│   add      Direct labour                                        x     │
│                                                                       │
│   add      Direct expenses                                      x     │
│                                                                     ─  │
│   equals   PRIME COST                                           x     │
│                                                                       │
│   add      Production overheads                                 x     │
│                                                                     ─  │
│   equals   PRODUCTION COST                                      x     │
│                                                                       │
│   add      Selling and distribution costs ┐                    x     │
│                                            │                          │
│   add      Administration costs  ──────────┤ non-production overheads  x │
│                                            │                          │
│   add      Finance costs  ─────────────────┘                   x     │
│                                                                     ─  │
│   equals   TOTAL COST                                           x     │
│                                                                    ══  │
└─────────────────────────────────────────────────────────────────────┘
```

Note that:

- *prime cost* is the direct cost of manufacturing products, before the addition of production overheads
- *production cost* is the factory cost of manufacturing the products, ie prime cost plus production overheads
- *total cost* is production cost plus non-production overheads

The cost structure above is especially appropriate for a manufacturing business; indeed a separate *manufacturing account* – which shows costs through to production cost – is prepared prior to the profit and loss account. Manufacturing accounts are covered in more detail in Chapter 8.

By taking total cost away from sales revenue we can create a profit statement. This shows the profitability of the business after all costs have been taken into account. The profit statement is:

```
┌─────────────────────────────────────────────────────────────────────┐
│                                                                       │
│            PROFIT STATEMENT                                           │
│                                                                 £     │
│                                                                       │
│            Sales                                                x     │
│                                                                       │
│   less     Total cost                                           x     │
│                                                                     ─  │
│   equals   PROFIT                                               x     │
│                                                                    ══  │
└─────────────────────────────────────────────────────────────────────┘
```

CHAPTER SUMMARY

- Cost accounting calculates how much it costs to produce a unit of goods or service.

- Costs can be classified by element, by function and by nature.

- The main elements of cost are
  - materials
  - labour
  - expenses

  Each of these can be direct or indirect.

- Costs can be classified by function, eg production, selling and distribution, administration, finance.

- By nature, costs are fixed, or semi-fixed, or variable.

- A total cost statement lists the direct costs and the overheads involved in producing the output of a business. Sales revenue minus total cost equals profit.

KEY TERMS

cost unit	unit of output to which costs can be charged
cost centre	section of a business to which costs can be charged
unit of output	the output of the business expressed in terms of units of production or service
direct costs	those costs that can be identified directly with each unit of output
indirect costs	all costs that cannot be identified directly with each unit of output
prime cost	the direct cost of materials, labour and expenses
overheads	the indirect costs of materials, labour and expenses

fixed costs	costs which remain fixed over a range of output levels
semi-fixed costs	costs which combine a fixed and variable element
variable costs	costs which vary directly with output
total cost statement	list of all the direct costs and the overheads involved in producing the output of the business

STUDENT ACTIVITIES

The answers to these Student Activities are printed in the back of this book. Further questions and more fully extended Student Activities and Assessments are to be found in the accompanying Osborne Books' text *Costing, Reports & Returns Workbook*.

1.1   Select an organisation – either where you work, or one with which you are familiar.

(a)   Prepare a diagram, similar to that shown on page 7, identifying the main functions of the organisation and the costs incurred by each section.

(b)   Describe the cost units and cost centres used by the organisation.

1.2   Suggest one cost unit and two cost centres for:

- a college of further education

- a mixed farm, growing crops and raising cattle

1.3   (a)   Why is it important to analyse costs in different ways, eg by element, by function and by nature?

(b)   Classify each of the following costs by nature (ie fixed, or semi-fixed, or variable):

- raw materials

- factory rent

- telephone

- direct labour, eg production workers paid on the basis of work done

- indirect labour, eg supervisors' salaries

- commission paid to sales staff

Taking the costs in turn, explain to a friend, who is about to set up a furniture manufacturing business, why you have classified each as fixed, or semi-fixed, or variable. Answer the comment, "What difference does it make anyway, they are all costs that have to be paid."

1.4   Severn Manufacturing Limited makes chairs for school and college use. The chairs have plastic seats, and tubular steel legs. You are to classify the manufacturing costs into:

- direct materials
- indirect materials
- direct labour
- indirect labour
- direct expenses
- indirect expenses

The cost items to be classified are:

COST ITEM	CLASSIFICATION (write your answer)
Tubular steel	
Factory supervisor's salary	
Wages of employee operating the moulding machine which produces the chair seats	
Works canteen assistant's wages	
Rates of factory	
Power to operate machines	
Factory heating and lighting	
Plastic for making chair seats	
Hire of special machinery for one particular order	
Cost of grease for the moulding machine	
Depreciation of factory machinery	
Depreciation of office equipment	

If you believe alternative classifications exist, argue the case and state if you need further information from the company.

1.5   Wyvern Water Limited bottles natural spring water at its plant at Walcoll at the base of the Wyvern Hills. The natural spring is on land owned by a local farmer to whom a royalty is paid for each bottle of water produced.

You are working in the costing section of Wyvern Water and are asked to analyse the following cost items into the appropriate columns and to agree the totals:

Cost item	Total cost	Prime cost	Production overheads	Admin costs	Selling and distribution costs
	£	£	£	£	£
Wages of employees working on the bottling line	6,025				
Wages of employees in the stores department	2,750				
Cost of bottles	4,050				
Safety goggles for bottling line employees	240				
Advertisement for new employees	125				
Depreciation of bottling machinery	500				
Depreciation of sales staff's cars	1,000				
Royalty paid to local farmer	750				
Cost of trade exhibition	1,500				
Computer stationery	210				
Sales staff salaries	4,095				
TOTALS	21,245				

1.6 The following figures relate to the accounts of Hughes Limited, a manufacturing business, for the year ended 31 December 1998:

	£
Raw materials used in the factory	118,830
Rent and rates of factory	16,460
Factory wages	117,315
Factory power	3,825
Factory heat and light	1,185
Factory expenses and maintenance	4,095
Salaries and wages of office staff	69,350
Advertising	11,085
Office expenses	3,930
Depreciation of factory plant and machinery	3,725
Sales revenue	426,350

You are to:

(a) Prepare a total cost statement for the year which shows:
- prime cost
- production cost
- total cost

Discuss any assumptions that you make and state if you need further information from the company.

(b) Prepare a profit statement for the year (on the assumption that all the goods manufactured have been sold).

2 MATERIALS COSTS

this chapter covers . . .

Businesses hold stocks of materials in the form of raw materials and components, products bought for resale, and service items. Often the value of such materials is high, representing a considerable investment of money. In this chapter we will look at:

- the purchasing and control of stocks of materials
- re-ordering procedures
- the records that a business keeps of its stocks of materials
- the purposes of stock taking and stock reconciliation
- the valuation of stock
- the use of stores ledger records

NVQ PERFORMANCE CRITERIA COVERED

unit 5: RECORDING COST INFORMATION

element 1

record and analyse information relating to direct costs

❑ *direct costs are identified in accordance with the organisation's costing procedures*

❑ *information relating to direct costs is clearly and correctly coded, analysed and recorded*

❑ *direct costs are calculated in accordance with the organisation's policies and procedures*

❑ *information is systematically checked against the overall usage and stock control practices*

❑ *queries are either resolved or referred to the appropriate person*

MATERIALS STOCKS

Materials is the cost of:

- raw materials and components bought for use by a manufacturing business
- products bought for resale by a shop or a wholesaler
- service items, such as stationery, bought for use within a business

In costing we need to distinguish between direct materials and indirect materials. Thus a manufacturer classifies the cost of materials from which the finished product is made as direct materials; other materials used – grease for machines, cleaning materials, etc – are classified as indirect materials, and form part of the overheads of the business.

The buying of materials is normally undertaken by a firm's Purchasing Department, although in smaller businesses the responsibility will be carried out by an individual or the owner. The job of the buyer(s) is to ensure that the purchases made by the business are bought at the lowest possible cost, consistent with quality and quantity.

At any time most businesses will hold materials in stock ready for use or resale:

- a manufacturer holds stocks of raw materials and components in order to reduce the risk of production delays that may arise if a supplier is unable to deliver on time
- a shop or a wholesaler holds stock of products in order to make it easier to respond to a sudden increase in demand; likewise a manufacturer holds stocks of finished goods
- a business holds stocks of service items to keep things running smoothly – for example, if there was no photocopying paper the teaching at a college would be severely disrupted

PLANNING OF PURCHASES AND CONTROL OF STOCKS

Planning for the purchase of materials and the control of stocks of materials is critical to the efficiency of a business. However, holding stocks is expensive:

- they have to be financed, possibly by using borrowed money (on which interest is payable)
- there are storage costs, including rent and rates, security, insurance

Within a business there are conflicting demands on its policy for stocks of materials. On the one hand, the finance department will want to minimise stock levels to keep costs as low as possible; on the other hand, production and marketing departments will be anxious to keep stocks high so that output can be maintained and new orders satisfied speedily before customers decide to buy elsewhere.

There are a number of methods of planning purchases and of stock control. Which is adopted will depend on the size and sophistication of the business. It is important that a business knows how much stock it has at any time – either by making a physical stock count, or by keeping computer records (which need physical verification at regular intervals) – and it must know when it will have to re-order more stocks. The business then needs to know the quantity that needs to be re-ordered. The methods used include:

estimation

Some small businesses do not keep much stock, and the owner may estimate the quantity and timing of materials purchases. This is not a recommended method for a well-managed business.

'two bin' system

The principle here is to keep two 'bins' of a stock unit. When the first bin has run out, new stocks of materials are ordered and will be supplied before the second 'bin' runs out. The term 'bin' is used loosely, and can apply to any measure of stock. This is a very basic principle, but it works well in many situations.

perpetual inventory

'Inventory' is another word for stock. This system records receipt and issue of stock as the items pass in and out of the business, and re-orders are made accordingly. Records of stock are kept manually, or more commonly now on computer file activated by reading of bar codes. Many supermarkets and manufacturing businesses work on this basis, and order stock on a 'Just-In-Time' basis (see page 25).

formulas

Businesses need to calculate when to order materials, and how much to order; formulas can be used to help with this. These are explained in the sections which follow.

MATERIALS PURCHASES: LEVEL METHOD OF RE-ORDERING

This method orders materials in fixed quantities, eg 100 reams of photocopying paper (a ream is 500 sheets). For such a system to operate, the business should know:

- the *lead time*, ie how long it takes for new stock to be delivered after being ordered

- the appropriate *re-order amount*

- the *minimum stock level,* ie the lowest level that stock should fall to before the new order from the supplier is delivered (the minimum stock level is also known as a *buffer stock* to meet unexpected emergencies)

- the *maximum stock level* that can be held – this will often be determined by the amount of storage space available in the warehouse, shop or office stationery 'cupboard'

- the *re-order level*, ie the point at which a new order is to be placed – this is often the most critical factor to determine

Many businesses use manual or computer stock control systems to keep a running record of the amount of each material held in stock, the lead time for re-ordering, and the minimum stock level. The level method of re-ordering is illustrated as follows:

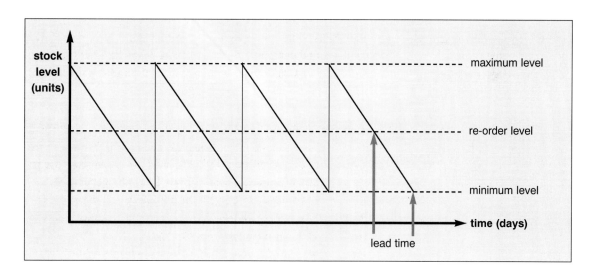

The re-order level is calculated so that replacement materials will be delivered before the stock level reaches the minimum level. The calculation of re-order level is:

(average daily issue of stock x number of days for delivery from supplier) + the minimum stock level

example

A4, white photocopying paper

average daily issue	300 reams (a ream is 500 sheets)
normal delivery	5 days
minimum stock	1,500 reams
maximum stock	10,000 reams

Re-order level = (300 daily issue x 5 number of days delivery)
+ 1,500 minimum stock

= (300 x 5) + 1,500

= 1,500 + 1,500

= 3,000 reams (re-order level)

When the balance of stock falls to 3,000 reams, a purchase order is forwarded to the suppliers of the paper.

MATERIALS PURCHASES: ECONOMIC ORDER QUANTITY (EOQ)

It is clear that the re-order quantity is critical to the stock-holding of a business:

- if re-order amounts are *too large*, too much stock will be held, which will be an expense to the business

- if re-order amounts are *too small*, the expense of constantly re-ordering will outweigh any cost savings of lower stock levels, and there will be the danger that the item might 'run out'

The most economic re-order quantity – *the economic order quantity (EOQ)* – is calculated by a mathematical formula which involves a number of different costs and other figures:

- *ordering cost* – the administration cost of placing each order, eg stationery, postage, wages, telephone

- *unit cost* – the cost of each unit or item of stock

- *stock holding cost* – the cost to the business of keeping the stock on the shelves expressed as a percentage of the average stock value for the year; examples of stock holding costs include rent and rates, insurance, wages, deterioration, obsolescence, security

- *annual usage* – the number of stock units used per year

The formula is:

$$Economic\ Order\ Quantity\ (EOQ) = \sqrt{\frac{2 \times annual\ usage \times ordering\ cost}{unit\ cost \times stock\ holding\ cost}}$$

On a calculator with a square root function, this formula can be worked out easily. Calculate the figures in the formula first, and then press the square root button ($\sqrt{}$).

If, for example, a stock item costs £10, the ordering cost of each order is £30, the stock holding cost is 20 per cent of average stock value, and annual usage is 2,000 units, the EOQ formula will be applied as follows:

$$Economic\ Order\ Quantity\ (EOQ) = \sqrt{\frac{2 \times 2,000 \times £30}{£10 \times 20/100}}$$

$$= \sqrt{\frac{120,000}{2}}$$

$$= \sqrt{60,000}$$

$$= 245\ units$$

As a result of using EOQ, a balance is struck between the cost of placing an order and the cost of holding stock; EOQ represents the most efficient level of order to place – in the example here it is 245 units.

MATERIALS PURCHASES: JUST-IN-TIME (JIT)

Just-In-Time is a system of materials purchasing favoured by manufacturing businesses and large supermarket chains. Using JIT, materials needed by a manufacturer are delivered to the production line, or – for retailers – delivered to the store, just as they are needed. The essentials of the successful operation of JIT are:

* the right quantities
* in the right place
* just-in-time

For JIT to operate effectively, the manufacturer or supermarket needs quality suppliers who can be contracted to deliver materials in accordance with demand schedules. In this way stock levels are kept to a minimum, with consequent savings in stock holding costs. The disadvantage is that the JIT system is susceptible to supply chain problems – eg bad weather or a labour dispute – there are no buffer stocks to absorb such difficulties.

Manufacturers who use JIT often try to attract component suppliers to the same area. The car manufacturer Fiat has gone a step further than this by building a car factory in southern Italy with the component firms on the same site.

Retailers who use JIT – such as major supermarket chains – have arrangements with their suppliers to supply goods more or less on demand. Information technology systems used by these businesses help them to anticipate the quantities they have to order: electronic tills provide up-to-the-minute stock usage for each product 'line' and so stock levels are constantly monitored. Orders are sent to suppliers, often through EDI (Electronic Data Interchange) systems, and delivered within a short space of time. If there is a run on a particular item – eg soft drinks in a heat wave – the system will ensure that new stock is delivered very rapidly.

Factors to consider in relation to JIT include:
- reliability of the supplier
- quality of goods supplied
- effect on the business of disruption of supplies caused by factors such as bad weather or strikes
- minimal stock taking requirements
- alternative uses for resources released, eg storage areas no longer needed
- overall efficiency of the JIT system in the context of maintaining the firm's output

STOCK RECORDS

Most businesses will have records of their stocks of materials. Such records may be kept either by using a computer stock control system, or manually on individual stock record cards. Under both methods – computer and manual – a separate record is maintained for each of the different materials kept in stock. The system is used whether the materials are held for resale by a retailer, or for use in production by a manufacturer. When supplies of the material are received they are entered in the stock record, and when items are sold (or issued to production) they are deducted from the stock record.

A typical stock record card is shown below. The stock item is A4 white photocopying paper which is used within the business.

STOCK RECORD CARD

Stock description ..A4 white photocopying paper..

Stock units ....reams..................................

Stock ref. No. ....P1026..........................

Location ....row A, bin 6......................

Minimum ....1,500 reams..........

Maximum ....10,000 reams..........

Re-order level ....3,000 reams.........

Re-order quantity ....5,000 reams...........

DATE	GOODS RECEIVED		GOODS ISSUED		BALANCE
	Reference	Quantity	Reference	Quantity	
1999					
1 Apr					3,000
2 Apr			MR 101	200	2,800
5 Apr			MR 104	300	2,500
6 Apr			MR 116	400	2,100
7 Apr			MR 121	250	1,850
8 Apr	GRN 17901	5,000			6,850
9 Apr	MRN 58	50			6,900

Note the following on the stock record card:

stock description	refers to the description of the stock, for example photocopying paper
stock units	refers to how the stock is stored or packed, eg photocopying paper is packed in reams (packets of 500 sheets)
stock reference no	refers to the identification number allocated to the stock by the business – often marked on the stock, and sometimes by means of a barcode
location	refers to where the stock can be found in the stores, eg row A, bin 6 refers to the location in the storeroom or warehouse
minimum	is the minimum level of the number of items to be kept in stock

maximum	is the maximum level of the number of items to be kept in stock
re-order level	is the level to which the stock falls before the business re-orders more items
re-order quantity	is the amount which is normally re-ordered
goods received	the two columns record the Goods Received Note (GRN) reference and the quantity of items received – or where goods are returned, the reference of the Materials Returns Note (MRN)
goods issued	the two columns record the Materials Requisition (MR) reference and the number of items issued
balance	is the number of items which remain in stock

STOCK TAKING AND STOCK RECONCILIATION

stock taking

A business will check regularly that the quantity of stock held is the same as the number recorded on the stock record cards. This is done by means of a stock take – counting the physical stock on hand to check against the balance shown by the records, and to identify any theft or deterioration.

Stock taking is carried out on either a periodic basis or continuously.

A *periodic basis* involves carrying out a stock take of all items held at regular intervals (often twice a year).

Continuous stock taking is a constant process where selected items are counted on a rotating basis, with all items being checked at least once a year (expensive, desirable or high-turnover items will need to be checked more frequently).

The number of items actually held is recorded on a stock list by the person doing the stock take. An extract from a stock list is shown on the next page; it shows the A4 paper seen in the stock record card. The stock list will, of course, contain many items when the stock take has been completed.

stock list as at *9 April 1999*					checker *H Ramsay*			
product code	item description	location	unit size	units counted	stock card balance	discrepancy	checker's initials
P1026	*A4 white photocopying paper*	*row A, bin 6*	*ream*	*6,900*	*6,900*	*nil*	*HR*

checker's signature *H Ramsay* .... **Authorised for write-off** ....

stock reconciliation

The object of the stock take is to see if the stock record cards accurately represent the level of stock held. The two columns on the stock list – 'units counted' and 'stock card balance' enable this comparison to be carried out; the process is known as a *stock reconciliation*. It is an important process because

- an accurate stock figure can then be used to value the stock
- it will highlight any discrepancies which can then be investigated

Discrepancies should be noted on the stock list and referred to the supervisor and any other people who may need to know, eg the storekeeper, or the firm's auditors who are organising the stock take. If the discrepancy is small it will be authorised for write-off. Larger discrepancies will need to be investigated, as they could have been caused by:

- an error on the stock record card, such as a failure to record a stock movement or an error in calculating the balance of stock
- theft of stock
- damaged stock being disposed of without any record having been made

VALUATION OF STOCK

The stock of materials held by a business invariably has considerable value and ties up a lot of money. At the end of the financial year, it is essential to value the stock for use in the calculation of profit in the final accounts. As we have just seen, a process of stock taking is used to make a physical check of the stock held, which is then compared with the stock records. The stock held is then valued as follows:

number of items held   x   cost per item   =   stock value at cost

The auditors of a business may make random checks to ensure that the stock value is correct.

Stock is valued at either:

- what it cost the business to buy the stock (including additional costs to bring the product or service to its present location or condition, such as delivery charges), or

- the net realisable value – the actual or estimated selling price (less any further costs such as selling and distribution)

This stock valuation is often described as being at the *lower of cost and net realisable value*. This valuation is taken from Statement of Standard Accounting Practice (SSAP) No 9, entitled 'Stocks and long-term contracts'; the valuation applies the prudence concept of accounting. It is illustrated as follows:

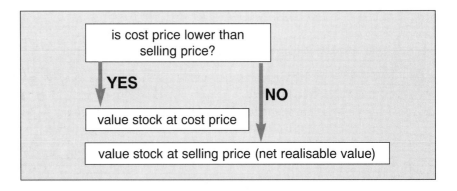

The difficulty in stock valuation is in finding out the cost price of stock – this is not easy when quantities of a particular stock item are continually being bought in – often at different prices – and then sold. Some businesses have stock in a number of different forms, eg manufacturing businesses have stocks of raw materials, work-in-progress and finished goods.

DIFFERENT METHODS USED IN STOCK VALUATION

Businesses use different methods to calculate the cost price of stock. Three commonly used methods are:

FIFO (first in, first out)   This method assumes that the first stocks acquired are the first to be sold or used, so that the valuation of stock on hand at any time consists of the most recently acquired stock.

LIFO (last in, first out)   Here it is assumed that the last stocks acquired are the first to be sold or used, so that the stock on hand is made up of earlier purchases.

AVCO (average cost)   Here the average cost of items held at the beginning of the year is calculated; as new stocks are bought a new average cost is calculated (based on a weighted average, using the number of units bought as the weighting).

The use of a particular method does not necessarily correspond with the method of physical distribution adopted in a firm's stores. For example, in a car factory one car battery of type X is the same as another, and no-one will be concerned if the storekeeper issues one from the last batch received, even if the FIFO system has been adopted. However, perishable goods are always physically handled on the basis of first in, first out, even if the accounting stock records use another method.

Having chosen a suitable stock valuation method, a business will continue to use that method unless there are good reasons for making the change. This is in line with the consistency concept of accounting.

STORES LEDGER RECORDS

In order to be able to calculate accurately the price at which stocks of materials are issued and to ascertain a valuation of stock, the following method of recording stock data, using a stores ledger record, is suggested (see next page):

STORES LEDGER RECORD

Date	Receipts			Issues			Balance		
	Quantity	Price	Value	Quantity	Price*	Value	Quantity	Price	Value
		£	£		£	£		£	£

*Note: this price is the cost price to the business, not the selling price – virtually all stock records are kept at cost price.

CASE STUDY

H RASHID COMPUTER SUPPLIES – STORES LEDGER RECORDS

situation

H Rashid runs a computer supplies company. One of the items he sells is the 'Zap' data disk.

To show how the stores ledger records would appear under FIFO, LIFO and AVCO, and the closing stock valuation at 31 May 1999, the following data is used for each method:

January	Opening stock of 40 units at a cost of £3.00 each
February	Bought 20 units at a cost of £3.60 each
March	Sold 36 units for £6 each
April	Bought 20 units at a cost of £3.75 each
May	Sold 25 units for £6 each

What will be the profit for the period using each stock valuation method?

FIFO

STORES LEDGER RECORD

Date	Receipts			Issues			Balance		
1999	*Quantity*	*Price*	*Value*	*Quantity*	*Price*	*Value*	*Quantity*	*Price*	*Value*
		£	£		£	£		£	£
Jan	Balance						40	3.00	120.00
Feb	20	3.60	72.00				40	3.00	120.00
							20	3.60	72.00
							60		192.00
March				36	3.00	108.00	4	3.00	12.00
							20	3.60	72.00
							24		84.00
April	20	3.75	75.00				4	3.00	12.00
							20	3.60	72.00
							20	3.75	75.00
							44		159.00
May				4	3.00	12.00			
				20	3.60	72.00			
				1	3.75	3.75	19	3.75	71.25

LIFO

STORES LEDGER RECORD

Date	Receipts			Issues			Balance		
1999	Quantity	Price	Value	Quantity	Price	Value	Quantity	Price	Value
		£	£		£	£		£	£
Jan	Balance						40	3.00	120.00
Feb	20	3.60	72.00				40	3.00	120.00
							20	3.60	72.00
							60		192.00
March				20	3.60	72.00			
				16	3.00	48.00	24	3.00	72.00
April	20	3.75	75.00				24	3.00	72.00
							20	3.75	75.00
							44		147.00
May				20	3.75	75.00			
				5	3.00	15.00	19	3.00	57.00

AVCO

STORES LEDGER RECORD

Date	Receipts			Issues			Balance		
1999	*Quantity*	*Price*	*Value*	*Quantity*	*Price*	*Value*	*Quantity*	*Price*	*Value*
		£	£		£	£		£	£
Jan	Balance						40	3.00	120.00
Feb	20	3.60	72.00				40	3.00	120.00
							20	3.60	72.00
							60	3.20	192.00
March				36	3.20	115.20	24	3.20	76.80
April	20	3.75	75.00				24	3.20	76.80
							20	3.75	75.00
							44	3.45	151.80
May				25	3.45	86.25	19	3.45	65.55

Note: Average cost is calculated by dividing the quantity held in stock into the value of the stock. For example, at the end of February, the average cost is £192 ÷ 60 units = £3.20.

The closing stock valuations at the end of May 1999 under each method show cost prices of:

FIFO	£71.25
LIFO	£57.00
AVCO	£65.55

There is quite a difference, and this has come about because different stock methods have been used.

effect on profit

In the example above, the selling price was £6 per unit. The effect on gross profit of using different stock valuations is as follows:

	FIFO	LIFO	AVCO
	£	£	£
Sales: 61 units at £6	366.00	366.00	366.00
Opening stock: 40 units at £3	120.00	120.00	120.00
Purchases: 20 units at £3.60 and 20 units at £3.75	147.00	147.00	147.00
	267.00	267.00	267.00
Less Closing stock: 19 units	71.25	57.00	65.55
Cost of sales	195.75	210.00	201.45
Gross profit	170.25	156.00	164.55
	366.00	366.00	366.00

In times of rising prices, FIFO produces the highest profit, LIFO the lowest, and AVCO between the other two. However, over the life of a business, total profit is the same in total, whichever method is chosen: the profit is allocated to different years depending on which method is used.

ADVANTAGES AND DISADVANTAGES OF FIFO, LIFO AND AVCO

FIFO (first in, first out)

advantages

- realistic, ie it assumes that goods are issued in order of receipt
- it is easy to calculate
- stock valuation comprises actual prices at which items have been bought
- the closing stock valuation is close to the most recent prices

disadvantages

- prices at which goods are issued are not necessarily the latest prices
- in times of rising prices, profits will be higher than with other methods (resulting in more tax to pay)

LIFO (last in, first out)

advantages

- goods are issued at the latest prices
- it is easy to calculate

disadvantages

- illogical, ie it assumes goods are issued in reverse order from that in which they are received
- the closing stock valuation is not usually at most recent prices
- when stocks are being run down, issues will 'dip into' old stock at out-of-date prices
- may not be acceptable to the Inland Revenue for taxation purposes as the method overstates cost of sales and understates profit

AVCO (average cost)

advantages

- over a number of accounting periods reported profits are smoothed, ie both high and low profits are avoided
- fluctuations in purchase prices are evened out so that issues do not vary greatly
- logical, ie it assumes that identical units, even when purchased at different times, have the same value
- closing stock valuation is close to current market values (in times of rising prices, it will be below current market values)

disadvantages

- difficult to calculate, and calculations may be to several decimal places
- issues and stock valuation are usually at prices which never existed
- issues may not be at current prices and, in times of rising prices, will be below current prices

The important point to remember is that a business must adopt a consistent stock valuation policy, ie it should choose one method of finding the cost price, and not change it without good reason. FIFO and AVCO are more commonly used than LIFO; in particular, LIFO usually results in a stock valuation for the final accounts which bears little relationship to recent costs – for this reason it is not favoured by SSAP 9.

CATEGORIES OF STOCK

Statement of Standard Accounting Practice No 9 requires that, in calculating the lower of cost and net realisable value, note should be taken of:

- separate items of stock, or
- groups of similar items

This means that the stock valuation 'rule' must be applied to each separate item of stock, or each group or category of similar stocks. The total cost cannot be compared with the total net realisable value, as is shown by the Case Study which follows.

CASE STUDY

PAINT AND WALLPAPER SUPPLIES

situation

The year-end stocks for the two main groups of stock held by the business Paint and Wallpaper Supplies are found to be:

	Cost	Net realisable value
	£	£
Paints	2,500	2,300
Wallpapers	5,000	7,500
	7,500	9,800

How will the stock be valued for the year-end accounts?

solution

The correct stock valuation is £7,300, which takes the 'lower of cost and net realisable value' for each group of stock, ie

	£
Paints (at net realisable value)	2,300
Wallpapers (at cost)	5,000
	7,300

You will also note that this valuation is the lowest possible choice, indicating that stock valuation follows the *prudence concept*.

STOCK VALUATION FOR MANUFACTURING BUSINESSES

We saw earlier that, under SSAP 9, stock is normally valued at the lower of cost and net realisable value. This principle applies to a manufacturer for the three types of stock that may be held at the year-end:

- raw materials
- work-in-progress
- finished goods

For raw materials, the comparison is made between cost (which can be found using techniques such as FIFO, LIFO, or AVCO) and net realisable value.

For stocks of both work-in-progress and finished goods, SSAP 9 requires that the cost valuation includes expenditure not only on direct materials but also on direct labour, direct expenses and production overheads. Thus for work-in-progress and finished goods, 'cost' comprises:

- direct materials
- direct labour
- direct expenses
- production overheads (to bring the product to its present location or condition)

Such 'cost' is then compared with net realisable value – less any further costs necessary to complete the item or get it in a condition to be sold – and the lower figure is taken as the stock valuation (remember that different items or groups of stock are compared separately).

CASE STUDY

ABC MANUFACTURING

situation

ABC Manufacturing started in business on 1 July 1998 producing security devices for doors and windows. During the first year 2,000 units were sold and, at the end of the year, on 30 June 1999, there were 200 units in stock which were finished and 20 units which were exactly half finished as regards direct materials, direct labour and production overheads.

Costs for the first year were:

	£
Direct materials used	18,785
Direct labour	13,260
Production overheads	8,840
Non-production overheads	4,420
Total cost for year	45,305

At 30 June 1999 it was estimated that the net realisable value of each completed security device was £35. There were no stocks of direct materials.

Calculate the stock valuation at 30 June 1999 for:

- work-in-progress
- finished goods

solution

WORK-IN-PROGRESS

To calculate the value of both work-in-progress and finished goods we need to know the production cost, ie direct materials, direct labour and production overheads. This is:

	£
Direct materials used	18,785
Direct labour	13,260
Production overheads	8,840
Production cost for year	**40,885**

All these costs are included because they have been incurred in bringing the product to its present location or condition. Non-production overheads are not included because they are not directly related to production.

Thus, a production cost of £40,885 has produced:

Units sold	2,000
Closing stock of completed units	200
Closing stock of work-in-progress –	
20 units exactly half-finished equals 10 completed units	10
Production for year	**2,210**

The **cost per unit** is:

$$\frac{£40,885}{2,210} = \textbf{£18.50 per unit}$$

The 20 half-finished units have a cost of (20 ÷ 2) x £18.50 = **£185**.
They have a net realisable value of (20 ÷ 2) x £35 = £350.
The value of work-in-progress will, therefore, be shown in the accounts as £185, which is the lower of cost and net realisable value.

FINISHED GOODS

The completed units in stock at the end of the year have a production cost of 200 x £18.50 = £3,700, compared with a net realisable value of 200 x £35 = £7,000. Applying the rule of lower of cost and net realisable value, finished goods stock will be valued at the cost price, **£3,700**.

OTHER STOCK VALUATION METHODS

As well as the FIFO, LIFO and AVCO methods used to determine the valuation of closing stock, other methods which could be used include:

standard cost

This uses a pre-determined cost – the standard cost (see Chapter 7) – based on the business' estimates of expected cost levels. SSAP 9 stresses that standard costs should be reviewed frequently, to ensure that they bear a reasonable relationship to actual costs during the period.

replacement cost

This method considers the price at which the items of stock can be replaced, either by purchase or by manufacture. SSAP 9 considers this method unacceptable because replacement cost is not necessarily the same as actual cost. For example, in times of rising prices, replacement cost will be higher than actual cost, which means that a profit is taken before the stock is sold.

CHAPTER SUMMARY

- Businesses hold stocks of raw materials and components bought for production, products bought for resale, and service items bought for use within the business.

- Two important stock costs are the ordering cost and the stock holding cost.

- Materials purchases can be made using techniques such as:
    - the level method of re-ordering
    - Economic Order Quantity (EOQ)
    - Just-In-Time (JIT)

- The level of stock is recorded on a stock record card, which also indicates
    - the level at which new stock should be ordered
    - the quantity of stock that should be re-ordered

- Stock levels of materials are monitored regularly by means of stock taking; stock reconciliation notes any discrepancies and reports them for further investigation.

- The normal valuation for stock is *at the lower of cost and net realisable value* (SSAP 9).

- Stock valuation methods include:
  - FIFO (first in, first out)
  - LIFO (last in, first out)
  - AVCO (average cost)
  - standard cost
  - replacement cost

- For a manufacturing business, cost comprises the direct manufacturing costs of materials, labour and expenses, together with the production overheads which bring the product to its present location or condition.

materials	the cost of:
	  – raw materials and components used in production
	  – products bought for resale
	  – service items bought for use within the business

level method of re-ordering	the re-ordering of materials in fixed quantities
Economic Order Quantity	a balance between ordering costs and stock holding costs; calculated by the formula: 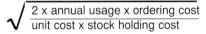 $$\sqrt{\frac{2 \times \text{annual usage} \times \text{ordering cost}}{\text{unit cost} \times \text{stock holding cost}}}$$
Just-In-Time (JIT)	the process of delivering goods in the right quantities, in the right place, just-in-time
stock record card	record held for each stock item which shows receipts of supplies and sales (or issues to production)
stock taking	the process of counting physical stock on hand
stock reconciliation	comparison of the physical stock on hand with the stock card balance and identification of the reason(s) for discrepancies

stock value	number of items held x stock valuation per item
cost	what it cost to buy the stock (including additional costs to bring the product to its present location or condition)
net realisable value	selling price (less any further costs such as selling and distribution)
stores ledger record	method of recording stock data in order to ascertain the price at which stocks of materials are issued, and to ascertain a valuation of stock using methods such as FIFO, LIFO and AVCO

STUDENT ACTIVITIES

The answers to these Student Activities are printed in the back of this book. Further questions and more fully extended Student Activities and Assessments are to be found in the accompanying Osborne Books' text *Costing, Reports & Returns Workbook*.

2.1   Calculate, for stock items D and E, the re-order stock level and the re-order quantity to replenish stock levels to the maximum level, from the following information:

- daily usage of D = 3 units, of E = 4 units
- total stock should never exceed 95 days' usage
- 10 days' stock should always be held
- there is space available in the store for 350 units of each item of stock
- normal delivery time is 7 days

2.2   (a)   Prepare a stock record card from the following information:

- *product:* A4 Yellow Card, code A4/Y3, location row 7, bin 5
- *units:* reams
- *maximum stock:* 35 days' usage
- *daily usage:* 3 units
- *normal delivery time:* 10 days
- *minimum stock:* 12 days' stock
- *opening balance on 1 May 1999:* 84 reams

Note: a blank stock record card, which may be photocopied, is provided in the Appendix.

(b)   Calculate maximum, minimum and re-order levels of stock, together with re-order quantity (to replenish stock to the maximum level)

(c)   Enter the following materials requisitions for May 1999 on the stock record card remembering to re-order when necessary and to show on the card the order arriving ten days later (Goods Received Note 4507):

4 May	Materials Requisition 184	18 reams
6 May	Materials Requisition 187	20 reams
10 May	Materials Requisition 188	10 reams
17 May	Materials Requisition 394	20 reams
20 May	Materials Requisition 401	11 reams
26 May	Materials Requisition 422	6 reams

2.3   Complete the following sentences:

(a)   Stock levels and movements are recorded on a ....

(b)   A person carrying out a stock check will record the stock on a ....

(c)   The process of comparing stock on the shelves with stock in the records is known as

....

(d)   The usual basis for stock valuation is at the lower of .... and ....

....

2.4 From the following information prepare stores ledger records for product X using (a) FIFO, (b) LIFO, (c) AVCO:

- 20 units of the product are bought in January 1999 at a cost of £3 each

- 10 units are bought in February at a cost of £3.50 each

- 8 units are sold in March

- 10 units are bought in April at a cost of £4.00 each

- 16 units are sold in May

Notes:

- a blank stores ledger record, which may be photocopied, is provided in the Appendix

- where appropriate, work to two decimal places

2.5 XY Limited is formed on 1 January 1999 and, at the end of its first half-year of trading, the stores ledger records show the following:

1999	TYPE X		TYPE Y	
	Receipts (units)	**Issues (units)**	**Receipts (units)**	**Issues (units)**
January	100 at £4.00		200 at £10.00	
February		80	100 at £9.50	
March	140 at £4.20			240
April	100 at £3.80		100 at £10.50	
May		140	140 at £10.00	
June	80 at £4.50			100

At 30 June 1999, the net realisable value of each type of stock is:

type X	£1,750
type Y	£1,950
	£3,700

You are to:

- Complete stores ledger records for products X and Y using (a) FIFO, (b) LIFO, (c) AVCO.

- The business has decided to use the FIFO method. Show the amount at which its stocks should be valued on 30 June 1999 in order to comply with standard accountancy practice.

Notes:

- a blank stores ledger record, which may be photocopied, is provided in the Appendix

- where appropriate, work to two decimal places

3 LABOUR COSTS

this chapter covers . . .

In this chapter we explain:

- the factors that affect labour costs
- the ways in which the direct labour employees of a business can be remunerated
- how payroll information is gathered
- the advantages and disadvantages of different labour remuneration methods
- overtime and idle time
- the use of a wages control account

NVQ PERFORMANCE CRITERIA COVERED

unit 5: RECORDING COST INFORMATION

element 1

record and analyse information relating to direct costs

❏ direct costs are identified in accordance with the organisation's costing procedures

❏ information relating to direct costs is clearly and correctly coded, analysed and recorded

❏ direct costs are calculated in accordance with the organisation's policies and procedures

❏ queries are either resolved or referred to the appropriate person

FACTORS THAT AFFECT LABOUR COSTS

There are many factors that need to be considered by a business when deciding how much to pay employees. The starting point will always be the amount that is paid by other businesses in the area for similar grades of employees but, at the same time, the wider economic implications of supply and demand will affect wage rates.

The factors to consider include:

* wage rates paid by other local businesses

* comparisons with national average wage rates

* the national minimum wage rate imposed by government

* any government incentives to take on additional employees, such as young people or the long-term unemployed

* local employment conditions – high unemployment in the area will drive down wage rates; conversely low unemployment, and especially a shortage of skilled labour, will increase wage rates

* for a new business, it might be prudent to choose to locate in an area of high unemployment – in addition to lower wage rates, there may be government incentives in the form of reduced rents and rates, training and other grants

Having taken on labour, a business must then decide how to remunerate its employees – the methods of labour remuneration are looked at in detail in the next section.

From time-to-time, employees will expect their pay rates to be reviewed and then, most probably, increased. Usually such a process takes place each year when wage rates are negotiated. In the negotiations, both the employer and the representatives of the employees will take into account such things as:

* the rise in the cost of living, for example, as measured by the Retail Price Index (RPI)

* the overall employment situation

* the profitability of the business – can it afford to pay increased wage rates?

While the employer will be seeking a package of measures that gives the business a more efficient workforce, employees will be looking for higher wages together with enhanced benefits.

LABOUR REMUNERATION

There are a number of ways in which the direct labour employees of a business can be remunerated. Remember that the direct labour cost is the wages paid to those who work on a production line, are involved in assembly, or are involved in the output of a service business.

The three main methods of direct labour remuneration are:

time rate   Time rate (sometimes known as a day rate) is where the employee is paid on the basis of time spent at work. Overtime may be paid for hours worked beyond a standard number of hours, or for work carried out on days which are not part of the working week, eg Saturdays or Sundays. Overtime is often paid at rates such as 'time-and-a-quarter', 'time-and-a-half', or even 'double-time'.

piecework rate   The employee is paid an agreed sum for each task carried out or for each unit of output completed.

bonus system   The employee is paid a time rate and then receives a bonus if output is better than expected. Such systems are often linked into standard costing – see Chapter 7 – where the quantity of work that can be achieved at a standard performance in an hour (a standard hour) is estimated; the bonus is then expressed as an agreed percentage of the standard hours saved.

Most other employees, eg factory supervisors, sales staff, office staff, are usually paid on a weekly or monthly basis. Such wages and salaries – classed as indirect labour costs – may be increased by bonus payments; for example, a production bonus for factory supervisors, commissions for sales staff, a profit-sharing scheme for all employees.

There are many variations on the three methods outlined above and, indeed, changing patterns of employment create different remuneration methods from those that would have been the norm just a few years ago. For example, the contracting out of many business support services – such as cleaning, security, computers – means that the costing of such services by the provider may incorporate time rates and bonus systems whereas previously the employees would have been paid on a weekly or monthly basis.

The process of gathering payroll information about work done in order to make payment to employees comes from a variety of sources. The most common of these are:

- *time sheets,* where employees record the hours they have worked
- *clock cards,* where employees 'clock in' at the start of work, and 'clock out' at the end – these are often computerised
- *piecework tickets,* completed by employees who work on a batch of output
- *job cards,* where each employee records the amount of time spent on each job
- *route cards* – which are used to follow a product through the production process – on which employees record the amount of time they spend working on the product
- *computer cards* – 'swipe' cards which link direct into the computerised payroll are increasingly being used by employers to record attendance

CASE STUDY

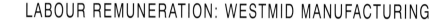

LABOUR REMUNERATION: WESTMID MANUFACTURING

situation

Westmid Manufacturing Company has three factories in the West Midlands making parts for the car industry. Each factory was bought from the previous owners and, as a result, each has a different method for remunerating its direct labour workforce. The details of the method of remuneration in each factory, together with data on two employees from each factory, are as follows:

Walsall factory

In this factory, which is involved in heavy engineering, employees are paid on the basis of a time rate. Employees are required to 'clock in' and 'clock out' each day.

John Brown is a machine operator and his clock card for last week shows that he worked 39 hours; his hourly rate of pay is £8 per hour.

Stefan Wozniak is a skilled lathe operator and his clock card shows that he worked 42 hours; his hourly rate of pay is £10 per hour, with overtime for hours worked beyond 40 hours at 'time-and-a-half'.

Dudley factory

This factory operates a number of light engineering production lines making car components such as windscreen wiper blades, headlamp surrounds, interior mirrors etc. The production line employees are all paid on a piecework basis; however, each employee receives a guaranteed time rate which is paid if the piecework earnings are less than the time rate. This may happen if, for example, there are machine breakdowns and the production line has to be halted.

Tracey Johnson works on the line making headlamp surrounds. For each one that passes through her part of the process, she is paid 30p; her guaranteed time rate is 37 hours each week at £6 per hour. Last week's production records show that she processed 870 units.

Pete Bronyah is on the line which makes interior mirrors. For his part of the process he receives £1.00 for each one, with a guaranteed time rate of 37 hours at £6 per hour. Last week there was a machine failure and he was only able to process 150 units.

Wolverhampton factory

In this factory a number of engineering production lines are operated. The direct labour force is paid on a time rate basis, but a bonus is paid if work can be completed faster than the standard performance. Thus a standard time allowance is given for each task and, if it can be completed in less time, a bonus is paid: the bonus in this factory is for the savings achieved to be shared equally between employer and employee. Wages are, therefore, paid on the following basis: time rate + 50% of (time saved x time rate). If no bonus is due, then the time rate applies.

Martin Lee worked a 38 hour work last week; his time rate is £10 per hour. He is allowed a standard time of 30 minutes to carry out his work on each unit of production; last week he completed 71 units.

Sara King has a time rate of £11 per hour; last week she worked 40 hours. She is allowed a standard time of 15 minutes to carry out her work on each unit of production; last week she completed 184 units.

What were the gross earnings of each employee?

solution

Walsall factory

John Brown:	39 hours x £8.00 per hour	=	£312.00
Stefan Wozniak:	40 hours x £10.00 per hour = £400		
	2 hours x £15.00 per hour = £30	=	£430.00

Dudley factory

Tracey Johnson:	Piecework rate, 870 units x 30p per unit	=	£261.00
	Guaranteed time rate, 37 hours x £6.00 per hour	=	£222.00
	Therefore piecework rate of £261.00 is paid.		
Pete Bronyah:	Piecework rate, 150 units x £1.00 per unit	=	£150.00
	Guaranteed time rate, 37 hours x £6.00 per hour	=	£222.00
	Therefore guaranteed time rate of £222.00 is paid.		

Wolverhampton factory

Martin Lee:	Time rate, 38 hours x £10.00 per hour	=	£380.00
	Bonus, time allowed 71 units x 30 minutes each = 35 hours 30 minutes		
	Therefore no time saved, so no bonus payable.		
	Time rate of £380 paid.		

Sara King:

Time rate, 40 hours x £11.00 per hour		=	£440.00
Bonus, time allowed 184 x 15 minutes each	= 46 hours		
Therefore time saved is 6 hours			
Bonus is 50% of (6 hours x £11.00)		=	£33.00
Therefore wages are £440.00 + £33.00		=	£473.00

The Case Study illustrates some of the direct labour remuneration methods in use, however it should be appreciated that there are many variations on these to be found.

DIRECT LABOUR REMUNERATION METHODS: ADVANTAGES AND DISADVANTAGES

time rate

Time rate is often used where it is difficult to measure output, and where quality is more important than quantity. Variations include a high time rate, used to motivate employees where a higher standard of work is required.

advantages:
- easy to understand and to calculate
- no requirement to establish time allowances and piecework rates
- the employee receives a regular wage, unaffected by fluctuations in output
- can be used for all direct labour employees
- quality of the finished product does not suffer as a result of hurried work

disadvantages:
- both efficient and inefficient employees receive the same wage
- no incentive is given to employees to work harder
- slower working will not affect basic wage, but may lead to overtime
- more supervisors are needed to ensure that output is maintained

piecework rate

Piecework rate is used where the quantity of output is important, and there is less emphasis on quality.

Variations include:

- piecework with guaranteed time rate, which ensures that employees are paid if production is stopped through no fault of their own, eg machine breakdown, or shortage of materials

- differential piecework system, where a higher rate is paid for all output beyond a certain level, eg 50p per unit for the first 100 units each day, then 60p per unit thereafter; used to motivate employees to produce more than a basic level of output

- attendance allowances, paid to encourage employees on piecework to attend each day, thus ensuring that the production-line can be staffed and operated every working day

advantages:

- payment of wages is linked directly to output

- more efficient workers earn more than those who are less efficient

- work is done quicker and less time is wasted

disadvantages:

- not suitable for all direct labour employees

- pay is reduced if there are production problems, eg machine breakdown or shortage of materials

- quality of the finished product may be low

- more inspectors may be needed

- control systems needed to check the amount produced by each worker

- more complex pay calculations

- may be difficulty in agreeing piecework rates with employees

bonus systems

Bonus systems are used to encourage employees to be more efficient in an environment where the work is not so repetitive. Variations include an accelerating premium bonus – which is an increased bonus paid for higher levels of output, and group bonuses paid to groups of employees who achieve increased output – the group could be as large as the entire workforce of a large company, or as small as a work team of two or three people.

advantages:
- wages linked to output, but minimum wage is guaranteed each week
- work is done quicker and less time is wasted
- more efficient workers earn more
- a bonus system can often be applied to the entire workforce

disadvantages:
- bonus is not paid if circumstances beyond employee's control prevent work, eg machine breakdown or shortage of materials
- quality of finished product may be low
- more inspectors may be needed
- control procedures needed/more complex pay calculations
- may be difficulty in agreeing bonus rates with employees

qualities of a good labour remuneration scheme

These include:
- reward should be related to effort and fair to all staff
- the scheme should be easy to manage and administer, and cheap and efficient to run
- it should be easy for employees to understand how pay is calculated
- payment should be made at regular intervals and soon after the event, eg employees on piecework should be paid in the week after the production has been achieved
- the principles of the scheme should remain constant, but there should be flexibility to deal with changes in production techniques

OVERTIME AND IDLE TIME

So far we have divided labour costs between:
- *direct costs*, labour costs of production-line employees
- *indirect costs*, labour costs of other employees, such as supervisors, office staff, etc

Whilst this distinction appears clear enough, there are times when a proportion of the labour costs of production-line employees is classed as an indirect cost (rather than a direct cost) and is included amongst the overheads of the business. Examples of this are:

overtime payments

When production-line employees work overtime they are usually paid at a rate above the time rate. For example, overtime might be paid at 'time-and-a-half'; thus an employee with a time rate of £8 an hour will be paid overtime at £12 an hour. For normal cost accounting purposes, any overtime worked is charged at £8 an hour to direct labour, and £4 an hour to indirect labour. In this way, the cost of overtime is spread across all output and is not charged solely to the output being worked on during the overtime period. As another issue, management will wish to know why there was the need to work overtime, and will seek to control such an increase in labour costs.

However, where a customer requests overtime to be worked to get a rush job completed, then the full overtime rate (£12 an hour in the above example) is charged as direct labour, and passed on as a cost to the customer.

idle time

Idle time occurs when production is stopped through no fault of the production-line employees – for example, a machine breakdown, or a shortage of materials. Employees paid under a piecework or a bonus system will receive time rate for the period of the stoppage. Such wages costs are normally charged to overheads as indirect labour.

WAGES CONTROL ACCOUNT

A wages control account – which may also include salaries – is used to charge the labour costs to the various cost centres of a business. In this way:

• direct labour costs are charged to work-in-progress

• indirect labour costs are charged to production overheads

• administration labour costs are charged to non-production overheads

For example, a manufacturing business has completed its payroll for the week and has the following amounts to pay:

		£
•	net wages to be paid to employees	5,000
•	income tax and National Insurance Contributions (NIC) to be paid to the Inland Revenue	1,000
•	pension contributions to be paid to the pension fund	500
	TOTAL PAYROLL FOR THE WEEK	6,500

The total payroll for the week is analysed as:

		£
•	direct labour costs	3,500
•	indirect labour costs	2,000
•	administration labour costs	1,000
		6,500

The wages control account is prepared as follows:

Dr	**Wages Control Account**	Cr

	£		£
Cash/bank (net wages)	5,000	Work-in-progress (direct labour)	3,500
Inland Revenue		Production overheads	
(income tax and NIC)	1,000	(indirect labour)	2,000
Pension contributions	500	Non-production overheads	
		(administration)	1,000
	6,500		6,500

By using the wages control account in this way, the total cost of the payroll is split between the various cost centres of the business. We shall look in more detail at the book-keeping for costing in Chapter 8.

CHAPTER SUMMARY

- Factors that affect labour costs include:
  - wage rates paid by other local businesses
  - comparisons with national average wage rates
  - the national minimum wage set by government
  - local employment conditions

- Employees will seek to negotiate increases in pay rates with reference to:
  - the cost of living
  - the overall employment situation
  - profitability of the business

- Main methods of direct remuneration include:
  - time rate
  - piecework rate
  - bonus systems

- Payroll information is gathered from a variety of sources, including:
  - time sheets
  - clock cards
  - piecework tickets
  - job cards
  - route cards
  - computer 'swipe' cards

- Amounts paid in overtime are classified as
  - a direct cost, where overtime is worked at the request of a customer
  - an indirect cost, for other overtime worked

- Idle time is usually classified as an indirect cost

KEY TERMS

time rate	hours worked x rate per hour
piecework rate	units produced x rate per unit
bonus systems	amount, usually calculated as a share of time saved, added to the time rate
standard hour	quantity of work that can be achieved at a standard performance in an hour
time sheet	method by which employees record the hours they have worked
clock card	where employees 'clock in' at the start of work, and 'clock out' at the end
piecework ticket	documentation completed by employees who work on a batch of output
job card	documentation completed by employees which records the amount of time spent on each job
route card	documentation which follows a product through the production process – employees record the amount of time they spend working on the product
overtime payments	amount paid when overtime is worked – depending on the circumstances, it could be either a direct or an indirect cost

idle time	period during which production is stopped through no fault of the production-line employees; employees usually receive time rate for idle time, and the cost is normally classified as an indirect cost
wages control account	used to charge labour costs to the various cost centres: – direct labour to work-in-progress – indirect labour to production overheads – administration labour to non-production overhead

STUDENT ACTIVITIES

The answers to these Student Activities are printed in the back of this book. Further questions and more fully extended Student Activities and Assessments are to be found in the accompanying Osborne Books' text *Costing, Reports & Returns Workbook*.

3.1 A manufacturing business pays its production workers on a time rate basis. A bonus is paid where production is completed faster than the standard hour output; the bonus is paid at half of the time rate for production time saved. How much will each of the following employees earn for the week?

Employee	Time rate	Hours worked	Standard hour output	Actual production
N Ball	£8.00 per hour	35	30 units	1,010 units
T Smith	£9.00 per hour	37	40 units	1,560 units
L Lewis	£10.00 per hour	40	20 units	855 units
M Wilson	£7.00 per hour	38	24 units	940 units

3.2 Harrison & Company is a manufacturing business. Currently it pays its production-line workers on a time rate basis. Recently the employee representatives have approached the management of the company with a view to seeking alternative methods of remuneration. Suggestions have been made that either a piecework system, or a time rate with a production bonus system would be more appropriate.

The office manager has asked you, as an Accounting Technician, to draft a memorandum to the management giving advantages and disadvantages of:

• time rate

• piecework

• time rate, plus production bonus

as methods of remunerating production-line employees. In particular, you are asked to describe two circumstances under which the piecework basis would not be in the interests of employees.

3.3 **(a)** A company pays its production-line employees on a piecework basis, but with a guaranteed time rate. How much will each of the following employees earn during the week?

Employee	Time rate	Hours worked	Production	Piecework rate
L Fry	£10.00 per hour	40	1,200 units	30p per unit
R Williams	£8.00 per hour	37	450 units	70p per unit
P Grant	£9.50 per hour	36	725 units	50p per unit

(b) What are the problems a company might face in operating a piecework system of remuneration?

3.4 Print 'n Go is a print shop that specialises in printing headed notepaper for businesses. It employs two printers, Steve Kurtin and Pete Singh. Both are paid a basic rate per hour for a 35-hour week with two overtime rates: time-and-a-third for weekdays (rate 1), and time-and-a-half for week-ends (rate 2). In addition, a production bonus is paid of 25p per 1,000 copies printed.

Details for last week are as follows:

	Steve Kurtin	Pete Singh
Basic rate per hour	£5.50	£6.50
Total hours worked	39	42
Overtime: rate 1	4	3
rate 2	–	4
Number of copies printed	45,000	57,000

You are to

• calculate the gross wages earned by each employee for last week

• calculate the piecework rate per 1,000 copies printed that would be equal to the gross wages earned by Steve Kurtin for the week, assuming the same output level of 45,000 copies.

3.5 Wyvern Fabrication Company has two departments – moulding and finishing. Data relating to labour for a four-week period is given on the labour cost card on the next page.

The company uses a bonus scheme whereby employees receive 50 per cent of the standard hours saved in each department paid at the actual labour rate per hour. This is not included in the actual wages cost (see next page), which shows actual hours multiplied by the actual wage rate.

LABOUR COST CARD for the four weeks ended 26 February 1999		
	MOULDING	FINISHING
Actual wages cost (£)	31,160	36,450
Standard hours	4,000	5,000
Actual hours	4,100	4,500
Standard hours saved		
Bonus (£)		
Total labour cost (£)		

You are to calculate the total labour cost for each department.

3.6 Last week the wages control account of Annabel's Bakery had three credit entries:

- work-in-progress   £2,100
- production overheads   £ 900
- non-production overheads £ 700

TOTAL PAYROLL FOR THE WEEK   £3,700

You are to explain the purpose of the three entries.

4 EXPENSES

this chapter covers . . .

In this chapter we examine:

- *expenses as an element of cost*
- *the distinction between capital expenditure and revenue expenditure*
- *the distinction between direct expenses and indirect expenses*
- *the nature and behaviour of fixed, semi-fixed and variable costs*

NVQ PERFORMANCE CRITERIA COVERED

unit 5: RECORDING COST INFORMATION

element 1

record and analyse information relating to direct costs

❏ *direct costs are identified in accordance with the organisation's costing procedures*

❏ *information relating to direct costs is clearly and correctly coded, analysed and recorded*

❏ *direct costs are calculated in accordance with the organisation's policies and procedures*

❏ *queries are either resolved or referred to the appropriate person*

EXPENSES – AN ELEMENT OF COST

The third main element of cost is that of expenses, ie any cost that cannot be classified as materials or labour. Expenses include items such as rent, rates, telephone, lighting, heating, royalties paid to the designer of a product, special items bought in for a particular product, etc.

It is important that expenses are categorised correctly in order that costs can be calculated accurately and accounting statements can show a true representation of the state of the business. To achieve this, as shown by the diagram below, we need to distinguish between:

- capital expenditure and revenue expenditure
- direct expenses and indirect expenses
- fixed costs and variable costs

Note that both direct and indirect expenses can be either fixed or variable in nature – see page 65.

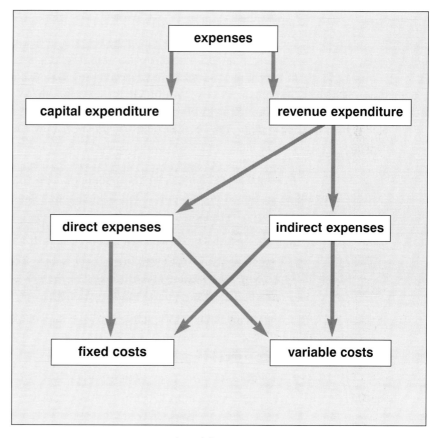

categorising expenses

CAPITAL EXPENDITURE AND REVENUE EXPENDITURE

Capital expenditure can be defined as *expenditure incurred on the purchase, alteration or improvement of fixed assets.* For example, the purchase of a car for use in the business is capital expenditure. Included in capital expenditure are costs such as:

• delivery of fixed assets

• installation of fixed assets

• improvement (but not repair) of fixed assets

• legal costs of buying property

Revenue expenditure is *expenditure incurred on running costs.* For example, the cost of petrol or diesel for the car (above) is revenue expenditure. Included in revenue expenditure are the running costs of:

• maintenance and repair of fixed assets

• making, selling and distributing the goods or products in which the business trades

• administration of the business

Capital expenditure is shown in the balance sheet, while revenue expenditure is a cost in the profit and loss account. It is important to classify these types of expenditure correctly in the accounting system. For example, if the cost of the car was shown in profit and loss account, then costs would be overstated and the net profit would be reduced considerably, or a net loss recorded; meanwhile, the balance sheet would not show the car as a fixed asset – clearly this is incorrect as the business owns the asset. Note, however, that there is a link between capital expenditure and the profit and loss account: as fixed assets are depreciated, the amount of depreciation is shown as a cost in the profit and loss account. Thus depreciation relates to the time period over which the fixed asset is used.

In some circumstances we must take care to distinguish between capital and revenue expenditure. For example:

• *cost of building an extension to the factory £30,000, which includes £1,000 for repairs to the existing factory*

   – capital expenditure, £29,000

   – revenue expenditure, £1,000 (because it is for repairs to an existing fixed asset)

• *a plot of land has been bought for £20,000, the legal costs are £750*

   Capital expenditure £20,750 (the legal costs are included in the capital expenditure, because they are the cost of acquiring the fixed asset, ie the legal costs are capitalised).

- *own employees used to install a new air conditioning system: direct labour £1,000, materials £1,500*

  Capital expenditure £2,500 (an addition to the property). Note that, in cases such as this, revenue expenditure, ie direct labour and materials purchases, will need to be reduced to allow for the transfer to capital expenditure.

- *own employees used to repair and redecorate the premises: direct labour £500, materials £750*

  Revenue expenditure £1,250 (repairs and redecoration are running expenses).

- *purchase of a new machine £10,000, payment for installation and setting up £250*

  Capital expenditure £10,250 (costs of installation and setting up of a fixed asset are capitalised).

Only by allocating capital expenditure and revenue expenditure correctly can costs be ascertained properly and the profit and loss account and balance sheet reflect accurately the financial state of the business. It is especially important to identify revenue expenditure in the costing of output; a product that is costed wrongly (for example at too high a price) may not sell well because the selling price is too expensive for buyers. Identification of capital expenditure is important for knowing the assets owned by a business, which are shown on the balance sheet.

DIRECT EXPENSES AND INDIRECT EXPENSES

For cost accounting purposes, revenue expenditure needs to be identified as either a direct expense or an indirect expense:

- direct expenses – those expenses which can be attributed to particular units of output
- indirect expenses – other expenses which cannot be attributed directly to particular units of output

direct expenses

Examples of direct expenses include:

- royalties payable to the designer of a product
- special items bought in for a particular product or job
- hire of specialist machinery/equipment for a particular product or job
- consultant's fees related to a particular product or job

- power costs of running machinery (provided that the machinery is separately metered and is used for a particular product or job)
- depreciation methods linked directly to output, eg units of output (or service) method

  The units of output (or service) method of depreciation estimates:

  - the number of units to be produced by a machine, or
  - the number of hours of operation of a machine, or
  - the number of miles/kilometres expected from a vehicle

  over its expected life. Depreciation for a given year is calculated by reference to the number of units/hours/miles for that year.

indirect expenses

Examples of indirect expenses include:

- factory and office rent and rates
- telephone costs
- power costs of running machinery (where machinery is used for a variety of products or jobs, or where power consumption is low and it is not worthwhile for the costing system to analyse the amount of the direct expense)
- heating and lighting
- insurance
- cost of running motor vehicles
- depreciation methods not linked directly to output, eg straight-line and reducing balance methods

straight-line depreciation

A fixed percentage is written off the original cost of the asset each year, calculated by reference to the useful economic life of the asset as follows:

$$\frac{\text{cost of asset – estimated residual (scrap or salvage) sale proceeds}}{\text{number of years' expected use of the asset}}$$

reducing balance depreciation

A fixed percentage is written off the reduced balance each year, the reduced balance being the cost of the asset less depreciation to date. The formula to calculate the percentage of reducing balance depreciation is:

$$r = 1 - \sqrt[n]{\frac{s}{c}}$$

where:

r = percentage rate of depreciation

n = number of years

s = salvage or scrap (residual) value

c = cost of asset

charging the cost of expenses

The cost of direct expenses – which is attributable to output – is charged to work-in-progress. The cost of indirect expenses is charged to overheads and split between:

- production overheads
- non-production overheads, such as
    - selling and distribution
    - administration
    - finance

Direct expenses are included with the costs of direct materials and direct labour to give a total of direct costs (prime cost). Indirect expenses are included in the total of indirect costs (overheads) of a business. For a service business, a major proportion of the costs are likely to be in the form of indirect costs; by contrast, a manufacturing business is likely to have a greater proportion of direct costs.

We shall look at the layout of the manufacturing account and the book-keeping for costing in Chapter 8.

FIXED AND VARIABLE COSTS

It is important in costing to appreciate the *nature of costs* – in particular to realise that not all costs increase or decrease in line with increases or decreases in output. As seen in Chapter 1 (page 9), all costs, by nature, are:

- fixed, or
- semi-fixed (also known as semi-variable), or
- variable

fixed costs

Fixed costs remain constant over a range of output levels, despite other changes – for example, insurance, rent, rates. In the form of a graph, they appear as follows:

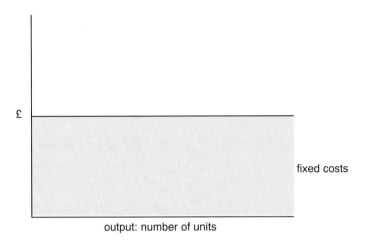

output: number of units

Note that money amounts are shown on the vertical axis and units of output on the horizontal axis.

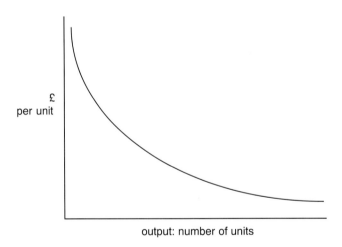

output: number of units

For fixed costs, the *cost per unit* falls as output increases, as follows:

For example, with rent of £40,000 per year:

- at output of 4,000 units, equals £10 per unit
- at output of 10,000 units, equals £4 per unit

Whilst it is sensible to seek to achieve maximum output in order to reduce the cost per unit, fixed costs do not remain fixed at all levels of production. For example, a decision to double production is likely to increase the fixed costs – an increase in factory rent, for example, because an additional factory may need to be rented. Fixed costs are often described as *stepped fixed costs*, because they increase by a large amount all at once; graphically, the cost behaviour is shown as a step:

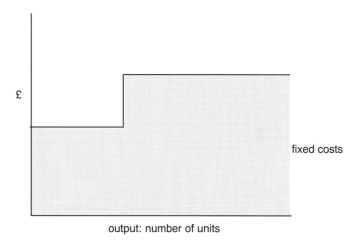

semi-fixed costs

These combine both a fixed and a variable element. For example, a telephone bill comprises the fixed rental for the line, together with the variable element of call charges. Such a *mixed cost* is expressed graphically as:

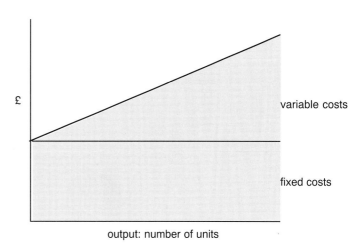

variable costs

Variable costs alter directly with changes in output levels, ie as activity increases, then the cost increases. Examples include direct materials, direct labour, direct expenses such as royalties. Graphically, variable costs appear as follows:

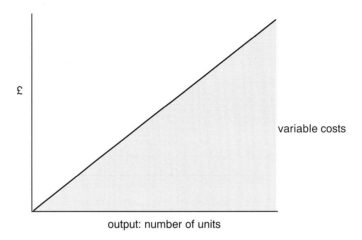

For example, a record company paying a royalty of £1 for each compact disc (CD) produced:

- at output of 1,000 CDs, equals variable cost of £1,000
- at output of 10,000 CDs, equals variable cost of £10,000

The cost per unit remains constant at all levels of output, as follows:

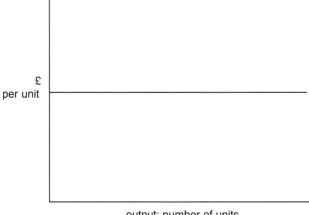

FIXED AND VARIABLE COSTS IN DECISION MAKING

Identifying costs as being fixed, semi-fixed or variable helps with decision making – the business might be able to alter the balance between fixed and variable costs in order to increase profits. A product could be made:

- either, by using a labour-intensive process, with a large number of employees supported by basic machinery
- or, by using expensive machinery in an automated process with very few employees

In the first case, the cost structure will be high variable costs (direct labour) and low fixed costs (depreciation of machinery – assuming that straight-line or reducing balance depreciation methods are used). In the second case, there will be low variable costs, and high fixed costs. Management will need to examine the relationship between the costs – together with the likely sales figures, and the availability of finance with which to buy the machinery – before making a decision.

More specifically, a knowledge of the nature of costs can be used to help management to:

- identify the element of fixed costs within total costs
- prepare schedules of budgeted production costs

IDENTIFYING THE ELEMENT OF FIXED COSTS

Where the total costs are known at two levels of output, the element of fixed costs can be identified using the 'high/low' technique.

example

- at output of 1,000 units, total costs are £7,000
- at output of 2,000 units, total costs are £9,000

What are the fixed costs?

Using the 'high/low' technique to identify the fixed costs:

- The high output and costs are deducted from the low output and costs, as follows:

	high output	2,000 units	£9,000
less	low output	1,000 units	£7,000
equals	difference	1,000 units	£2,000

- The amount of the variable cost per unit is now calculated as:

$$\frac{\text{change in cost}}{\text{change in units}} \quad = \quad \frac{£2,000}{1,000} \quad = \quad £2 \text{ variable cost per unit}$$

- Therefore, at 1,000 units of output the cost structure is:

	total cost	£7,000
less	variable costs (1,000 units x £2 per unit)	£2,000
equals	fixed costs	£5,000

- Check this now at 2,000 units of output when the cost structure is:

	variable costs (2,000 units x £2 per unit)	£4,000
add	fixed costs (as above)	£5,000
equals	total costs	£9,000

Note that the 'high/low' technique can only be used when variable costs increase by the same money amount for each extra unit of output (ie there is a linear relationship), and where there are no stepped fixed costs.

SCHEDULES OF BUDGETED PRODUCTION COSTS

Where fixed and variable costs are known for the three elements of costs – materials, labour and expenses – at a particular level of output, it is relatively simple to calculate what the costs will be at changed levels of output. For example, if variable materials costs at an output of 1,000 units are £2,000 then, at an output of 1,100 units, they will be £2,200 (ie a 10 per cent increase in both output and cost). By contrast, the fixed expense of factory rent of, say, £5,000 will be unchanged if output increases by 10 per cent. (Note that such calculations assume a linear relationship for variable costs and that there are no stepped fixed costs.)

Such changes in costs can be incorporated, as part of a business' planning process, into a formal schedule of *budgeted production costs*. This calculates total production cost and the cost per unit at changed (either increased or decreased) levels of output, as shown in the Case Study which follows.

SPEEDPEN LTD: BUDGETED PRODUCTION COSTS

situation

Speedpen Limited, which manufactures quality rollerball pens, has budgeted its production costs for 1999 on the basis of an output of 100,000 units as follows:

			£
•	variable costs	– materials	75,000
		– labour	50,000
		– expenses	10,000
•	fixed costs	– labour	22,500
		– overheads	33,500

The sales department thinks that demand for the product is more likely to be 110,000 units, or could be as high as 125,000 units.

You have been asked to prepare a budgeted cost schedule based on outputs of 100,000 units, 110,000 units and 125,000 units. The cost schedule is to show total production cost and the cost per unit at each level of output.

solution

1999	BUDGETED PRODUCTION COSTS		
UNITS	100,000	110,000	125,000
COSTS	£	£	£
Variable costs			
Materials	75,000	82,500	93,750
Labour	50,000	55,000	62,500
Expenses	10,000	11,000	12,500
	135,000	148,500	168,750
Fixed costs			
Labour	22,500	22,500	22,500
Overheads	33,500	33,500	33,500
	56,000	56,000	56,000
TOTAL PRODUCTION COST	191,000	204,500	224,750
COST PER UNIT	£1.91	£1.86	£1.80

Notes:

- Variable costs per unit are:

  –   materials, £0.75 (ie £75,000 ÷ 100,000 units)

  –   labour, £0.50

  –   expenses, £0.10

- At the higher levels of output simply multiply the unit costs by 110,000 and 125,000

- Fixed costs remain fixed at the higher levels of output

- Total production cost is total variable costs plus total fixed costs

- Cost per unit is total production cost divided by output (note that cost per unit has been rounded to the nearest penny)

- The costs at higher levels of output assume that:

  –   there is a linear relationship for variable costs

  –   there are no stepped fixed costs

- The fall in cost per unit as output increases occurs because the fixed costs are being spread over a greater number of units, ie the fixed cost per unit falls

CHAPTER SUMMARY

- Expenses, together with materials and labour, form the three main elements of cost.

- Expenses are categorised between:

  – capital expenditure and revenue expenditure

  – direct expenses and indirect expenses

  – fixed costs and variable costs

- Identification of revenue expenditure is important in the costing of output; identification of capital expenditure is important for knowing the assets owned by a business.

- Direct expenses are charged to work-in-progress.

- Indirect expenses are charged to overheads and split between:

  – production overheads

  – non-production overheads, such as selling and distribution, administration

KEY TERMS

- The nature of costs means that not all costs increase or decrease in line with increases or decreases in output; all costs, by nature, are:
  - fixed, or
  - semi-fixed, or
  - variable

- A knowledge of the nature of costs enables:
  - identification of the element of fixed costs within total costs
  - preparation of a schedule of budgeted production costs

capital expenditure	expenditure incurred on the purchase, alteration or improvement of fixed assets
revenue expenditure	expenditure incurred on running costs
direct expenses	those expenses that are attributable to particular units of output
indirect expenses	all other expenses which are not attributable directly to particular units of output
overheads	the indirect costs of materials, labour and expenses
fixed costs	costs which remain fixed over a range of output levels
semi-fixed costs	costs which combine a fixed and variable element
variable costs	costs which vary directly with output
'high/low' technique	method used to identify the element of fixed costs within total costs
budgeted production costs	schedule which shows the calculation of total production cost and cost per unit at particular levels of output

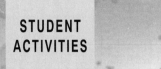

The answers to these Student Activities are printed in the back of this book. Further questions and more fully extended Student Activities and Assessments are to be found in the accompanying Osborne Books' text *Costing, Reports & Returns Workbook*.

STUDENT ACTIVITIES

4.1 Define:

(a) capital expenditure

(b) revenue expenditure

Give two examples of each.

4.2 Define:

(a) direct expenses

(b) indirect expenses

Give two examples of each.

4.3 Fred Jarvis normally works as a production-line employee of Wyevale Plastics. However, for the past four weeks he has been building an extension to the company's warehouse.

How should his wages for this period be dealt with in the accounts? Why is this?

4.4 Explain the nature of the costs, as shown by the following graphs:

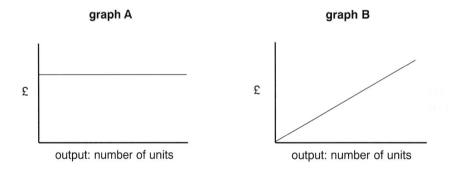

graph A

graph B

£

output: number of units

£

output: number of units

Graph (a) shows the cost of the rent of a factory.

Graph (b) shows the wages of production-line employees who are paid on a piecework basis.

4.5 Classify the following costs (tick the appropriate column):

		capital expenditure	revenue expenditure
(a)	purchase of motor vehicles		
(b)	depreciation of motor vehicles		
(c)	payment of office rent		
(d)	salaries of office staff		
(e)	legal fees relating to the purchase of property		
(f)	re-decoration of office		
(g)	installation of air-conditioning in office		
(h)	wages of own employees used to build extension to the stockroom		
(i)	installation and setting up of a new machine		

4.6 Classify the following costs (tick the appropriate column):

		direct expenses	indirect expenses	either*
(a)	hire of machinery for a particular job			
(b)	office rent			
(c)	cleaning materials			
(d)	power costs			
(e)	royalty paid to designer for each unit of output			
(f)	sales staff car expenses			
(g)	depreciation of production machinery			
(h)	consultant's fees relating to a particular job			
(i)	heating and lighting			

*explain (on a separate sheet of paper) your reasons for classifying costs in this column

4.7 Classify the following costs (tick the appropriate column):

		fixed	semi-fixed	variable
(a)	rates of business premises			
(b)	royalty paid to designer for each unit of output			
(c)	car hire with fixed rental and charge per mile			
(d)	employees paid on piecework basis			
(e)	straight-line depreciation			
(f)	units of service depreciation			
(g)	direct materials			
(h)	telephone bill with fixed rental and charge per unit			
(i)	office salaries			

4.8   Eveshore Pottery Limited manufactures a range of 'souvenir' mugs, cups and saucers, plates, etc, which sell well to visitors from abroad who are seeking a memento of 'Olde England'. A number of different costs have been incurred during the last month, and you are asked to classify them into:

- direct materials

- indirect materials

- direct labour

- indirect labour

- direct expenses

- indirect expenses

The costs are:

(a)   cleaning materials for the machines

(b)   wages of factory supervisor

(c)   clay from which the 'pots' are made

(d)   10p royalties payable to the designer for each 'Eveshore Plate' made

(e)   salary of office clerk

(f)   electricity used to heat the kilns

(g)   rates of factory

(h)   depreciation of office equipment

(i)   wages of production-line workers

(j)   salesperson's salary

(k)   interest charged on bank overdraft

If you believe alternative classifications exist, argue the case and state if you need further information from the company.

Of the overhead costs, ie indirect materials, indirect labour and indirect expenses, you are to indicate which would be classified as:

- production overheads

- selling and distribution overheads

- administration overheads

- finance overheads

4.9 The management accountant of Nerca Manufacturing Limited has provided you with the following information:

- at 10,000 units of output, total costs are £50,000

- at 15,000 units of output, total costs are £65,000

You are to use the 'high/low' technique to identify the element of fixed costs. The accountant tells you that variable costs have a linear relationship, and that there are no stepped fixed costs.

4.10 Monica Manufacturing has budgeted the production costs for 1999 on the basis of an output of 250,000 units as follows:

		£
variable costs	– materials	400,000
	– labour	325,000
	– expenses	100,000
fixed costs	– labour	96,500
	– overheads	107,500

The sales department thinks that demand for the product is more likely to be 300,000 units, or could be as high as 350,000 units.

You are to prepare a schedule of budgeted production costs based on outputs of 250,000 units, 300,000 units and 350,000 units. The schedule is to show total production cost and the cost per unit at each level of output. (Note: you may assume that there is a linear relationship for variable costs, and that there are no stepped fixed costs.)

Briefly describe and explain the trend in costs per unit for the three budgeted levels of production.

5 OVERHEADS

NVQ PERFORMANCE CRITERIA COVERED

unit 5: RECORDING COST INFORMATION

element 2

record and analyse information relating to the allocation, apportionment and absorption of overhead costs

❏ *data are correctly coded, analysed and recorded*

❏ *overhead costs are established in accordance with the organisation's procedures*

❏ *information relating to overhead costs is accurately and clearly recorded*

❏ *overhead costs are correctly attributed to producing and service cost centres in accordance with agreed methods of allocation, apportionment and absorption*

❏ *adjustments for under or over recovered overhead costs are made in accordance with established procedures*

❏ *methods of allocation, apportionment and absorption are reviewed at regular intervals in discussions with senior staff, and agreed changes to methods are implemented*

❏ *staff working in operational departments are consulted to resolve any queries in the data*

OVERHEADS

The overheads of a business comprise:

- indirect materials
- indirect labour
- indirect expenses

Overheads do not relate to particular units of output but must, instead, be shared amongst all the cost units (units of output to which costs can be charged) to which they relate. For example, the cost of the factory rent must be included in the cost of the firm's output. We will see how the overheads are charged to output, and some of the difficulties that may occur.

The important point to remember is that all the overheads of a business, together with the direct costs (materials, labour and expenses) must be covered by money flowing in from sales of the firm's output.

Overheads are usually classified by function under headings such as:

- *factory or production*, eg factory rent and rates, indirect factory labour, indirect factory materials, heating and lighting of factory
- *selling and distribution,* eg salaries of sales staff, vehicle costs, delivery costs
- *administration,* eg office rent and rates, office salaries, heating and lighting of office, indirect office materials
- *finance,* eg bank interest

In order to determine how much has been spent on overheads, it will be necessary to use the accounting records: for example, the amount for rent, rates, salaries, wages, heating, lighting, vehicle costs, etc. Some figures, such as those for wages, and for purchases of materials, will need to be analysed to see which part of the total cost is a direct expense (to be charged directly to the appropriate cost units), and which is the indirect expense (to be charged to overheads).

Once the various overheads have been classified, they are then either *allocated* or *apportioned* to cost centres (sections of a business to which costs can be charged).

ALLOCATION AND APPORTIONMENT OF OVERHEADS

Allocation of overheads is the charging to a cost centre of those overheads that have been directly incurred by that cost centre.

For example, in a large organisation a whole factory might be a cost centre and so the rent and rates of that factory will be allocated to it as a separate cost centre. Another example is where a department is the cost centre; here the costs of a supervisor working solely within one department are allocated to that department.

Apportionment of production overheads is where cost centres are charged with a proportion of overheads.

For example, a department which is a cost centre within a factory will be charged a proportion of the factory rent and rates. Another example is where a supervisor works within two departments, both of which are separate cost centres: the indirect labour cost of employing the supervisor is shared between the two cost centres.

With apportionment, a suitable basis must be found to apportion production overheads between cost centres; the basis selected should be related to the responsibility for the cost being incurred. Different methods might be used for each overhead, for example:

OVERHEAD	BASIS OF APPORTIONMENT
rent, rates	floor area (or volume of space) of cost centres
heating, lighting	floor area (or volume of space) of cost centres
buildings insurance	floor area (or volume of space) of cost centres
buildings depreciation	floor area (or volume of space) of cost centres
machinery insurance	cost or net book value of machinery and equipment
canteen	number of employees (or full-time equivalents) in each cost centre
supervisory costs	number of employees, or labour hours worked by supervisors, in each cost centre

Note that apportionment is used for those overheads that cannot be allocated directly to a cost centre. For example, a college's Business Studies Department occupies a building in another part of town from the main college building: the rates for the building can be allocated to the Business Studies cost centre. By contrast, the rates for the main college building must be apportioned amongst the cost centres on the main campus.

LASER ENGINEERING LIMITED: OVERHEAD ALLOCATION AND APPORTIONMENT

situation

Laser Engineering Limited, which makes car engine components, uses some of the latest laser equipment in one department, while another section of the business continues to use traditional machinery. Details of the factory are as follows:

Department X is a 'hi-tech' machine shop equipped with laser-controlled machinery which cost £80,000. This department has 400 square metres of floor area. There are three machine operators: the supervisor spends one-third of the time in this department.

Department Y is a 'low-tech' part of the factory equipped with machinery which cost £20,000. The floor area is 600 square metres. There are two workers who spend all their time in this department: the supervisor spends two-thirds of the time in this department.

The overheads to be allocated or apportioned are as follows:

1	Factory rates	£12,000
2	Wages of the supervisor	£21,000
3	Factory heating and lighting	£2,500
4	Depreciation of machinery	£20,000
5	Buildings insurance	£2,000
6	Insurance of machinery	£1,500
7	Specialist materials for the laser equipment	£2,500

How should each of these be allocated or apportioned to each department?

solution

The recommendations are:

1 Factory rates – apportioned on the basis of floor area, ie 40% to Department X, and 60% to Department Y.

2 Supervisor's wages – apportioned on the basis of time spent, ie one-third to Department X, and two-thirds to Department Y. If the time spent was not known, an alternative basis could be established on the number of employees.

3 Factory heating and lighting – apportioned on the basis of floor area.

4 Depreciation of machinery – apportioned on the basis of machine value, ie four-fifths to Department X, and one-fifth to Department Y.

5 Buildings insurance – apportioned on the basis of floor area.

6 Insurance of machinery – apportioned on the basis of machine value.

7 Specialist materials for the laser equipment – allocated to Department X, the cost centre which directly incurred the cost.

It is important to note that there are no fixed rules for the apportionment of overheads – the only proviso is that the basis used should be equitable, ie that a fair proportion of the overhead is charged to the department which has responsibility for the cost being incurred.

The apportionment of overheads for Laser Engineering Limited is as follows:

overhead	basis of apportionment	total £	dept X £	dept Y £
Factory rates	Floor area	12,000	4,800	7,200
Wages of supervisor	Time spent	21,000	7,000	14,000
Heating and lighting	Floor area	2,500	1,000	1,500
Dep'n of machinery	Machine value	20,000	16,000	4,000
Buildings insurance	Floor area	2,000	800	1,200
Machinery insurance	Machine value	1,500	1,200	300
Specialist materials	Allocation	2,500	2,500	–
		61,500	33,300	28,200

Note that overhead apportionment is often, in practice, calculated using a computer spreadsheet.

SERVICE DEPARTMENTS

Many businesses have departments which provide services within the business; for example, maintenance, transport, stores or stationery, etc. Each service department is likely to be a cost centre, to which a proportion of overheads is charged. As service departments do not themselves have any cost units to which their overheads may be charged, the costs of each service department must be re-apportioned to the production departments (which do have cost units to which overheads can be charged). A suitable basis of re-allocation must be used, for example:

- the overheads of a maintenance department might be re-apportioned to production departments on the basis of value of machinery or equipment, or on the basis of time spent in each production department

- the overheads of a stores or stationery department could be re-apportioned on the basis of value of goods issued to production departments

- the overheads of a subsidised canteen could be re-apportioned on the basis of the number of employees

Re-apportionment of service department overheads is considered in the next section.

The diagram below summarises the ways in which overheads are allocated or apportioned to production cost centres, together with the re-apportionment of the service department's costs.

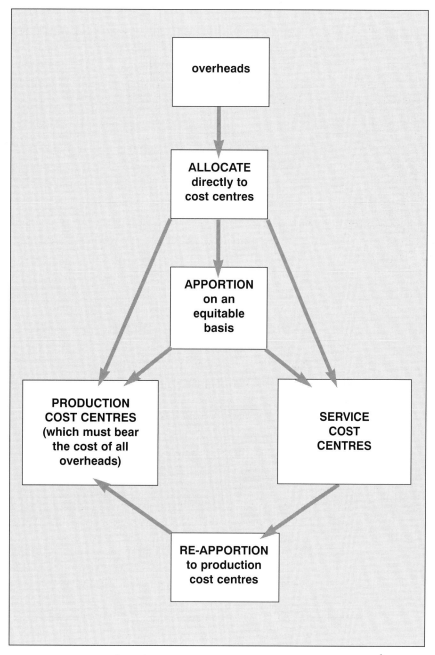

allocation and apportionment of overheads

RE-APPORTIONMENT OF SERVICE DEPARTMENT OVERHEADS

The overheads of service departments are charged to production cost centres using different techniques depending on the complexity of the business:

- direct apportionment is used where service departments provide services to production departments only

- the step-down method is used where service departments provide services to both production departments and to some other service departments

- the reciprocal method is used where service departments provide services to both production departments and to all other service departments

To illustrate these we will apply the techniques to a business with two production departments, A and B, and two service departments, stores and maintenance. After allocation and apportionment of production overheads, the totals are:

	total	production dept A	production dept B	stores	maintenance
	£	£	£	£	£
Overheads	20,400	10,000	5,000	2,400	3,000

direct apportionment

Here the service departments do not provide services to one another. Their costs are directly apportioned to production departments using a suitable basis. In the example above:

- stores overheads are re-apportioned on the basis of the number of stores requisitions – department A has made 150 requisitions; department B has made 50

- maintenance overheads are re-apportioned on the value of machinery – department A has machinery with a net book value of £20,000, department B's machinery has a value of £10,000

Using direct apportionment, the overheads of the service departments are re-apportioned as shown on the next page:

	total	production dept A	production dept B	stores	maintenance
	£	£	£	£	£
Overheads	20,400	10,000	5,000	2,400	3,000
Stores	–	1,800	600	(2,400)	–
Maintenance	–	2,000	1,000	–	(3,000)
	20,400	13,800	6,600	–	–

Thus all the overheads have now been charged to the production departments where they can be absorbed into the cost units which form the output of each department.

step-down method

This is used where, as well as to production departments, one service department provides services to another, but there is no reciprocation of services. Using the example, the stores department deals with requisitions from the maintenance department, but no maintenance work is carried out in the stores department. Under the step-down method we re-apportion firstly the overheads of the stores department (because it does not receive any reciprocal services from the maintenance department), and secondly the overheads of the maintenance department:

- stores requisitions – department A, 150; department B, 50; maintenance, 50
- value of machinery – department A, £20,000; department B, £10,000

The re-apportionment of the production overheads of the service departments, using the step-down method, is as follows:

	total	production dept A	production dept B	stores	maintenance
	£	£	£	£	£
Overheads	20,400	10,000	5,000	2,400	3,000
Stores	–	1,440	480	(2,400)	480
				–	3,480
Maintenance	–	2,320	1,160	–	(3,480)
	20,400	13,760	6,640	–	–

All of the overheads have now been charged to the production departments.

reciprocal method

This is used where service departments provide services to all other departments, including other service departments. Thus, in the example, the stores department deals with requisitions from the maintenance department, and there is a reciprocal service of maintenance provided to stores. The apportionment of production overheads to production departments is carried out by repeating the re-apportionment of service department overheads:

- stores requisitions – department A, 150; department B, 50; maintenance, 50
- value of machinery – department A, £20,000; department B, £10,000; stores, £10,000

The re-apportionment, using the reciprocal method, can be calculated *manually* (shown below) or by using *formulas* (see opposite page).

	total	production dept A	production dept B	stores	maintenance
	£	£	£	£	£
Overheads	20,400	10,000	5,000	2,400	3,000
Stores	–	1,440	480	(2,400)	480
				–	3,480
Maintenance	–	1,740	870	870	(3,480)
Stores	–	522	174	(870)	174
Maintenance	–	87	44	43	(174)
Stores	–	32	11	(43)	–
	20,400	13,821	6,579	–	–

All of the overheads have now been charged to the production departments:

	£
department A	13,821
department B	6,579
	20,400

Inevitably, with the reciprocal method, some rounding of money amounts is necessary. Once the repeated re-apportionment brings service department overheads to small amounts, it is best to make one final re-apportionment to production departments only (as has been done here with stores).

reciprocal method using formulas

1 The overheads of each department (production and service) are set out as formulas:

Production department A: £10,000 + 0.6 stores + 0.5 maintenance

Production department B: £5,000 + 0.2 stores + 0.25 maintenance

Stores service department: £2,400 + 0.25 maintenance

Maintenance department: £3,000 + 0.2 stores

Note: the proportions for stores and maintenance are based respectively on the number of stores requisitions and the value of machinery.

2 The amount of stores overheads is calculated as:

£2,400 + 0.25 (£3,000 + 0.2 stores) = £2,400 + £750 + 0.05 stores

Therefore 0.95 stores = £3,150

So stores = £3,316 (ie £3,150 ÷ 0.95)

3 Knowing the amount of stores overheads, the amount of maintenance overheads can now be calculated as:

£3,000 + 0.2 stores = £3,000 + (0.2 x £3,316) = £3,000 + £663 = £3,663

4 Thus the amounts of overhead charged to the production departments are:

Department A: £10,000 + (0.6 x £3,316) + (0.5 x £3,663)
= £10,000 + £1,990 + £1,831 = £13,821

Department B: £5,000 + (0.2 x £3,316) + (0.25 x £3,663)
= £5,000 + £663 + £916 = £6,579

As can be seen, all of the overheads are now charged to the production departments. Note that there are often small rounding differences between the two methods of calculation explained here.

OVERHEAD ABSORPTION

Once overheads have been allocated or apportioned to production cost centres, the final step is to ensure that the overheads are charged to cost units. In the language of cost accounting this is known as *absorption,* ie the cost of overheads is charged to the cost units which pass through that particular production department. Thus the overheads are passed to the customer in a two-stage process:

1   the overheads are transferred from the cost centre to the cost units

2   the cost of each cost unit forms part of the selling price (non-production overheads – see page 99 – and profit form the other part)

There are plenty of examples of overhead absorption in everyday life – it is not something used solely by manufacturing businesses. For example, if you take a car to be repaired at a garage, the bill will be presented as follows:

Parts	£70.00
Labour: 3 hours at £30 per hour	£90.00
Total	£160.00

Within this example bill are the three main elements of cost: materials (parts), labour and overheads. The last two are combined as labour – the garage mechanic is not paid £30 per hour; instead the labour rate might be £10 per hour, with the rest, ie £20 per hour, being a contribution towards the overheads and profit of the garage. Other examples are accountants, solicitors, etc who charge a 'rate per hour', part of which is used to contribute to the cost of overheads and profit.

In order to absorb the overheads of a department, there are two steps to be followed:

1   calculation of the overhead absorption rate (OAR)

2   application of this rate to cost units

Although there are a variety of methods available to a business, three traditionally used (and still popular) overhead absorption rates are based on:

•   units of output

•   direct labour hour

•   machine hour

units of output

Using this method, production overhead is absorbed on the basis of each unit of output.

1   *Calculation of the overhead absorption rate:*

$$\frac{\text{total cost centre overheads}}{\text{total cost units}} = \text{cost per unit}$$

2   *Application of the rate:*

cost units x overhead absorption rate = overhead absorbed

Example

Department A   total cost centre overheads for year   £100,000

expected total output for year   20,000 units

output in March   1,500 units

1   *Overhead absorption rate:*

$$\frac{£100,000}{20,000 \text{ units}} = £5.00 \text{ per unit}$$

2   *Application of the rate:*

1,500 units x £5.00 = £7,500 of overhead absorbed in March

direct labour hour

With this method, production overhead is absorbed on the basis of the number of direct labour hours worked.

1   *Calculation of the overhead absorption rate:*

$$\frac{\text{total cost centre overheads}}{\text{total direct labour hours (in cost centre)}} = \text{cost per direct labour hour}$$

2   *Application of the rate:*

direct labour hours worked x overhead absorption rate = overhead absorbed

Example

Department B   total cost centre overheads for year   £40,000

expected direct labour for year   5,000

actual direct labour hours in March   450

1   *Overhead absorption rate:*

$$\frac{£40,000}{5,000 \text{ hours}} = £8 \text{ per direct labour hour}$$

2   *Application of the rate:*

450 hours x £8 = £3,600 of overhead absorbed in March

machine hour

Here the production overhead is absorbed on the basis of machine hours.

1 *Calculation of the overhead absorption rate:*

$$\frac{\text{total cost centre overheads}}{\text{total machine hours (in cost centre)}} = \text{cost per machine hour}$$

2 *Application of the rate:*

machine hours worked x overhead absorption rate = overhead absorbed

Example

Department C	total cost centre overheads for year	£216,000
	expected machine hours for year	36,000
	actual machine hours in March	3,500

1   *Overhead absorption rate:*

$$\frac{£216,000}{36,000 \text{ hours}} = £6 \text{ per machine hour}$$

2   *Application of the rate:*

3,500 hours x £6 = £21,000 of overhead absorbed in March

which method to use?

Only one overhead absorption rate will be used in a particular department, and the method selected must relate to the reason why the costs are incurred. For example, a cost centre which is machine based, where most of the overheads incurred relate to machinery, will use a machine hour basis.

Where units of production are identical, eg in a factory, the units of output method is appropriate. However, it would be entirely unsuitable where different types and sizes of products pass through the same department, because each unit would be charged the same rate.

The direct labour hour method is a very popular method (eg the garage mentioned earlier) because overheads are absorbed on a time basis. Thus the cost unit that requires twice the direct labour of another cost unit will be charged twice the overhead. However this method will be inappropriate where some units are worked on by hand while others quickly pass through a machinery process and require little direct labour time.

A machine hour rate is particularly appropriate where expensive machinery is used in the department. However, it would be unsuitable where not all products pass through the machine but some are worked on by hand: in the latter case, no overheads would be charged to the cost units.

It is important to select the best method of overhead absorption for the particular business, otherwise wrong decisions will be made on the basis of the costing information. As overheads are often incurred on a time basis, they are traditionally absorbed in this way, eg by direct labour hour and machine hour rates. Activity based costing (see pages 94 to 99) is a costing system which adopts a different approach to overhead absorption: it relates overheads to output on the basis of activities.

Alternative overhead absorption methods can be based on a percentage of certain costs such as direct materials, direct labour, prime cost, eg 20 per cent of prime cost.

PRE-DETERMINED OVERHEAD RATES

Overhead absorption rates are set *in advance* by making forecasts of production and costs. However, it is quite likely that actual overhead absorbed will be different from the estimates made at the beginning of the year. Thus overhead will be either *under-absorbed*, or *over-absorbed;* under-absorption means that less overhead has been recovered than has been incurred; over-absorption means that more overhead has been recovered than incurred.

Example
Department D

overhead absorption rate (based on units of output)	£6.00 per unit
expected total output for year	6,000 units
actual output in year	6,300 units

- Total overheads for the department are 6,000 units x £6.00 per unit = £36,000
- Actual overhead absorbed: 6,300 units x £6.00 per unit = £37,800
- Over-absorption of overhead: £37,800 - £36,000 = £1,800

Where there is over-absorption of overheads, the amount is

- debited to production overheads account
- credited to profit and loss account

Thus over-absorption of overheads seems, on first impressions, to be a 'bonus' for a business – profits will be higher; however, it should be remembered that the overhead rate may have been set too high. As a consequence, sales might have been lost because the selling price has been too high.

Under-absorption of overheads is

- credited to production overheads account
- debited to profit and loss account

Here the amount of under-absorbed overheads adds to the total cost of production, and so to reduced profits.

We shall look in more detail at the book-keeping for over-absorption and under-absorption of overheads in Chapter 8.

ACTIVITY BASED COSTING

Activity based costing (ABC) charges production overheads to output on the basis of activities.

As we have seen, traditional costing systems usually charge production overheads to output on the basis of methods such as units of output, direct labour hours (or labour cost), machine hours, etc. While this method may be suitable for production-line industries which are labour intensive, or where production requires the use of heavy machinery, it is not always appropriate for today's capital intensive, low-labour industries, as demonstrated in the example which follows.

Example

A company manufactures two products, Dexet and Exet. Dexet is produced on a labour-intensive production line, using basic machinery; Exet is produced using the latest 'state of the art' computer-controlled machinery, which requires few employees.

The company's elements of cost are:

direct materials

Dexet	£250,000
Exet	£250,000
Total	£500,000

direct labour

Dexet	£200,000	(20,000 hours at £10 per hour)
Exet	£50,000	(5,000 hours at £10 per hour)
Total	£250,000	

overheads (fixed)   £250,000

Note: a major proportion of the overheads relates to maintenance and depreciation of the computer controlled machinery used to make Exet.

The company uses direct labour hours as the basis by which to charge overheads to production. Therefore, the overheads will be split between the two products as:

overhead for Dexet = four-fifths (ie 20,000/25,000 hours) of total overheads of £250,000 = £200,000

overhead for Exet = one-fifth (ie 5,000/25,000 hours) of total overheads of £250,000 = £50,000

Thus, the majority of the overhead is charged to the labour-intensive production line (Dexet), and relatively little to the capital intensive line (Exet). As a major proportion of the costs relates to Exet, this has the effect of undercosting this product (and overcosting Dexet). Instead, activity based costing, with its use of cost drivers, will provide an alternative to traditional overhead absorption methods.

the framework of activity based costing

Activity based costing (ABC) charges overheads to output by means of cost pools and cost drivers.

Cost pools are collections of costs linked to particular activities.

Cost drivers are activities which cause costs to be incurred.

In the example looked at above, the cost driver used to charge overheads to output was – inappropriately – direct labour hours; this caused the product Dexet to bear a higher proportion of overheads than it had incurred. Instead of using a cost driver linked to the number of hours, activity based costing uses cost drivers linked to the way in which the business is conducted and, hence, the activities that cause costs to be incurred.

The framework of ABC is a two-stage process:

- Stage 1 is to collect together overhead costs into an appropriate activity cost pool, eg materials procurement (purchasing), materials handling, setting up of machines.

- Stage 2 is to select an appropriate cost driver and to calculate a cost driver rate – eg cost per purchase order, cost per materials movement, cost per set up – at which to charge to the output on the basis of the number of activities incurred.

The diagram below shows these stages of ABC, with examples of activity cost pools and cost driver rates.

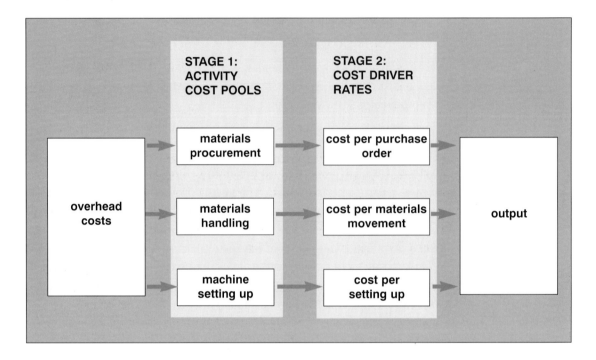

activity based costing, with examples of cost pools and cost driver rates

Cost driver rates are calculated as follows:

$$\frac{\text{activity cost pool (£s)}}{\text{cost drivers (number)}} = \text{cost driver rate}$$

For example, if the overhead costs of procurement are £30,000 to process 1,000 purchase orders, then the cost driver rate is:

$$\frac{£30,000}{1,000} = £30 \text{ per purchase order}$$

In ABC, the selection of cost drivers is important as they must have a close relationship with activities, which can then be charged to output through the cost driver rate. Examples of activities and their cost drivers are shown on the next page.

activity	cost driver
materials procurement (purchasing)	number of purchase orders
processing sales invoices	number of invoices
machine setting up	number of set-ups
machine maintenance	number of maintenance hours
canteen/restaurant	number of meals served
hotel housekeeping (accommodation)	number of guests
car park	number of vehicles parked
parcel delivery	number of parcels
trains/boats/planes	number of passengers

As these examples show, activity based costing is applicable to both manufacturing and service businesses. By using ABC, the emphasis is placed on which activities cause costs. It answers the question why costs are incurred, instead of simply stating the amount of the cost for a given period. By using ABC, the responsibility for the cost is established and so steps can be taken to minimise it for the future.

The limitations of activity based costing are that common overhead costs, which are applicable to the whole business, are still absorbed on traditional lines; for example, the rent of business premises will be absorbed on the basis of floor area. It is also important to ensure that the costs of obtaining data for ABC do not outweigh the benefits of the method.

The Case Study which follows demonstrates the use of ABC.

CASE STUDY

EVESHORE ENGINEERING: ACTIVITY BASED COSTING

situation

Eveshore Engineering manufactures two products, Alphatron and Betatron. Alphatron is produced in batches of 500 units of output; Betatron is produced in batches of 100 units of output. Each unit of production – whether Alphatron or Betatron – requires one direct labour hour.

Production of each batch of Alphatron and Betatron requires the following overheads:

• the machinery to be set-up at a cost of £400 per batch (to cover the engineer's time, test running of the machinery, etc)

• quality inspection at a cost of £200 per batch (to cover the inspector's time, cost of rejects, etc)

In a typical week the company produces 500 units of Alphatron, ie one batch of 500 units, and 500 units of Betatron, ie five batches of 100 units. Thus the set-up and quality inspection costs for the six batches produced each week will be:

6 set-ups at £400 each	=	£2,400
6 quality inspections at £200 each	=	£1,200
TOTAL		£3,600

Note: each 'box' represents one set-up and one quality inspection

As each unit of output requires one direct labour hour, ie Alphatron 500 hours, Betatron 500 hours, the overhead costs of set-ups and quality inspection, using traditional costing systems, will be charged to output as follows:

Alphatron	=	£1,800
Betatron	=	£1,800
TOTAL		£3,600

The company has recently appointed a new accountant; she questions whether the company is using the correct basis on which to charge overheads to output. The problem is that Alphatron requires just one set-up and one quality inspection each week, while Betatron requires five set-ups and five quality inspections.

solution

By using activity based costing, with set-ups and inspections as cost drivers, the accountant shows that overheads can be charged as follows:

Alphatron

1 set-up at £400	=	£400
1 quality inspection at £200	=	£200
TOTAL		£600

Betatron

5 set-ups at £400	=	£2,000
5 quality inspections at £200	=	£1,000
TOTAL		£3,000

By using activity based costing, there is a more accurate reflection of the cost of demand on the support functions of set-up and quality inspection: it reduces the cost of 500 units of Alphatron by £1,200 (ie £1,800 – £600) and increases the cost of 500 units of Betatron by £1,200 (ie from £1,800 to £3,000). This may have implications for the viability of Betatron, and for the selling prices of both products.

ABSORPTION OF NON-PRODUCTION OVERHEADS

This chapter has focussed on the allocation and apportionment of production overheads so that they are absorbed into the units of output. However, all businesses also have non-production overheads incurred by cost centres, eg:

- selling and distribution
- administration
- finance
- marketing
- research and development

The overheads of these cost centres must also be recovered through the selling price. However, there is often a difficulty in relating these non-production overheads to units of output. Instead they are usually absorbed by relating them to the production cost, or the sales value, of the output.

Example

	£
Production cost of output	100,000
Non-production overheads	20,000

- Non-production overheads will be absorbed by adding 20 per cent (£20,000 ÷ £100,000) to production cost.
- Thus, if a particular batch of output had a production cost of £5,000, then the total cost would be calculated as:

	£	
Production cost of output	5,000	
Non-production overheads	1,000	(20 per cent of £5,000)
Total cost	6,000	

Note that, as with production overheads, absorption rates for non-production overheads are set in advance; thus a pre-determined rate is used for their recovery.

- Overheads are the indirect costs of a business which do not relate to particular units of output. They are classified by function, such as:
  - factory, or production
  - selling and distribution
  - administration
  - finance

- Production overheads are allocated to cost centres that have directly incurred the overhead.

- Production overheads are apportioned between cost centres, using a suitable basis, eg floor area, value of machinery, number of employees.

- Service department overheads are re-apportioned to production departments using different techniques:
  - direct apportionment
  - step-down method
  - reciprocal method

- Cost centre overheads are charged to cost units by means of an overhead absorption rate (OAR) such as:
  - units of output
  - direct labour hour
  - machine hour

- The objective of an OAR is to ensure that overheads are recovered by the cost units which pass through the cost centre.

- With pre-determined overhead rates, there may be:
  - either under-absorption of overheads
  - or over-absorption of overheads

- Activity based costing (ABC) is used to charge production overheads to output on the basis of cost drivers.

overheads	indirect materials + indirect labour + indirect expenses
allocation of overheads	the charging to a cost centre of those overheads that have been directly incurred by that cost centre
apportionment of overheads	the charging to a cost centre of a proportion of overheads
service department	a cost centre that provides services within the business to other cost centres

re-apportionment of overheads	the charging of service department overheads to production departments
overhead absorption	the charging of overheads to cost units
overhead absorption rate (OAR)	the rate used to charge overheads to cost units; may be based on: — units of output — direct labour hour — machine hour — other methods
pre-determined overhead rate	an OAR that is set in advance by making forecasts of production and costs
activity based costing (ABC)	the charging of overheads to output on the basis of activities
cost pools	collections of costs linked to particular activities
cost drivers	activities which cause costs to be incurred

STUDENT ACTIVITIES

The answers to these Student Activities are printed in the back of this book. Further questions and more fully extended Student Activities and Assessments are to be found in the accompanying Osborne Books' text *Costing, Reports & Returns Workbook*.

5.1 Distinguish between:
- allocation of overheads
- apportionment of overheads

5.2 Wyvern Fabrication Company has two production departments – moulding and finishing.

The company charges overheads on the basis of machine hours and the following overhead analysis information is available to you (note that service department overheads have already been apportioned to production departments):

OVERHEAD ANALYSIS SHEET		
	MOULDING	FINISHING
Budgeted total overheads (£)	9,338	3,298
Budgeted machine hours	1,450	680
Budgeted overhead absorption rate (£)		

Details of a particular job of work are as follows:

JOB OVERHEAD ANALYSIS SHEET		
	MOULDING	FINISHING
Job machine hours	412	154
Budgeted overhead absorption rate (£)		
Overhead absorbed by job (£)		

You are to:

(a) Calculate the overhead absorption rate for each of the two departments and complete the overhead analysis sheet.

(b) Calculate the production overhead absorbed by the job and complete the job overhead analysis sheet.

(c) Suggest two other overhead absorption rates that the company might use and comment on the circumstances that would make them appropriate.

5.3 ABC Limited is a manufacturing business with three cost centres: Departments A, B and C. The following are the expected factory expenses for the forthcoming year:

Rent and rates	£7,210
Depreciation of machinery	£10,800
Supervisor's salary	£12,750
Insurance of machinery	£750

Departmental information is:

	Dept A	Dept B	Dept C
Floor area (sq m)	300	150	250
Value of machinery	£25,000	£15,000	£10,000
Number of production-line employees	8	4	3

You are to:

(a) Apportion the expenses to the cost centres, stating the basis of apportionment.

(b) Calculate the overhead absorption rate (to two decimal places) of each department, based on direct labour hours. Note that the factory works a 37 hour week for 48 weeks in a year.

5.4 Wye Engineering Limited offers specialist engineering services to the car industry. It has two production departments – machining and finishing – and a service department which maintains the machinery of both departments. Expected production overheads for the forthcoming year are:

	£
Rent and rates	5,520
Buildings insurance	1,320
Insurance of machinery	1,650
Lighting and heating	3,720
Depreciation of machinery	11,000
Supervisory salaries	30,000
Maintenance department salary	16,000
Factory cleaning	4,800

The following information is available:

	Machining	Finishing	Maintenance
Floor area (square metres)	300	200	100
Number of employees	6	3	1
Value of machinery	£40,000	£15,000	–

The factory works a 35 hour week for 47 weeks each year.

You are to:

(a) Prepare an analysis of production overheads showing the basis of allocation and apportionment to the three departments of the business.

(b) Re-apportion the service department overheads to production departments on the basis of value of machinery.

(c) Calculate an overhead absorption rate based on direct labour hours for each of the two production departments.

(d) Discuss alternative overhead absorption rates that the company could use.

5.5 Mercia Tutorial College has two teaching departments – business studies and general studies – and two service departments – administration and technical support. The overheads of each department are as follows:

	£
• business studies	40,000
• general studies	20,000
• administration	9,600
• technical support	12,000

The basis for re-apportioning the overheads of the service departments is:

- administration, on the number of students in the teaching departments – business studies, 500; general studies, 250

- technical support, on the value of equipment in each department – business studies, £50,000; general studies, £25,000; administration, £25,000

You are to use the step-down method to re-apportion the two service department overheads to the two teaching departments.

5.6 Cradley Cider Company has two production departments – Triple X and Scrumpy – and two service departments – stores and maintenance. The overheads of each department are as follows:

	£
Triple X	20,000
Scrumpy	10,000
Stores	5,000
Maintenance	6,000

The basis for re-apportioning the overheads of the service departments is:

- stores, on the number of requisitions – Triple X, 120; Scrumpy, 40; maintenance, 40

- maintenance, on the value of equipment in each department – Triple X, £25,000; Scrumpy, £20,000; stores, £5,000

You are to use the reciprocal method* to re-apportion the two service department overheads to the two production departments.

* use either method, as explained in the chapter

5.7 Rossiter and Rossiter is a firm of chartered accountants, with two partners. Overhead costs for next year are estimated to be:

	£
Office rent	10,000
Secretarial salaries	30,000
Rates	4,800
Heating and lighting	2,400
Stationery	2,000
Postage and telephone	5,100
Car expenses	5,600

The two partners plan to work for 47 weeks next year. They will each be in the office for 40 hours per week, but will be working on behalf of their clients for 35 hours per week.

(a)   What is the overhead absorption rate per partner hour?

(b)   If each partner wishes to earn a salary of £30,000 per year, what is the combined hourly rate per partner, which includes overheads and their salaries?

(c)   If both partners actually work on their clients' behalf for 37 hours per week, what will be the total over-absorption of overheads for the year?

5.8 A friend of yours is about to start in business making garden seats. She plans to make two different qualities – 'Standard' and 'De Luxe'. Costs per unit for direct materials and labour are expected to be:

	Standard	De Luxe
	£	£
Direct materials	12.50	20.00
Direct labour:		
3 hours at £8.00 per hour	24.00	–
3.5 hours at £10.00 per hour	–	35.00
	36.50	55.00
Machine hours	1	2.5

Production overheads are expected to be £1,000 per month.

Production is expected to be 80 'Standard' seats and 40 'De Luxe' seats per month.

(a) Suggest three different methods by which overheads can be absorbed.

(b) Calculate the production cost of each of the two qualities of garden seats using the three different methods of overhead absorption.

(c) Compare the results of your calculations and suggest to your friend the most appropriate method of overhead absorption for this business.

5.9 Define:

(a) cost pools

(b) cost drivers

Give two examples of each.

5.10 Mereford Manufacturing makes two products, Exe and Wye. Product Exe is made in batches of 10,000 units and Product Wye is made in batches of 1,000 units. Each batch has the following set-up and quality inspection costs:

- set-up £250

- quality inspection £150

Each week, the company produces 50,000 units of Exe and 50,000 units of Wye. At present the company charges overheads to output on the basis of labour hours which are 500 hours per week for Exe and 500 hours for Wye.

(a) calculate the overheads charged to Exe and Wye each week, on the basis of labour hours

(b) calculate the overheads charged to Exe and Wye each week, using activity based costing with the cost drivers of set-up and quality inspection

(c) write a memorandum advising which is the more appropriate method of absorbing overheads

6 METHODS OF COSTING

this chapter covers . . .

In this chapter we examine:

- the methods of costing used by businesses to collect costs and to calculate the total cost of their output
- the costing methods of:
  - job costing
  - batch costing
  - contract costing
  - service costing
- the calculation of work-in-progress valuations

NVQ PERFORMANCE CRITERIA COVERED

unit 5: RECORDING COST INFORMATION

element 1

record and analyse information relating to direct costs

❏ direct costs are calculated in accordance with the organisation's policies and procedures

element 2

record and analyse information relating to the allocation, apportionment and absorption of overhead costs

❏ overhead costs are correctly attributed to producing and service cost centres in accordance with agreed methods of allocation, apportionment and absorption

COSTING METHODS

The *costing methods* used by business to collect costs and to calculate the total cost of their output include:

- job costing
- batch costing
- contract costing
- service costing

Each of these is used in conjunction with absorption costing to recover the cost of overheads. Remember that businesses must recover their overheads in the total price charged to their customers – this applies both to manufacturing businesses and to service industries, such as banks, shops, transport companies.

JOB COSTING

Job costing is used where:

- each job can be separately identified from other jobs
- costs are charged to the job

Thus the job becomes the cost unit to which costs are charged. Examples of job costing include engineering firms that produce 'one-offs' to the customer's specifications, printing businesses, vehicle repairs, jobbing builders, painters and decorators, etc.

The diagram on the next page shows the main steps involved in job costing. The important points are:

- each job is given a number, in order to identify it

- a separate *job cost card* (or *sheet*) is prepared for each job, listing the estimates of direct materials, direct labour, direct expenses and overheads (most businesses nowadays use a computer system to help with their costing and, in practice, the job cost card is held as a computer record on a database)

- the actual costs incurred are compared with the estimated costs, and variances between the two are analysed (there is more on variance analysis in Chapter 7); action can then be taken to correct the variances, which will help when preparing future estimates

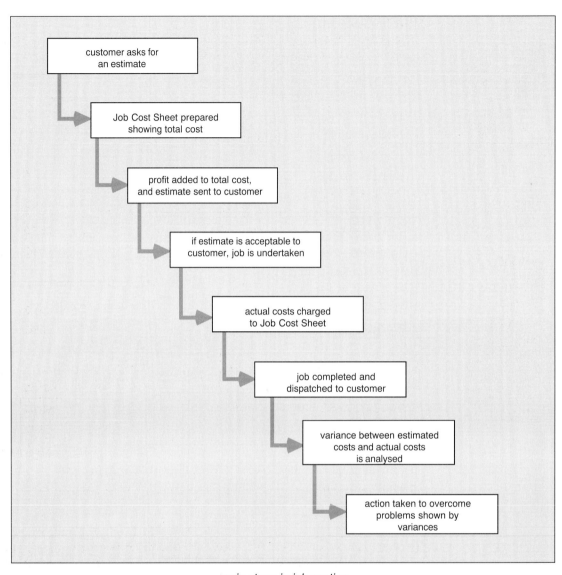

main steps in job costing

CASE STUDY

'FASHIONAID' – A CHARITY PROGRAMME

situation

The youth group at a local church has decided to organise an evening fashion show, to be called 'FashionAid'. The objective of the show is to raise money to send to a children's charity working in Central Africa. One of the organisers has asked for your help in arranging the printing of a programme for the evening's events. You approach Pearshore Printers for an estimate of the cost of printing 750 copies of a sixteen page programme.

solution

From their point of view, Pearshore Printers will allocate a number to the job. They prepare a Job Cost Sheet on their computer database as follows:

JOB NO. 6789
'FashionAid' Programme: 750 copies

	£
Direct Materials	
Paper for text: white glossart paper 135g (per square metre)	82.00
Paper for cover: coated board 200g (per square metre)	55.00
Printing plates	15.00
Direct Labour	
Printing: 5 hours at £10.00 per hour	50.00
Finishing: 2 hours at £9.00 per hour	18.00
Overheads (based on direct labour hours)	
7 hours at £20.00 per hour	140.00
TOTAL COST	360.00
Profit (15% of total cost)	54.00
SELLING PRICE	414.00

These estimated costs will be obtained as follows:

• *direct materials,* from the stores ledger records for materials already in stock, and from the firm's Purchasing Department for items that need to be bought in especially for this job

• *direct labour,* from the payroll records of the different grades of labour to be employed on this job

• *overheads,* from the pre-determined overhead absorption rate based, for this job, on direct labour hours

Assuming that the price is acceptable to the customer, the job will go ahead and Pearshore Printers will charge the actual costs to the job, and will calculate any variances, as follows:

JOB NO. 6789
'FashionAid' Programme: 750 copies

	ESTIMATE	ACTUAL	VARIANCE*	
	£	£	£	
Direct Materials				
Paper for text	82.00	90.00	8	ADV
Paper for cover	55.00	50.00	5	FAV
Printing plates	15.00	15.00	–	
Direct Labour				
Printing: actual 6 hours at £10.00 per hour	50.00	60.00	10	ADV
Finishing: actual 2 hours at £9.00 per hour	18.00	18.00	–	
Overheads				
8 hours at £20.00 per hour	140.00	160.00	20	ADV
TOTAL COST	360.00	393.00	33	ADV
Profit	54.00	21.00	33	ADV
SELLING PRICE	414.00	414.00	–	

* The variances are either *adverse* or *favourable:*

– a favourable variance is where the actual cost is lower than the estimate

– an adverse variance is where the actual cost is higher than the estimate

Pearshore Printers would need to analyse the reason for the variances (see Chapter 7), and to take corrective steps to overcome the problems caused by them.

BATCH COSTING

This form of costing is used where the output consists of a number of identical items which are produced together as a batch. Examples include a bakery producing a batch of standard white loaves, and then a batch of croissants; or a clothing factory producing a batch of jackets, and then a batch of trousers. Each batch is the cost unit to which the costs are charged. Once the batch has been produced, the cost per unit is calculated as follows:

$$\frac{\text{total batch cost}}{\text{number of units of output}} \quad = \quad \text{cost per unit}$$

In essence, batch costing is very similar to job costing – in a batch a number of identical units are produced.

CONTRACT COSTING

Contract costing is used by the construction industry and major engineering companies to cost large, complex projects which last for a long period of time (usually more than a year). The principles followed are those of job costing but the length and complexity of contract work causes financial differences:

- a large contract will often itself comprise a considerable number of smaller jobs (some of which may be sub-contracted) to be costed

- invariably building contracts are based at the construction site – this means that many costs that would otherwise be indirect become direct costs, eg supervisors' wages, site power and telephones, fuel for vehicles, depreciation of equipment

- as many contracts run for longer than one year, there is a need to calculate the profit or loss on the contract at the end of the financial year of the construction company, and to value the contract for balance sheet purposes; the contract is valued at either:

  - *if an overall profit is expected*, costs to date plus attributable profit (depending on how far through the contract is); or

  - *if an overall loss is expected,* costs to date, less the whole of the expected loss

Clearly the costing of a contract is a major task and one which can go spectacularly wrong as a number of companies have found in the past.

SERVICE COSTING

This method of costing applies to service industries. By using service costing the cost per passenger mile of a bus or train service, the cost of clearing a cheque, and the cost per student hour at a school or college can be calculated. (However, a bus company quoting for a trip to the seaside for a pensioners' group, or a college tendering for an in-house course, would use job costing.)

Example

A nursing home has capacity for twenty residents at any one time. The home achieves an occupancy rate of 90%, ie an average of eighteen beds are occupied at any one time. Costs for last year were:

		£
direct costs		
food and other supplies		27,290
nursing and medical staff		116,340
other support services		22,650
indirect costs		
overheads		29,410
		195,690

The cost per day of each resident is calculated as follows:

• The occupancy in days is (20 residents x 365 days) x 90% = 6,570 days

• Cost per day per resident is:

$$\frac{\text{total cost}}{\text{number of days}} = \frac{£195,690}{6,570} = \underline{£29.79 \text{ per day}}$$

WORK-IN-PROGRESS

In most manufacturing activities it is likely that, at any one time, there will be some units which are partly completed. For example, the production line at a car factory will always have cars which vary from being only just started, to those nearing the end of the line which are almost complete.

In calculating the cost per unit, it is necessary to take into account the degree of completeness of the work-in-progress. This is done by making equivalent unit calculations:

number of units in progress x percentage of completeness = equivalent units

Thus, 100 units which are exactly 40% complete are equal to 40 completed units.

The formula for calculating the cost per unit now becomes:

$$\frac{\textit{total cost of production}}{\textit{number of units of output + equivalent units-in-progress}} = \textit{cost per unit}$$

Example

Cradley Cider Company brews a popular local cider at its cider house in rural Herefordshire. The figures for the first month of the new season's production of its award-winning 'Triple X' variety are:

total cost of production	£8,500
units completed	800 barrels
units in progress	100 barrels

The units in progress are exactly half-finished. The equivalent units-in-progress, and the cost per barrel, for the month are as follows:

completed units		=	800 barrels
equivalent units	100 x 50%	=	50 barrels
cost per unit	$\dfrac{£8,500}{800 + 50}$	=	£10 per barrel

work-in-progress: different cost elements

Although in the example above, it was assumed that the work-in-progress was exactly half-finished, this may well not be the case for all the elements of cost. For example, while direct materials might be 100% complete, direct labour, and overheads might be 50% complete. Allowance has to be made for these differences in the calculation of the valuation of work-in-progress, and the layout used in the example below is one way in which the calculations can be made.

Example

The Toy Manufacturing Company makes a plastic toy called a 'Humber-Wumber'. The figures for the first month's production are:

direct materials	£6,600
direct labour	£3,500
production overheads	£4,000
units completed	900
units in progress	200

The units in progress are complete as regards materials, but are 50% complete for direct labour and overheads.

Cost element	Costs	Completed Units	Work-in-progress			Total Equivalent Units	Cost per Unit	WIP valuation
			Units	% complete	Equivalent Units			
	A	B	C	D	E	F	G	H
					C x D	B + E	A ÷ F	E x G
	£			%			£	£
Direct materials	6,600	900	200	100	200	1,100	6.00	1,200
Direct labour	3,500	900	200	50	100	1,000	3.50	350
Production overheads	4,000	900	200	50	100	1,000	4.00	400
Total	14,100						13.50	1,950

Note: columns are lettered to show how calculations are made.

Using an average cost basis, the cost per unit of the first month's production, and the month-end valuation figure for work-in-progress (WIP) is as follows:

900 completed units at £13.50 each = £12,150
work-in-progress valuation = £ 1,950
total costs for month = £14,100

Note that the above calculation uses an average cost basis; an alternative approach is to follow the principles of 'first in, first out'.

opening work-in-progress

When there is opening work-in-progress, the values of the different cost elements are added to the input costs of the period. For example, if in the month which follows the example above, direct labour costs are £4,000, the figure shown in the column costs for direct labour will be:

work-in-progress at start = £ 350
input costs (month's costs) = £4,000
total costs for the month = £4,350

The calculation of costs per unit and work-in-progress valuation at the month-end can then be made as follows:

$$\frac{opening\ work\text{-}in\text{-}progress\ +\ input\ costs\ for\ period}{number\ of\ units\ of\ output\ +\ equivalent\ units\text{-}in\text{-}progress} = cost\ per\ unit$$

**CHAPTER
SUMMARY**

- Methods of costing include:
  - job costing
  - batch costing
  - contract costing
  - service costing
- Job costing is used where each job can be separately identified from other jobs; the job becomes the cost unit to which costs are charged.
- Batch costing is used where the output consists of a number of identical items which are produced together as a batch.
- Contract costing is used to cost large, complex projects which last for a long period of time.
- Service costing is used in the service sector, such as transport services, banks, schools and colleges, hotels and restaurants, etc.
- The methods of costing enable the calculation of a cost per unit of output or service.

**KEY
TERMS**

costing method	technique used to collect costs and to calculate the total cost of output
job/batch/contract costing	a form of specific order costing which applies costs to jobs/batches/contracts
service costing	a form of costing for service industries; costs are averaged to find the cost per unit
job cost card/sheet	card/sheet (or record on a computer database) which shows the estimated and actual direct and indirect costs for a particular job
favourable variance	where the actual cost is lower than the estimate
adverse variance	where the actual cost is higher than the estimate
work-in-progress	partly completed goods at a particular time
equivalent units	number of units in progress x percentage of completeness

cost per unit

$$\frac{\text{total costs}}{\text{number of units (including equivalent units)}}$$

6.1 Discuss the method of costing that would be appropriate for:

- an accountant
- a bus company
- a baker
- a sports centre
- an hotel
- a construction company

6.2 A clothing manufacturer has been asked to give a quotation for the supply of a batch of uniforms for a band. Materials for the uniforms will be:

- 100 metres of cloth at £7.50 per metre
- 75 metres of braiding at £4.00 per metre

It is estimated that the job will take the machinists a total of 35 hours. They are paid at the rate of £6.00 per hour. The overhead absorption rate is £8.50 per direct labour hour.

You are to:

(a) Calculate the cost of the job

(b) Calculate the selling price if the company is to make a profit of 20% on the cost price

6.3 Rowcester Engineering Limited is asked to quote for the supply of a replacement cylinder head for a large stationary engine installed in a local factory. The item will need to be cast in the foundry and then passed to the finishing shop for machining to specification.

Materials needed will be a 100 kg ingot of high-strength steel, which costs £10 per kg.

Direct labour will be 10 hours in the foundry, and 15 hours in the finishing shop, of which 12 hours will be machine hours. Foundry workers are paid £10 per hour, while machine operators in the finishing shop are paid £12 per hour.

Overheads are charged on the basis of 80% of direct labour cost in the foundry, and on the basis of £20 per machine hour in the finishing shop.

Profit is to be 25% of cost price.

You are to:

(a) Prepare a Job Cost Sheet which shows the estimated cost of the job, and the selling price.

(b) Prepare an *actual cost statement* on the basis of the following:

- the cost of materials was £11 per kg
- the job took 12 labour hours in the foundry (of which 11 were machine hours)
- the job took 14 labour hours in the finishing shop

- machine operators in the finishing shop are now paid £12.50 per hour
- machine time in the finishing shop was 11 hours

(c) Show the variances (and whether they are adverse or favourable) and the actual profit (or loss) made on this job.

6.4 City Transit plc is a small train operating company which runs passenger rail services on a commuter line in a large city. The line links the docks area, which has been redeveloped with flats and houses, with the city centre, and then runs on through the suburbs. An intensive service is operated from early morning to late at night carrying people to and from work, schoolchildren, shoppers and leisure travellers.

The tracks that City Transit uses are leased from the track owner, Trakrail plc. The modern fleet of six diesel trains is owned and maintained by City Transit.

The following information is available in respect of last year's operations:

	cost	estimated life
Diesel trains	£650,000 each	20 years

Depreciation is on a straight-line basis, assuming a residual value of £50,000 for each train.

Leasing charges for track	£500,000 pa
Maintenance charges for trains	£455,000 pa
Fuel for trains	£105,000 pa
Wages of drivers and conductors	£240,000 pa
Administration	£260,000 pa

There were 2.5 million passenger journeys last year with an average distance travelled of five miles.

You are to calculate the cost per passenger mile of operating the railway for last year.

6.5 A manufacturer of plastic toys has the following information concerning the first month of production:

Direct materials	£11,500
Direct labour	£9,000
Production overheads	£18,000
Toys completed	20,000
Toys in progress	5,000

The work-in-progress is complete as regards materials, but is 50% complete as regards direct labour and production overhead.

You are to:

(a) Calculate the cost per toy of the first month's production

(b) Calculate the month-end valuation for work-in-progress

Note: use the average cost basis for your calculations

7 STANDARD COSTING

NVQ PERFORMANCE CRITERIA COVERED

unit 5: RECORDING COST INFORMATION

element 1

❑ standard costs are compared against actual costs and any variances are analysed

element 2

❑ standard costs are compared against actual costs and any variances are analysed

element 3

prepare and present standard cost reports

❑ standard cost reports with variances clearly identified are presented in an intelligible form

❑ unusual or unexpected results are identified and reported to managers

❑ any reasons for significant variances from standard are identified and the explanations presented to management

❑ the results of the analysis and explanations of specific variances are produced for management

❑ staff working in operational departments are consulted to resolve any queries in the data

WHAT IS STANDARD COSTING?

Standard costing sets a pre-determined cost for materials, labour, expenses and overheads in advance of production.

All businesses need methods of controlling the costs of materials, labour, expenses and overheads that go to make up the finished product. Imagine a car factory where the cost and amount of materials to make the car is not known; where the hours of work and rates of pay are not known, where the cost of overheads is not known. Under such circumstances, the costs could not be controlled, and it would be impossible to quote a price for the product to a customer. To overcome this problem many businesses establish a standard cost for their output. Thus a standard cost can be calculated for things as diverse as a product manufactured in a factory, a hospital operation, servicing a car, a meal in a restaurant, a passenger-mile on a bus.

The standard cost for units of output is pre-determined in advance of production and working on the assumptions of:

- either *ideal standard,* which is the standard that can be attained under the most favourable conditions; no allowances are made for poor quality materials, idle time and machine breakdowns

- or *attainable standard,* which is attained if the work is carried out efficiently, machines are operated properly, and materials are used properly; allowances are made for normal losses, waste and machine breakdowns.

Standard costs are set for:

- **materials**

  The quantity and quality of each type of material to be used in producing the output, and the price of such materials is pre-determined. Standard materials cost is the expected quantity and quality of materials multiplied by the expected material price.

- **labour**

  The labour hours required to manufacture a quantity of goods or provide a service, together with the cost of the labour is pre-determined. Standard labour cost is the expected labour hours multiplied by the expected wage rates.

- **expenses**

  The amount of any direct expenses, such as royalties payable to an author or designer, are pre-determined in order to establish the standard cost.

- **overheads**

  The expected quantity of output within a time period divided into the expected overheads will determine the standard overhead cost.

Once a standard cost has been established, it can be used by a business as part of the decision-making, planning, and control processes:

- **decision-making**

  The business can use the standard cost when making pricing decisions, and to consider the effect of using different qualities of materials and grades of labour on the standard cost of the output.

- **planning**

  The production of its goods or services can be planned for the next accounting period, and schedules prepared of the requirements for materials, labour and overheads.

- **control**

  The progress of the business can be monitored on a regular basis; costs can be controlled through variance analysis (see later in this chapter).

Note that standard costing is used in conjunction with absorption costing or activity based costing, ie the standard cost is set in advance of production.

setting standards

In standard costing, it is important that care should be taken over the setting of standards. Loosely set standards will be of no help to the management of a business when the figures are used in further analysis. It is a sign of well-set standards when there are few differences from standard.

The main departments within an organisation which can provide information to enable standards to be set are:

- **purchasing, or buying**

  The buying department of a business will be able to determine prices of materials used, and the expected price trends.

- **human resources, or personnel**

  This department will have current wage and salary rates, together with piecework, bonus and overtime details, of the various grades of employees; forecasts of changes can also be ascertained.

- **management services**

  Often called work study, this department will determine the standard amount of time that each work-task in the production process should take. From this can be calculated the *standard hour* (or minute) – the quantity of work that can be achieved at a standard performance in an hour (or minute).

- **production**

  This department has overall responsibility for production and will know the quantities of raw materials required for each unit of production, and the value of production that will be linked to the overhead costs.

standard costing in service industries

The principles of standard costing can be applied to service industries. For example, the standard cost of service can be calculated in terms of:

- passenger-mile, for bus and train companies
- guest night, for hotels
- in-patient days, for hospitals
- cost per case, for hospital outpatients
- cost per meal, in a restaurant

There are two specific problems for service industries:

- because demand for the service is on an 'as and when' basis (unlike a manufacturer which is able to plan production), it is more difficult to pre-determine the standard cost
- it is difficult to define the quality of service to be attained (by contrast, a manufacturer is able to set standards for its products and to employ inspectors to maintain such standards)

CASE STUDY

AMC ENGINEERING LIMITED: STANDARD COST

situation

This company manufactures car bumper mouldings. It has been asked by its major customer, Ikassa (Japan) Limited to prepare a quotation for mouldings for a new car, which is code-named "OK10". The elements of cost for 100 mouldings have been calculated by AMC Engineering as:

materials: polycarbonate (of specified quality), 200 kgs at £1.10 per kg
matt black finishing material, 10 litres at £5.40 per litre

labour: 10 hours at £5.75 per hour

3 hours at £8.50 per hour

overheads: 13 hours at £20 per hour

What is the standard cost of producing 100 bumper mouldings?

solution

	£	£
materials		
polycarbonate: 200 kgs at £1.10 per kg	220.00	
finishing material: 10 litres at £5.40 per litre	54.00	
		274.00

labour

10 hours at £5.75 per hour	57.50
3 hours at £8.50 per hour	25.50
	83.00
	357.00

overheads

13 hours at £20 per hour	260.00
STANDARD COST	617.00

The standard cost will then be used by AMC Engineering to help establish the selling price to the customer, ie standard cost + profit = selling price

STANDARD COSTING AND VARIANCE ANALYSIS

A particular feature of standard costing is its use as a method of cost control by comparing standard cost with the actual cost of the output in order to establish the variance, ie

standard cost	*minus*	**actual cost**	*equals*	**variance**

Variances can be either *favourable* (FAV) or *adverse* (ADV):

- a favourable variance is where the actual cost is lower than the standard cost
- an adverse variance is where the actual cost is higher than the standard cost

The variances – which we will study in detail later in the chapter – cover the main elements of cost:

- materials variances (pages 130–131): price variance, usage variance
- labour variances (pages 132–133): rate variance, efficiency variance
- overheads variances (pages 136–139): fixed overhead variances, variable overhead variances

management by exception

The control systems of a business will set down procedures for acting on variances, but only for significant variances. This type of system is known as *management by exception,* ie acting on variances that are exceptional.

Managers will normally work to *tolerance limits* imposed on costs. A tolerance limit is an acceptable percentage variance on the standard cost. If the cost exceeds the tolerance limit, the variance will be significant and investigative action will need to be taken. For example, the standard labour cost for a production department is £50,000 a month, with a tolerance limit of 5 per cent set. If labour costs in any one month exceed £50,000 x 5%, ie a variance of £2,500, action will have to be taken and the cause investigated, as shown in the diagram below.

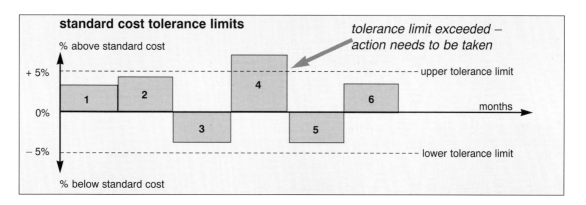

who needs to know about variances?

Variances against standard cost need to be reported to the *appropriate* level of management within the business. This level will depend on the significance of the variance, as shown in the two extreme examples which follow:

- **the cost of the materials used is going up by 1 per cent**

The managing director is unlikely to be interested – it will be up to the purchasing department to see if there is a way around the increase.

- **a major failure in an automated process has cut output by 50 per cent**

This is a matter to bring to the attention of higher management and the directors of the company: production patterns, purchasing and staffing will have to be re-organised so that production can be increased.

motivating employees

As a means of motivating employees, standard costs are an example of *responsibility accounting*. Managers and supervisors are made responsible for their own costs but, in order to be effective, managers must participate in the standard-setting process. As a method of motivation, standard costing can be seen by employees as either a 'carrot' or a 'stick', ie as a form of encouragement to achieve the costs set, or as a form of punishment if pre-determined costs are exceeded.

Often it is better if standards are set in terms of quantities of materials or hours of labour, rather than in money amounts. Non-financial managers and supervisors can then relate to the volume of inputs rather than their value, and can then seek to achieve the standards set.

reporting and investigating variances

The variances for each cost element are summarised on a *standard cost report*. Such reports reconcile the standard cost and the actual cost for each cost element (materials, labour, expenses and overheads), and show the variances. An example of a standard cost report is shown below. Note that the standard costs are based on the actual output (in the example, output of 1,200 walling blocks) and not the budgeted output (here 1,000 blocks).

STANDARD COST REPORT

product	garden walling blocks			**date**	08.11.1999
budgeted output	1,000 blocks			**period**	week 3
actual output	1,200 blocks				October 1999

	standard cost			actual cost	variance
	cost per unit	output	total cost		
	£		£	£	£
materials	0.25	1,200	300.00	270.00	30.00 FAV
labour	0.30	1,200	360.00	325.00	35.00 FAV
overheads:					
fixed	0.30	1,200	360.00	403.00	43.00 ADV
variable	0.10	1,200	120.00	117.00	3.00 FAV
TOTAL	0.95	1,200	1,140.00	1,115.00	25.00 FAV

---

format of a standard cost report

The standard cost report shows the variances for each cost element by comparing the standard cost of the actual output with the actual cost. A favourable variance is a positive amount, eg for materials £300 – £270 = £30 FAV. Because actual costs are lower than standard, a favourable variance increases profits. By contrast, an adverse variance, eg fixed overheads £360 – £403 = £43 ADV, increases costs and so reduces profits.

The order for investigating variances shown by the standard cost report is usually as follows:

• large variances – favourable and adverse

• other adverse variances

• any remaining favourable variances

Note that small variances may not be worth investigating – the cost of the investigation might outweigh the benefits.

The variances need to be investigated by the appropriate level of management:

• less significant variances are dealt with by managers and supervisors

• significant variances need to be referred to a higher level of management who will decide what further investigation is required

Note that constant adverse or favourable variances need to be investigated as the standard costs may have been set incorrectly.

reporting cycle

For standard costing to be used effectively it is essential that employees are trained to record information accurately about actual costs. This forms the first part of the reporting cycle, which will go on to produce the standard cost report. As with all reporting procedures, the quality of the information must be:

– accurate

– timely

– in the appropriate format, highlighting the major features

The reporting cycle of the standard cost report will depend on the time periods used. For example, if a business establishes standard costs and planned (or budgeted) output on the basis of monthly – or four-weekly – periods, then variances are likely to be reported within the first two weeks of the next period – often in the form of a computer printout from the finance department. Generally a senior manager will call a meeting at a fixed point in each production period – with the staff responsible for the costs – in order to review variances from the previous period. This date establishes the reporting cycle, for example:

> **WEEK 1**
>
> all costs from the previous period must have been
> produced by the beginning of week 2

> **WEEK 2**
>
> actual figures from the previous period must be analysed by the
> end of week 2 so that the standard cost report can be completed

> **WEEK 3**
>
> the review meeting can then be held at the beginning of week 3
> of each period

revision of standards

At regular intervals – annually, or more often – the standard costs need to be revised to take note of:

- cost increases caused by inflation, which will affect materials, labour and overheads (although not necessarily to the same extent)

- changes to the specifications and quality of materials, eg an improvement in quality may lead to less wastage and easier, faster, production

- changes to work practices, eg an increase in automation may lead to reduced labour costs, or the employment of different grades of employees

controllable and non-controllable costs

When investigating variances, it is important to appreciate that not all of the costs in a standard cost can be controlled directly by managers and supervisors in the short-term. For example, the cost of rent paid on the premises is outside the control of the purchasing manager – the rent being negotiated by the property services manager. Nevertheless, a proportion of rent will be included amongst the overheads when calculating the standard cost. By contrast the purchasing manager has control over the cost of raw materials (unless there is a world price – eg for coffee or crude oil – over which he or she can have no influence). Thus we can distinguish between:

- *controllable costs* – costs which can be influenced by the manager/supervisor

- *non-controllable costs* – costs which cannot be influenced by the manager/supervisor in the short-term

Note that, in the longer-term, all costs are controllable. For example, a business may decide to move to premises where the rent is cheaper, or to close its operations at one location, or even – in the extreme – to cease trading altogether.

MONITORING OF STANDARD COSTS

A business using the standard costing system will monitor the outcomes by comparing the standard costs set with the results that actually occurred. An outline of the monitoring process is shown in the diagram below.

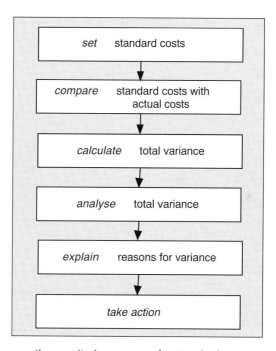

the monitoring process for standard costs

VARIANCES AND SUB-VARIANCES

The full amount by which the actual cost of a product differs from the standard cost is known as the total cost variance. It is calculated by deducting actual cost from standard cost, for example:

cost of making 1,200 garden walling blocks

	£
standard cost	1,140
actual cost	1,115
TOTAL COST VARIANCE	25 FAV

The total cost variance is made up of the variances for each of the main elements of cost:

- materials
- labour
- overheads

The variance for each element can be further analysed into a number of *sub-variances* which are used to identify the *reasons* for the variance.

The main variances and sub-variances for a manufacturing business are as follows.

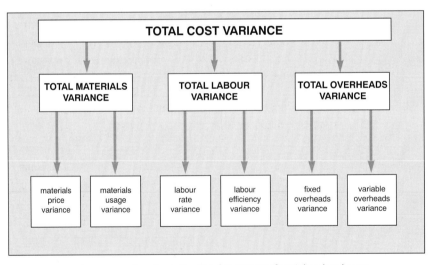

variances and sub-variances for a manufacturing business

As the diagram shows, the total cost variance can result from a combination of factors:

- *total materials variance*
  - price variance, caused by a price rise (or price fall) in the cost of materials
  - usage variance, caused by a change in the amount of materials used

- *total labour variance*
  - rate variance, caused by an unexpected rise in pay rates, or the need to use a different grade of employee (at a higher or lower wage rate)
  - efficiency variance caused by a higher or lower output than expected
- *total overheads variance*
  - fixed overhead variance, caused by an unexpected change in fixed costs, eg an increase in the rent of the factory
  - variable overhead variance, caused by a change in the cost or use of a variable overhead, eg the rise in the cost per unit.of electricity

The principle of variance analysis is that variances and sub-variances are identified and calculated until they can be seen to be the responsibility of an individual employee, or small section within the business. For example, a materials price variance, where the cost of materials is different from the standard cost, is the responsibility of the buying department; it is this department that will have to explain to management the reason(s) for any variance. Note that a variance can only identify that a problem exists; it is for the appropriate section of the business to identify the *cause* of the variance.

The illustration below shows how the standard cost report for 1,200 garden walling blocks (on page 124) can be developed to show the sub-variances. The specific calculations for these sub-variances are shown in the Case Studies which follow each of the next two sections. Overhead variances are discussed on pages 136-139, and are illustrated in a Case Study (page 139).

	standard cost of making 1,200 blocks	actual cost of making 1,200 blocks	sub-variances		
	£	£		£	£
materials	1,200 kilos at 25p per kg 300	900 kilos at 30p per kg 270	price usage	45 75	ADV FAV
				30	FAV
labour	60 hours at £6.00 per hour 360	65 hours at £5.00 per hour 325	rate efficiency	65 30	FAV ADV
				35	FAV
overheads fixed variable	360 120	403 117		43 3	ADV FAV
TOTAL COST	1,140	1,115		25	FAV

standard cost report, showing sub-variances for materials and labour
(sub-variances for overheads are discussed on pages 136-139)

From this report, the materials and labour sub-variances will certainly cause the management to investigate the reasons for both the favourable and adverse variances.

THE CALCULATION OF MATERIALS VARIANCES

The variances and sub-variances for materials costs are:

variance

• total materials variance, which is caused by

sub-variances

• materials price variance – the actual price paid compared with the standard price
• materials usage variance – the actual amount used compared with the standard quantity

The money amounts of these are calculated from the areas indicated in the diagram set out below. Note that, for clarity of presentation, both the actual price and the actual quantity used are greater than standard, ie they are adverse variances.

The variances are calculated as follows:

total materials variance =

(standard quantity x standard price) – (actual quantity x actual price)

This variance can then be analysed further by calculating the sub-variances:

materials price sub-variance =

(standard price – actual price) x actual quantity

materials usage sub-variance =

(standard quantity – actual quantity) x standard price

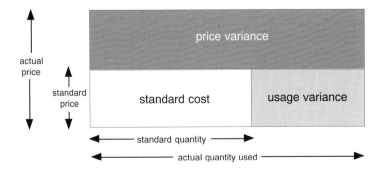

Note from this diagram:

- The change in the price of materials, based on the quantity actually used, forms the materials price variance – shaded  in the diagram. This variance is the responsibility of the *buying department.*

- The change in the actual quantity used, based on the standard price, forms the materials usage variance – shaded  in the diagram. This variance is the responsibility of the *production department.*

- The variances can also be favourable, ie less than the standard cost.

when are materials price variances calculated?

Please see page 371 (after the index) for a note on this subject.

CASE STUDY

WYVERN WALLING: MATERIALS VARIANCES

situation

Wyvern Walling is a manufacturer of garden wall blocks. The management accountant has prepared the following costs for a batch of 1,200 garden walling blocks:

- the standard price of concrete is 25p per kg

- the standard usage is 1,200 kg

The results achieved are:

- the actual price of concrete used was 30p per kg

- the actual usage was 900 kg

In short, the concrete has cost more, but less has been used for each wall block. What are the variances and sub-variances for materials costs?

solution

Here both the price and usage have differed from the standard to give the following total materials variance:

(standard quantity x standard price) – (actual quantity x actual price)

(1,200 kgs x 25p per kg) – (900 kgs x 30p per kg)   =

£300 – £270 = ⟶ £30 FAVOURABLE

While the total materials variance is favourable by £30, as both price and usage differ from standard, the sub-variances must be calculated:

materials price sub-variance

(standard price – actual price) x actual quantity

(25p – 30p) x 900 kgs = ⟶ £45 ADVERSE

materials usage sub-variance

(standard quantity – actual quantity) x standard price

(1,200 kgs – 900 kgs) x 25p = ⟶ £75 FAVOURABLE

TOTAL MATERIALS VARIANCE ⟶ £30 FAVOURABLE

Notes:

The materials price sub-variance is based on the actual quantity used, and is the difference between:

- the amount that would have been charged at the standard price
- the actual amount charged

The materials usage sub-variance is based on the standard price, and is the difference between:

- the standard quantity that should have been used
- the actual amount used

For this batch of 1,200 wall blocks, the materials variance is £30 FAV. This agrees with the standard cost report shown on page 124. As a consequence, the rise in price (the adverse sub-variance) must be investigated, together with the reason for the reduced usage of materials (the favourable sub-variance).

THE CALCULATION OF LABOUR VARIANCES

The variances and sub-variances for labour costs are:

variance

- total labour variance, which is caused by

sub-variances

- labour rate variance – the actual rate of wages paid compared with the standard rate
- labour efficiency variance – the actual level of efficiency of the workforce compared with the standard level

The money amounts of these are calculated from the areas indicated in the diagram set out below. Note that for clarity of presentation, both actual labour rate and the actual hours worked are greater than standard, ie they are adverse variances:

The variances are calculated as follows:

total labour variance =

(standard hours x standard rate) – (actual hours x actual rate)

This variance can then be analysed further by calculating the sub-variances:

labour rate sub-variance =

(standard rate – actual rate) x   actual hours

labour efficiency sub-variance =

(standard hours – actual hours) x   standard rate

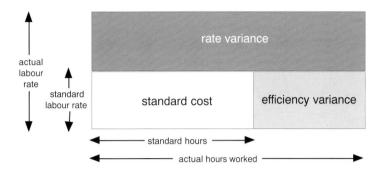

Note from this diagram:

- The change in the labour rate, based on the actual hours worked, forms the labour rate variance – shaded ▬▬▬ in the diagram. This variance is the responsibility of the *human resources, or personnel department.*

- The change in the actual hours worked, based on the standard hours, forms the labour efficiency variance – shaded ▭ in the diagram. This variance is the responsibility of the *production department.*

CASE STUDY

WYVERN WALLING: CALCULATING LABOUR VARIANCES

situation

The management accountant of Wyvern Walling has prepared the following labour costs for a batch of 1,200 garedn walling blocks:

- the standard cost of direct labour is £6.00 per hour
- the standard efficiency is 60 hours per batch

The results achieved are:

- the actual cost of direct labour was £5.00 per hour
- the actual production took 65 hours

In short, the wage rates are lower, but the employees have not worked as efficiently. What are the variances and sub-variances for labour costs?

solution

Here both the rate and efficiency have differed from the standard to give the following *total labour variance:*

(standard hours x standard rate) – *(actual hours x actual rate)*

(60 hours x £6.00 per hour) – (65 hours x £5.00 per hour)

£360 – £325 = ⟶ £35 FAVOURABLE

Note: The calculation gives a positive figure of £35; this means that the actual cost is less than the standard cost, ie it is favourable, and profits will increase. By contrast, an adverse cost variance is a negative figure, ie the actual cost is greater than the standard cost, and profits will decrease.

While the total labour variance is favourable by £35, as both rate and efficiency differ from standard, the sub-variances must be calculated:

labour rate sub-variance

(standard rate – actual rate) x actual hours

(£6.00 – £5.00) x 65 hours = ⟶ £65 FAVOURABLE

labour efficiency sub-variance

(standard hours – actual hours) x standard rate

(60 hours – 65 hours) x £6.00 = ⟶ £30 ADVERSE

TOTAL LABOUR VARIANCE = ⟶ £35 FAVOURABLE

Notes:

The labour rate sub-variance is based on the actual hours, and is the difference between:

• the amount that would have been paid at the standard rate

• the actual amount paid

The labour efficiency sub-variance is based on the standard rate, and is the difference between:

• the standard hours that should have been taken for the work

• the actual hours taken

For this batch of 1,200 wall blocks, the labour variance is £35 FAV. This agrees with the standard cost report shown on page 124. The management of Wyvern Walling will wish, no doubt, to investigate the reasons for both sub-variances.

IDLE TIME VARIANCE

The labour efficiency sub-variance is traditionally used to measure the efficiency of the workforce. However, sometimes a lack of efficiency is caused by factors outside the control of the workforce – for example, a machine breakdown. Such factors are measured by the *idle time variance*. It is calculated as:

idle time hours x standard rate

example

The labour for making 500 units of product Exe is expected to be:

- the standard cost of direct labour is £6.00 per hour
- the standard efficiency is 25 hours

The actual results are found to be:

- the cost of direct labour is £6.00 per hour
- the production took 35 hours, including 5 hours of idle time caused by a machine breakdown

total labour variance

(25 hours x £6.00 per hour) – (35 hours x £6.00 per hour)

= £150 – £210 = £60 ADVERSE

This is analysed as follows:

labour rate sub-variance

(£6.00 – £6.00) x 35 hours = NIL

As the standard labour rate is the same as the actual rate, the variance is nil.

idle time variance

5 hours x £6.00 (the standard cost of direct labour) = £30 ADVERSE

labour efficiency sub-variance

(25 hours – 30 hours) x £6.00 = £30 ADVERSE

Although production took a total of 35 hours, as 5 of these were idle time, productive hours are taken as 30. Thus the total labour variance of £60 is made up of

labour rate sub-variance	nil	
idle time variance	£30	ADVERSE
labour efficiency sub-variance	£30	ADVERSE
	£60	ADVERSE

When there has been a period of idle time, the idle time variance is calculated to ensure that the labour efficiency variance reflects actual productive hours against standard hours.

OVERHEAD VARIANCES

The standard cost for overheads distinguishes between fixed overheads and variable overheads. The objective of setting a standard cost for overheads is to absorb the amount of the overheads into the overall cost of the output. Inevitably, actual costs often vary somewhat from standard costs; managers use overhead variances to understand why there has been over-absorption or under-absorption of overheads.

The diagram below shows the total variances and sub-variances for production overheads. The sub-variances are based on changes in expenditure, volume of output, and efficiency.

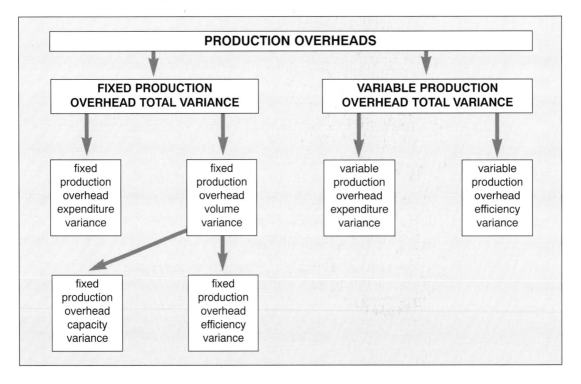

production overheads variances and sub-variances for a manufacturing business

The production overheads total variances can result from a combination of factors:

- **fixed production overhead total variance**

  - expenditure variance, where the actual cost of the overhead is different from the standard cost that has been planned, or budgeted

  - volume variance, where there is a difference between the standard hours for actual output and the budgeted hours (where overheads are absorbed on the basis of standard labour hours)

The *volume variance* can be further analysed into:

- – capacity variance, where actual hours for actual output differ from the budgeted hours
- – efficiency variance, where the actual hours for the actual output differ from the stnadard hours for the actual output, ie the workforce has been either more efficient or less efficient
- • **variable production overhead total variance**
  - – expenditure variance, where actual cost of the overhead is different from the standard cost
  - – efficiency variance, caused by a difference between the standard hours worked and the actual hours worked for the actual output

An *adverse* overhead variance shows that more has been spent on overheads than has been charged to production (ie overheads are under-absorbed); thus profit will be reduced. A favourable overhead variance shows that overheads have been over-absorbed, and will increase profits. However, as we saw in Chapter 5, over-absorption of overheads on a regular basis means that the overhead rate may have been set too high; this will lead to the selling price being set high and, as a consequence, sales may have been lost.

THE CALCULATION OF OVERHEAD VARIANCES

Note

When calculating overhead variances, do not include idle time in actual time: 'actual hours' is the amount of productive hours.

fixed overheads

As we have seen, the variances and sub-variances for fixed overheads are:

variance

fixed production overhead total variance, *which is caused by:*

sub-variances

- • fixed production overhead *expenditure* variance – the cost difference
- • fixed production overhead *volume* variance – the difference in output

The volume variance can be analysed further between:

- • fixed production overhead *capacity* variance – the difference between the actual hours for actual output and the budgeted hours
- • fixed production overhead *efficiency* variance – the efficiency of the workforce measured by the difference between the standard hours for actual output and the actual hours worked

The variances are calculated as follows:

fixed production overhead total variance =

(standard hours for actual output x standard overhead rate) –

(actual hours for actual output x actual overhead rate)

Note that this variance uses the standard hours for actual output, rather than planned or budgeted output. Thus, if the standard hours for budgeted output was 100 hours, but 10 per cent more was produced, then 'standard hours for actual output' will be 110 hours.

This variance can then be analysed further by calculating the sub-variances:

fixed production overhead expenditure variance =

(standard hours for budgeted output x standard overhead rate) –

(actual hours for actual output x actual overhead rate)

fixed production overhead volume variance =

(standard hours for budgeted output x standard overhead rate) –

(standard hours for actual output x standard overhead rate)

Note that this sub-variance can also be calculated as either:

• fixed overheads x percentage increase/decrease in output from budgeted, or

• (budgeted output – actual output) x overhead absorption rate per unit

The fixed production overhead volume variance can itself be analysed into two further sub-variances, calculated as follows:

fixed production overhead capacity variance =

(standard hours for budgeted output – actual hours for actual output) x

standard overhead rate

fixed production overhead efficiency variance =

(standard hours for actual output – actual hours for actual output) x

standard overhead rate

The Case Study on page 139 shows how these fixed production overhead variances are calculated.

variable overheads

As we have seen, the variances and sub-variances for variable overheads are:

variance

- variable production overhead total variance, which is caused by:

sub-variances

- variable production overhead expenditure variance – the cost difference
- variable production overhead efficiency variance – the efficiency of the workforce

The variances are calculated as follows:

variable production overhead total variance =

(standard hours for actual output x standard overhead rate) –

(actual hours for actual output x actual overhead rate)

As with fixed overheads, note that this variance uses the standard hours for actual output, rather than planned or budgeted output.

This variance can then be analysed further by calculating the sub-variances:

variable production overhead expenditure variance =

(actual hours for actual output x standard overhead rate) –

(actual hours for actual output x actual overhead rate)

variable production overhead efficiency variance =

(standard hours for actual output – actual hours for actual output) x

standard overhead rate

The Case Study which follows shows how both fixed and variable production overhead variances are calculated.

CASE STUDY

WYVERN WALLING: OVERHEAD VARIANCES

situation

The standard cost report for garden walling blocks made by Wyvern Walling is shown on page 124. The company had budgeted to make 1,000 blocks during week 3 of October 1999 with production overhead costs of:

fixed overheads   £0.30 per unit
variable overheads   £0.10 per unit

Note: overheads are absorbed on the basis of the number of direct labour hours.
Thus the standard overhead cost of 1,000 blocks is budgeted to be:

STANDARD COST (1,000 BLOCKS)

fixed production overheads

      50 hours at £6.00 per hour   = £300.00

variable production overheads

      50 hours at £2.00 per hour   = £100.00

                                       £400.00

As the overhead absorption rate is based on the number of direct labour hours:

– fixed overheads: 20 blocks per hour at £0.30 per unit = £6.00 per hour

– variable overheads: 20 blocks per hour at £0.10 per unit = £2.00 per hour

---

Once production is completed, it is found that 1,200 blocks were produced during the period. The actual cost of the overheads was:

ACTUAL COST (1,200 BLOCKS)

fixed production overheads

      65 hours at £6.20 per hour   = £403.00

variable production overheads

      65 hours at £1.80 per hour   = £117.00

                                       £520.00

Clearly both fixed and variable overheads have cost more but output was up by 200 blocks (or 20 per cent) and overhead hours were up by 15 hours (or 30 per cent).

What are the variances and sub-variances for overheads?

solution

Based on the actual output of 1,200 blocks, the extract from the standard cost report for overheads is as follows:

	standard cost			actual cost	variance
	cost per unit £	output	total cost £	£	£
overheads					
fixed	0.30	1,200	360.00	403.00	43.00 ADV
variable	0.10	1,200	120.00	117.00	3.00 FAV
					40.00 ADV

FIXED PRODUCTION OVERHEADS

The number of hours worked and the overhead cost have both differed from the standard cost to give the following fixed production overhead total variance:

(standard hours for actual output x standard overhead rate) minus

(actual hours for actual output x actual overhead rate)

(60 hours* x £6) – (65 hours x £6.20) =
£360 – £403 = ⟶ £43 ADVERSE

* The standard hours for budgeted output was 50 hours for 1,000 blocks; as 20% more blocks were made, the standard hours for actual output is:

50 hours x 120 per cent = 60 hours

While the total overhead variance is adverse by £43, as the number of hours worked and the cost both differ from standard, the sub-variances must be calculated:

fixed production overhead expenditure variance

(standard hours for budgeted output x standard overhead rate) <u>minus</u>

(actual hours for actual output x actual overhead rate)

(50 hours x £6) – (65 hours x £6.20) =
£300 – £403 = ⟶ £103 ADVERSE

fixed production overhead volume variance

(standard hours for budgeted output x standard overhead rate) <u>minus</u>

(standard hours for actual output x standard overhead rate)

(50 hours x £6) – (60 hours x £6) =
£300 – £360 = ⟶ £60 FAVOURABLE

Notes:
- this sub-variance is favourable because £60 of fixed overhead has been over-absorbed; the effect of this is to increase profits
- this sub-variance can also be calculated by multiplying the amount of fixed overheads by the percentage increase or decrease in output from budgeted – here, £300 x 20% increase = £60 FAVOURABLE

FIXED PRODUCTION OVERHEAD TOTAL VARIANCE = ⟶ £43 ADVERSE

Thus actual expenditure on fixed overheads has been £103 more than the standard cost, but this is reduced by a favourable volume variance of £60.

The fixed production overhead volume variance of £60 favourable can be further analysed between:

fixed production overhead capacity variance
(standard hours for budgeted output – actual hours for actual output)
x standard overhead rate

(50 hours – 65 hours) x £6 =
15 hours x £6 = —————————————————▶ £90 FAVOURABLE

fixed production overhead efficiency variance
(standard hours for actual output – actual hours for actual output)
x standard overhead rate

(60 hours – 65 hours) x £6 =
5 hours x £6 = —————————————————▶ £30 ADVERSE

FIXED PRODUCTION OVERHEAD VOLUME VARIANCE ▶ £60 FAVOURABLE

It can be seen that the favourable volume variance of £60 comprises a favourable capacity variance of £90 and an adverse efficiency variance of £30.

VARIABLE PRODUCTION OVERHEADS

The number of hours worked and the overhead have differed from the standard cost to give the following variable production overhead total variance:
(standard hours for actual output x standard overhead rate) <u>minus</u>
(actual hours for actual output x actual overhead rate)

(60* hours x £2) – (65 hours x £1.80) =
£120 – £117 = —————————————————▶ £3 FAVOURABLE

* As with fixed overheads, the standard hours have been adjusted to allow for the 20 per cent increase in output.

The total overhead variance is favourable by £3 – which means that overhead has been over-absorbed. As both the number of hours worked and the overhead cost differ from standard, the sub-variances must be calculated.

variable production overhead expenditure variance
(actual hours for actual output x standard overhead rate) <u>minus</u>
(actual hours for actual output x actual overhead rate)

(65 hours x £2) – (65 hours x £1.80)
£130 – £117 = —————————————————▶ £13 FAVOURABLE

variable production overhead efficiency variance
(standard hours for actual output – actual hours for actual output)
x standard overhead rate

(60 hours - 65 hours) x £2 =
5 hours x £2 = —————————————————▶ £10 ADVERSE

VARIABLE PRODUCTION OVERHEAD TOTAL VARIANCE ▶ £ 3 FAVOURABLE

These two sub-variances demonstrate how the over-absorption or under-absorption of variable overhead, shown by the total variance of £3 favourable is made up. Here the cost difference shown by the expenditure variance is favourable by £13 (because overhead has been over-absorbed). By contrast the efficiency variance is adverse by £10 (because 65 hours was taken to do 60 hours of work).

The following diagram illustrates how each main overhead variance from the Case Study is analysed between sub-variances:

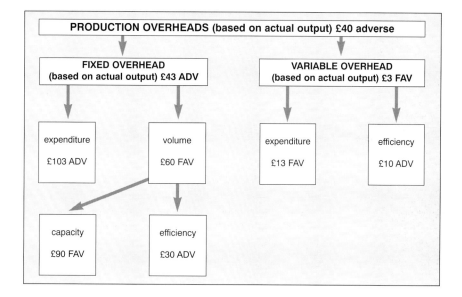

CAUSES OF VARIANCES

Standard costs are set in order to give individual departmental managers, who are responsible for aspects of the business' output, suitable targets to aim for. When actual costs are compared with standard costs, an investigation can be carried out to find out the causes of the variances and sub-variances, and to see what can be done about them for the future. Note, in particular, the way in which variances and sub-variances are calculated down to a responsibility level of an individual employee, or a small section within the business – *responsibility accounting*.

The main causes of variances are listed below and on the next page.

materials	*price*	*usage*
inflation	✓	
change in exchange rates	✓	
alternative materials used	✓	✓

theft	✓	
change in specifications	✓	✓
labour	*rate*	*efficiency*
pay rise	✓	
poor supervision		✓
different grade of labour used	✓	✓
change in machine speeds		✓

Note the inter-relationship between variances. For example, poor quality materials may give a favourable price variance but will often lead to an adverse usage variance; this may also cause an adverse labour efficiency variance because of problems caused in the manufacturing process.

fixed overheads	*expenditure*	*volume*
inflation	✓	
change in exchange rates	✓	
stepped fixed cost	✓	
lack of sales		✓
reduced stock levels		✓
idle time		✓
machine breakdown		✓

variable overheads	*expenditure*	*efficiency*
inflation	✓	
change in exchange rates	✓	
change in method of production		✓
change in machine speeds		✓
change in quality of materials		✓

VARIANCE SCHEDULES

In Student Activities and Assessments you will often be asked to prepare a variance schedule which lists the variances and sub-variances for materials, labour and overheads. Such a schedule forms a major part of a standard cost report (which will be studied in more detail at level 4 of NVQ in Accounting).

The variance schedule also incorporates a report section where

- significant variances can be noted

- the causes of variances can be highlighted

- the reasons for under- or over-absorption of overheads can be explained

The variance schedule for production of 1,200 walling blocks used in the Case Studies in this chapter (see pages 131,133 and 139) is as follows:

VARIANCE SCHEDULE

PRODUCT: 1,200 garden walling blocks   **Period:** week 3, October 1999

		£		£	
Materials variances					
Price				45	ADV
Usage				75	FAV
				30	FAV
Labour variances					
Rate				65	FAV
Efficiency				30	ADV
				35	FAV
Variable overhead variances					
Expenditure				13	FAV
Efficiency				10	ADV
				3	FAV
Fixed overhead variances					
Expenditure				103	ADV
	Capacity	90	FAV		
	Efficiency	30	ADV		
Volume				60	FAV
				43	ADV
TOTAL VARIANCE				25	FAV

REPORT

❑ The total materials, labour, and variable overhead variances are all favourable.

❑ The total fixed overhead variance is adverse.

❑ The most significant variances are materials price, materials usage, labour rate, fixed overhead expenditure and volume.

❑ The materials variances may well be inter-linked – although the materials have cost more, they may well be of better quality, leading to more efficient usage. If this proves to be the case, it might be appropriate to continue using the better quality materials.

❑ The labour variances may also be inter-linked – although the labour rate has been lower, labour efficiency has deteriorated. This suggests that a lower grade of labour has been used, which is less efficient in working practices.

❑ The variable overhead variances are not significant.

❑ The adverse fixed overhead variance means that fixed overheads were under-absorbed by £43. The main reason for this is the adverse expenditure variance of £103, indicating that actual overheads were greater than those budgeted. The favourable capacity variance of £90 is caused by a higher level of production than that budgeted; however, the effect of this is reduced by an adverse efficiency variance of £30, giving a total volume variance of £60 favourable.

Note that the variance schedule:
- details the variances and sub-variances for materials, labour and overheads
- concludes with the total variance
- includes a report which notes significant variances, highlights the causes of variances, and explains the under- or over-absorption of overheads

A blank layout of a variance schedule is included in the Appendix at the end of this book. It is suggested that you use this layout when preparing variance schedules; unless instructed otherwise, you should always complete the 'report' section of the schedule.

CONTROL RATIOS

As well as variance analysis, there are a number of control ratios which can be used by managers to measure the performance of the business. Such ratios, which are expressed as percentages, include:

$$\text{efficiency ratio} = \frac{\text{standard hours for actual output}}{\text{actual hours for actual output}} \times \frac{100}{1}$$

$$\text{capacity ratio} = \frac{\text{actual hours for actual output}}{\text{budgeted hours}} \times \frac{100}{1}$$

$$\text{activity ratio*} = \frac{\text{standard hours for actual output}}{\text{budgeted hours}} \times \frac{100}{1}$$

* a combination of the efficiency and capacity ratios

Example

During June 1999, Jason Manufacturing plans to make 1,000 units of output with 2,000 labour hours (ie 2 hours for each unit). The actual output for the month is 990 units made in 1,800 hours.

$$\text{efficiency ratio} = \frac{(990 \text{ units} \times 2 \text{ hours})}{1,800 \text{ hours}} \times \frac{100}{1} = 110\%$$

$$\text{capacity ratio} = \frac{1,800 \text{ hours}}{2,000 \text{ hours}} \times \frac{100}{1} = 90\%$$

$$\text{activity ratio} = \frac{(990 \text{ units} \times 2 \text{ hours})}{2,000 \text{ hours}} \times \frac{100}{1} = 99\%†$$

† efficiency ratio x capacity ratio: 110% x 90% = 99%

Thus while the activity is 99%, the efficiency of the workforce (at 110%) has compensated for the lower use of capacity of 90%.

In terms of responsibility accounting:

- the efficiency ratio measures how the production manager is organising the output of the business

- the capacity ratio shows senior management whether or not the business is achieving the targets set in terms of hours available

- the activity ratio is an indicator for senior management of the overall performance of the business

The control ratios may reveal the need for management to review the standard hours that have been set for output.

CHAPTER SUMMARY

- Standard costs are established for the main elements of cost: materials, labour and overheads.

- Actual costs are recorded and a comparison is made in a standard cost report between standard costs and actual costs.

- Variances – the difference between standard costs and actual costs – are calculated and are acted upon if they are significant.

- Total materials variance is analysed between
  - price variance
  - usage variance

- Total labour variance is analysed between
  - rate variance
  - efficiency variance

  An idle time variance is also calculated where there has been non-productive time.

- Overhead variances are calculated for
  - fixed overhead variance
  - variable overhead variance

  which are analysed between changes in expenditure, volume of output and efficiency.

- A favourable cost variance indicates that profit will be higher; an adverse cost variance means that profit will be lower.

- Control ratios measure the performance of a business in terms of
  - efficiency ratio
  - capacity ratio
  - activity ratio

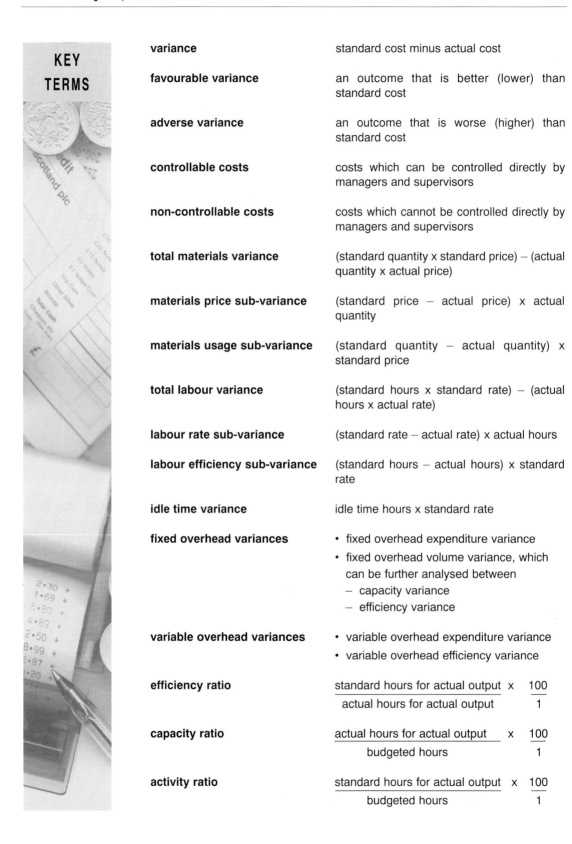

KEY TERMS

variance	standard cost minus actual cost
favourable variance	an outcome that is better (lower) than standard cost
adverse variance	an outcome that is worse (higher) than standard cost
controllable costs	costs which can be controlled directly by managers and supervisors
non-controllable costs	costs which cannot be controlled directly by managers and supervisors
total materials variance	(standard quantity x standard price) – (actual quantity x actual price)
materials price sub-variance	(standard price – actual price) x actual quantity
materials usage sub-variance	(standard quantity – actual quantity) x standard price
total labour variance	(standard hours x standard rate) – (actual hours x actual rate)
labour rate sub-variance	(standard rate – actual rate) x actual hours
labour efficiency sub-variance	(standard hours – actual hours) x standard rate
idle time variance	idle time hours x standard rate
fixed overhead variances	• fixed overhead expenditure variance • fixed overhead volume variance, which can be further analysed between – capacity variance – efficiency variance
variable overhead variances	• variable overhead expenditure variance • variable overhead efficiency variance
efficiency ratio	$\dfrac{\text{standard hours for actual output}}{\text{actual hours for actual output}} \times \dfrac{100}{1}$
capacity ratio	$\dfrac{\text{actual hours for actual output}}{\text{budgeted hours}} \times \dfrac{100}{1}$
activity ratio	$\dfrac{\text{standard hours for actual output}}{\text{budgeted hours}} \times \dfrac{100}{1}$

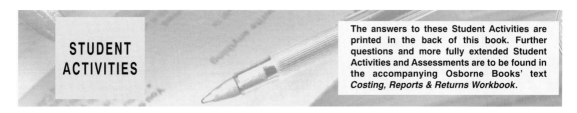

7.1 Rowcester Engineering Limited makes engine castings for a specialist car manufacturer. The castings are made in the foundry and are then sent to the machine shop for machining to the customer's specifications.

As a cost clerk, you have been asked to prepare a standard cost based on budgeted output of 1,000 castings. The following information is available to you:

materials for each casting

– 5.5 kg of ordinary steel at £3.50 per kg

– 2.0 kg of high tensile steel at £10.00 per kg

labour for each casting

– 1 hour of foundry-workers' wages at £10.50 per hour

– 1.5 hours in the machine shop at £12.75 per hour

overheads

– fixed production overheads, £5.00 per casting

– variable production overheads, £4.50 per casting

You are to calculate the standard cost of producing 1,000 castings.

7.2 From the following information prepare a standard cost report for week 3 of October 1999 (use a layout similar to that shown on page 124).

product: cardboard boxes, size 750 mm x 400 mm x 300 mm
budgeted output: 5,000 boxes
actual output: 4,500 boxes

standard cost (per unit)	£
materials	0.06
labour	0.10
fixed production overheads	0.03
variable production overheads	0.02

actual costs	
materials	280.00
labour	425.00
fixed production overheads	150.00
variable production overheads	85.00

(a)   What factors do you think may have caused the variances?

(b)   What further analysis of the cost information would you advise?

7.3   The following extract from the standard cost report for the manufacture of ornamental clay garden pots, showing sub-variances for materials and labour, has been passed to you for further action:

	standard cost of making 600 pots		actual cost of making 600 pots		sub-variances			
		£		£		£	£	
materials	900 kilos		800 kilos		price	40		ADV
	at 75p per kg	675	at 80p per kg	640	usage	75		FAV
							35	FAV
labour	150 hours		140 hours		rate	70		ADV
	at £5.00 per hour	750	at £5.50 per hour	770	efficiency	50		FAV
							20	ADV
overheads								
fixed		300		308			8	ADV
variable		150		126			24	FAV
TOTAL COST		1,875		1,844			31	FAV

You are to:

(a)   show how the sub-variances for materials and labour have been calculated

(b)   explain how you will use the variances and sub-variances as part of the process of monitoring costs

7.4   From the following data you are to calculate:

(a)   materials price variance

(b)   materials usage variance

(c)   total materials variance

(Indicate whether each variance is adverse or favourable)

	Standard Price	Standard Usage	Actual Price	Actual Usage
Material A	£5 per kg	100 kgs	£4 per kg	120 kgs
Material B	£20 per unit	120 units	£22 per unit	100 units
Material C	£10 per litre	600 litres	£9 per litre	500 litres
Material D	£2 per metre	300 metres	£3 per metre	250 metres

7.5 From the following data you are to calculate:

(a)   labour rate variance

(b)   labour efficiency variance

(c)   total labour variance

(Indicate whether each variance is adverse or favourable)

	Standard Hours	Standard Wage Rate	Actual Hours	Actual Wage Rate
Product 1	8	£5.00	7	£5.50
Product 2	3	£4.50	4	£5.00
Product 3	24	£6.00	30	£5.75
Product 4	12	£8.00	15	£8.50

7.6 The labour cost for making 2,000 units of a product is expected to be:

• the standard cost of direct labour is £6.50 per hour

• the standard efficiency is 60 hours

The actual results are found to be:

• the actual cost of direct labour is £6.75 per hour

• the production took 65 hours, including 6 hours of idle time caused by a machine breakdown

You are to calculate:

(a)   labour rate variance

(b)   idle time variance

(c)   labour efficiency variance

(d)   total labour variance

7.7 The management accountant of Wyvern Foods Limited is concerned about the cost of chocolate used in the production of 'choc-chip cookies'. She has called a meeting with the production manager and the purchasing manager to discuss the results for November 1998, which are:

• actual production	600,000 cookies
• actual chocolate used	6,500 kgs
• actual cost of chocolate used	£5,460

The budget set out the following:

• standard price of chocolate	£0.80 per kg
• standard usage at production level of 600,000 cookies	6,000 kgs

You are to:

(a)   detail the variances for November 1998

(b)   suggest possible reasons for the cause of these variances

7.8   The management accountant of Wyvern Foods Limited is concerned about the direct labour costs in the production of 'choc-chip cookies'. She has called a meeting with the production manager and the human resources manager to discuss the results for November 1998, which are:

- actual production   600,000 cookies
- actual direct labour hours   840 hours
- actual direct labour cost   £4,368

The budget set out the following:

- standard direct labour cost   £5.00 per hour
- standard direct labour hours at production
  level of 600,000 cookies   850 hours

You are to:

(a)   detail the variances for November 1998

(b)   suggest possible reasons for the cause of these variances

7.9   Pershore Pots makes ornamental clay garden pots. The company budgeted to make 680 pots during October 1999 with production overhead costs of:

fixed overheads   £0.50 per pot

variable overheads   £0.25 per pot

Overheads are absorbed on the basis of the number of direct labour hours.

The standard overhead cost of making 680 pots is budgeted to be:

STANDARD COST (680 POTS)

fixed production overheads
170 hours at £2.00 per hour   =   £340.00
variable production overheads
170 hours at £1.00 per hour   =   £170.00
                                                        £510.00

As the overhead absorption rate is based on the number of direct labour hours:

- fixed overheads: 4 pots per hour at £0.50 per pot = £2.00 per hour
- variable overheads: 4 pots per hour at £0.25 per pot = £1.00 per hour

---

Once production is completed, it is found that 600 pots were produced during the period. The actual cost of the overheads were:

ACTUAL COST (600 POTS)		
fixed production overheads		
140 hours at £2.20 per hour	=	£308.00
variable production overheads		
140 hours at £0.90 per hour	=	£126.00
		£434.00

You are to:

(a)   show the extract from the standard cost report for fixed and variable production overheads, based on an output of 600 pots

(b)   calculate the variances and sub-variances for overheads

(c)   write a brief note for each variance and sub-variance to explain what it means

7.10   Agchem (Western) Limited makes chemicals for the agricultural industry. One of its production lines makes a product under the trade name 'Zeta'. For June 1999 production of Zeta was budgeted at 5,000 bags; actual production was 6,000 bags. The standard and actual cost details for June were as follows:

STANDARD COST PER BAG			
	Quantity	**Unit price**	**Cost per bag**
Materials	10 kgs	£2	£20
Labour	2 hours	£5	£10
Prime cost			£30

ACTUAL COST – JUNE 1999		
	Quantity	**Total cost**
Materials	61,000 kgs	£128,100
Labour	11,850 hours	£ 61,620
Prime cost		£189,720

You are to:

   (a)   Calculate the following cost variances

- materials price variance

- materials usage variance

- labour rate variance

- labour efficiency variance

   (b)   Complete a table of variances and prepare a report that

- summarises the variances for materials and labour

- notes any significant sub-variances of £2,000 or more

- highlights the causes of all materials and labour variances from the information given

Note: For the table of variances, use the layout of the variance schedule in the Appendix at the end of this book.

7.11   The Chester Carpet Company makes quality carpets; one of its popular carpets is the 'Aztec' range. The standard cost of a square metre of 'Aztec' carpet is:

	£
materials, 0.5 kgs at £3.00 per kg	1.50
labour, 30 minutes at £5.00 per hour	2.50
fixed production overheads, 30 minutes at £6.00 per hour	3.00
	7.00

Budget output (square metres) for the month of February 1999	10,000
Actual output (square metres)	9,500

Actual costs for the month were:	£
materials, 4,800 kgs at £3.10 per kg	14,880
labour, 4,700 hours at £5.20 per hour	24,440
fixed production overheads, 4,700 hours at £5.90 per hour	27,730
	67,050

From this data, a colleague has already calculated the fixed overhead variances as:

- fixed production overhead expenditure variance   £2,270 favourable
- fixed production overhead capacity variance   £1,800 adverse
- fixed production overhead efficiency variance   £ 300 favourable

You are to:

(a)   Calculate the following cost variances

- materials price variance

- materials usage variance

- labour rate variance

- labour efficiency variance

(b)   Complete a table of variances and prepare a report that

- summarises the variances for materials, labour, and overheads

- notes any significant sub-variances in excess of £500 or more

- highlights the causes of all material and labour variances from the information given

- derives the under/over-absorption of overheads from the variances calculated and explains how the under/over-absorption has come about

Note: for the table of variances, use the layout of the variance schedule in the Appendix.

7.12   During May 1999, Cradley Castings planned to make 2,000 units of output with 1,000 labour hours. The actual output for the month is 1,890 units made in 1,050 hours.

You are to calculate:

(a)   efficiency ratio

(b)   capacity ratio

(c)   activity ratio

Write a short memorandum on your findings.

8 BOOK-KEEPING FOR COSTING

this chapter covers . . .

This chapter explains:

- the use of
  - a manufacturing account to show production cost
  - a profit and loss account to show net profit
- the importance of identification and coding of costs
- how an integrated book-keeping system incorporates the accounts for both costing and financial accounting
- the book-keeping to record under-absorption and over-absorption of overheads
- the book-keeping to record variances, including the use of a variance account

NVQ PERFORMANCE CRITERIA COVERED

unit 5: RECORDING COST INFORMATION

element 1

record and analyse information relating to direct costs

❏ information relating to direct costs is clearly and correctly coded, analysed and recorded

element 2

record and analyse information relating to the allocation, apportionment and absorption of overhead costs

❏ information relating to overhead costs is accurately and clearly recorded

❏ adjustments for under- or over-recovered overhead costs are made in accordance with established procedures

THE USE OF A MANUFACTURING ACCOUNT

As we saw in Chapter 1, a business brings together all of the costs involved in producing its output in the form of a *total cost statement:*

		£
	Direct materials	x
add	Direct labour	x
add	Direct expenses	x
equals	PRIME COST	x
add	Production overheads	x
equals	PRODUCTION COST	x
add	Non-production overheads, eg	
	• selling and distribution expenses	x
	• administration expenses	x
	• finance expenses	x
equals	TOTAL COST	x

A total cost statement can be prepared on the basis of a single cost unit, or a batch, or a whole production unit such as a factory. However, overall, a business needs to have an accounting system that records its costs and its sales for all its output, and then shows the profit or loss that has been made for the accounting period. For a business such as a retailer that buys and sells goods, without carrying out any production processes, the accounting system is relatively simple – the figure for sales is deducted from the amount of purchases (after allowing for changes in the value of opening and closing stock) and the amount of overheads; a profit is made when sales exceed the total costs. For a manufacturer, though, the costs are more complex as they comprise the direct and indirect costs of materials, labour and expenses; also, a manufacturer will invariably have opening and closing stock in three different forms – direct materials, work-in-progress and finished goods.

In its year-end (or final) accounts a manufacturer uses the layout of the total cost statement and prepares:

• a manufacturing account, which shows production cost

• a profit and loss account, which shows net profit for the accounting period

The final accounts use the following outline:

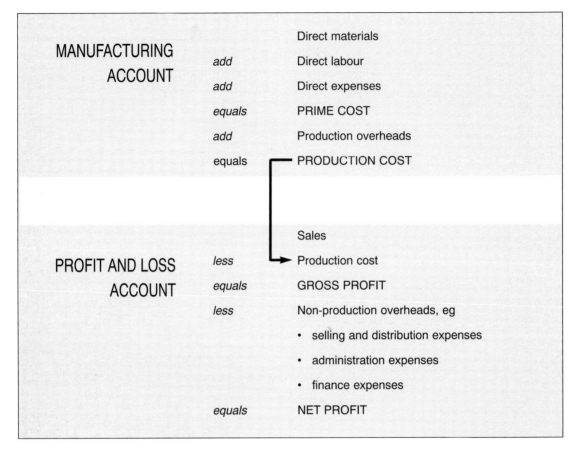

MANUFACTURING ACCOUNT

		Direct materials
add		Direct labour
add		Direct expenses
equals		PRIME COST
add		Production overheads
equals		PRODUCTION COST

PROFIT AND LOSS ACCOUNT

		Sales
less		Production cost
equals		GROSS PROFIT
less		Non-production overheads, eg
		• selling and distribution expenses
		• administration expenses
		• finance expenses
equals		NET PROFIT

notes

- Adjustments have to be made to allow for changes in the value of stock at the start of the accounting period (opening stock) and at the end of the accounting period (closing stock) for:
  - direct materials, in the manufacturing account
  - work-in-progress (or partly manufactured goods), in the manufacturing account
  - finished goods, in the profit and loss account
- The profit and loss account shows two levels of profit:
  - gross profit, the difference between selling price and production cost (after allowing for changes in the value of opening and closing stock)
  - net profit, the profit after all costs have been deducted and which belongs to the owner(s) of the business
- Certain expenses might be apportioned on an appropriate basis between the manufacturing account and the profit and loss account – for example, rates might be apportioned two-thirds to the factory (production overheads) and one-third to the office (non-production overheads)

An example of a manufacturing and profit and loss account is shown below:

ALPHA MANUFACTURING COMPANY

MANUFACTURING AND PROFIT AND LOSS ACCOUNT

for the year ended 31 December 1999

	£	£
Opening stock of direct materials		5,000
Add Purchases of direct materials		50,000
		55,000
Less Closing stock of direct materials		6,000
COST OF DIRECT MATERIALS USED		49,000
Direct labour		26,000
Direct expenses		2,500
PRIME COST		77,500
Add Production (factory) overheads:		
Indirect materials	2,000	
Indirect labour	16,000	
Indirect expenses:		
Rent of factory	5,000	
Depreciation of factory machinery	10,000	
Factory light and heat	4,000	
		37,000
		114,500
Add Opening stock of work-in-progress		4,000
		118,500
Less Closing stock of work-in-progress		3,000
PRODUCTION COST OF GOODS COMPLETED		115,500
Sales		195,500
Opening stock of finished goods	6,500	
Production cost of goods completed	115,500	
	122,000	
Less Closing stock of finished goods	7,500	
COST OF SALES		114,500
Gross profit		81,000
Less Non-production overheads:		
Selling and distribution expenses	38,500	
Administration expenses	32,000	
Finance expenses	3,500	
		74,000
Net profit		7,000

IDENTIFICATION AND CODING OF COSTS

In order to be able to prepare the final accounts of manufacturing account and profit and loss account, a business must use a detailed book-keeping system which enables accurate information to be extracted. For the book-keeping system to be accurate, as costs are incurred they must be charged to the correct account in the system. This is achieved by a system of:

- identification of the cost unit or cost centre to which the cost is to be charged
- coding the cost so that it is charged to the correct book-keeping account of the cost unit or cost centre

Systems of coding have been discussed earlier (page 6). Here we are concerned with the place of the coding system as a part of the book-keeping process. This is illustrated as follows:

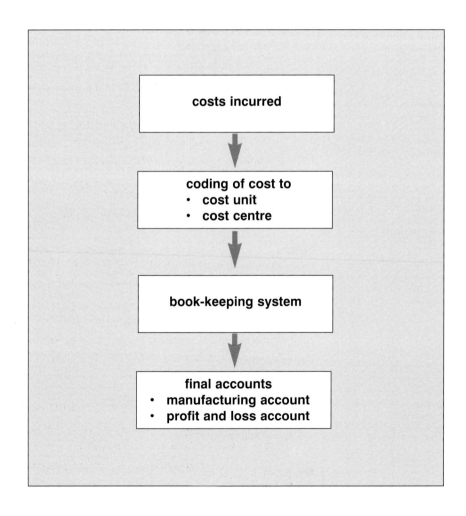

INTEGRATED BOOK-KEEPING SYSTEM

The book-keeping system for costing contains the double-entry accounts which record transactions about the cost of a product or service, and the sales revenues. An *integrated book-keeping system* incorporates the accounts of the business for both costing and financial accounting, ie the book-keeping for the two types of accounting is combined together in one ledger rather than being kept in separate, non-integrated, ledgers. The principles of double-entry book-keeping are followed in that:

- a debit entry records a gain in value, an asset or an expense
- a credit entry records the giving of value, a liability or an income item

We will see how an integrated book-keeping system is used by considering three separate stages:

stage 1 – manufacturing costs and profit and loss account

stage 2 – direct and indirect costs

stage 3 – receipts and payments

Using the diagram on the next page, we will focus on each of the three stages.

stage 1 – manufacturing costs and profit and loss account (on the right-hand side of the diagram)

- this stage incorporates the manufacturing costs of materials, labour and production overheads
- these costs are debited to work-in-progress account
- from work-in-progress account the cost of those goods that are completed is transferred to finished goods account
- cost of sales is the manufacturing cost of those goods that have been sold
- profit and loss account incorporates the non-production overheads
- profit is sales minus cost of sales and non-production overheads
- transfers out of materials, work-in-progress and finished goods are for the amount taken to the next stage of production; for example, with materials, only those materials used in production will be transferred to work-in-progress – any balance remaining on materials account represents the stock held at the end of the accounting period

stage 2 – direct and indirect costs (on the left-hand side of the diagram)

- this shows how the direct and indirect costs are built up on the debit side of each account
- amounts are then transferred to manufacturing costs and profit and loss account

direct and indirect costs

manufacturing costs and profit and loss account

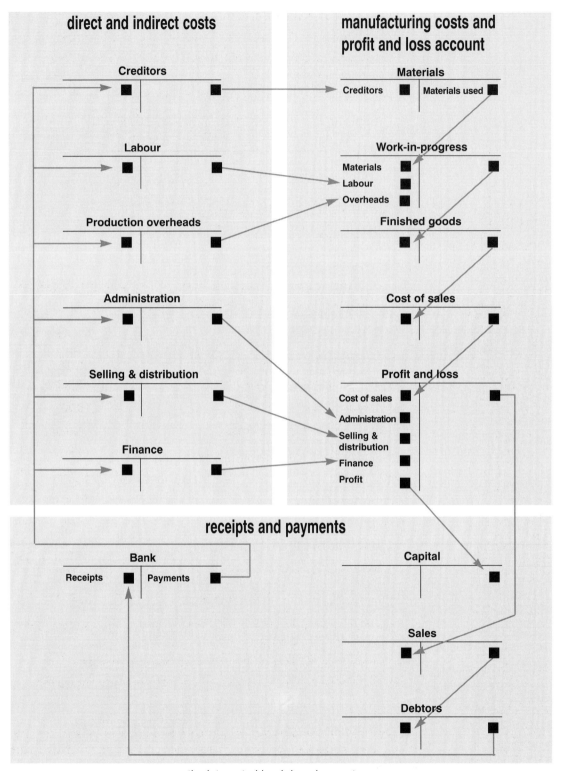

the integrated book-keeping system

stage 3 – receipts and payments (at the bottom of the diagram)

- here profit for the accounting period is transferred to capital
- the sales account is linked to profit and loss account and to the debtors' accounts
- receipts from debtors are debited in bank account
- payments are made from bank account to settle creditors and the direct and indirect costs of the business, so completing the book-keeping 'loop'

CASE STUDY

MARTLEY MANUFACTURING: INTEGRATED BOOK-KEEPING SYSTEM

situation

Martley Manufacturing started in business making wooden toys on 1 January 1999. During January the following transactions took place:

	£
Opening capital paid in to bank	10,000
Direct materials bought on credit	5,000
Direct labour costs paid by cheque	6,000
Production overheads paid by cheque	3,000
Non-production overheads paid by cheque	2,000
Credit sales	15,000
Receipts from debtors	12,000
Payments to creditors	3,500
Direct materials transferred to work-in-progress	4,000
Work-in-progress transferred to finished goods	11,000
Finished goods transferred to cost of sales	10,000

The above transactions are to be recorded in the integrated book-keeping system of Martley Manufacturing. Note that:

- the full cost of direct labour is to be transferred to work-in-progress
- the full cost of production overheads is to be transferred to work-in-progress

solution

It is suggested that you 'audit' the month's transactions to the double-entry accounts; in particular, ensure that you can understand the debit and credit entry for each transaction.

STAGE 1: MANUFACTURING COSTS AND PROFIT AND LOSS ACCOUNT

Dr		**Materials Account**		Cr
	£			£
Creditors	5,000	Work-in-progress		4,000
		Balance c/d		1,000
	5,000			5,000
Balance b/d	1,000			

Dr		**Work-in-Progress Account**		Cr
	£			£
Direct materials	4,000	Finished goods		11,000
Direct labour	6,000	Balance c/d		2,000
Production overhead	3,000			
	13,000			13,000
Balance b/d	2,000			

Dr		**Finished Goods Account**		Cr
	£			£
Work-in-progress	11,000	Cost of sales		10,000
		Balance c/d		1,000
	11,000			11,000
Balance b/d	1,000			

Dr		**Cost of Sales Account**		Cr
	£			£
Finished goods	10,000	Profit and loss		10,000

Dr		**Profit and Loss Account**		Cr
	£			£
Cost of sales	10,000	Sales		15,000
Non-production overhead	2,000			
Net profit (to capital account)	3,000			
	15,000			15,000

STAGE 2: DIRECT AND INDIRECT COSTS

Dr		**Creditors' Account**		Cr
	£			£
Bank	3,500	Materials		5,000
Balance c/d	1,500			
	5,000			5,000
		Balance b/d		1,500

Dr		**Labour Costs Account**		Cr
	£			£
Bank	6,000	Work-in-progress		6,000

Dr		**Production Overheads Account**		Cr
	£			£
Bank	3,000	Work-in-progress		3,000

Dr		**Non-Production Overheads Account**		Cr
	£			£
Bank	2,000	Profit and loss		2,000

STAGE 3: RECEIPTS AND PAYMENTS

Dr		**Capital Account**		Cr
	£			£
Balance c/d	13,000	Bank		10,000
		Profit and loss		3,000
	13,000			13,000
		Balance b/d		13,000

Dr		**Sales Account**		Cr
	£			£
Profit and loss	15,000	Debtors		15,000

Dr	**Debtors Account**		Cr
	£		£
Sales	15,000	Bank	12,000
		Balance c/d	3,000
	15,000		15,000
Balance b/d	3,000		

Dr	**Bank Account**		Cr
	£		£
Capital	10,000	Creditors	3,500
Debtors	12,000	Labour	6,000
		Production overheads	3,000
		Non-production overheads	2,000
		Balance c/d	7,500
	22,000		22,000
Balance b/d	7,500		

In bank account the transactions have been listed in the order in which they appear in the book-keeping, and are not necessarily in chronological order.

Note the following points:

• At the end of January the book-keeping system balances, as shown by the following trial balance:

	Dr	Cr
	£	£
Materials	1,000	
Work-in-progress	2,000	
Finished goods	1,000	
Creditors		1,500
Capital		13,000
Debtors	3,000	
Bank	7,500	
	14,500	14,500

• As the business has stocks of materials, work-in-progress and raw materials at the end of the month, transfers from the accounts to the next stage of production are reduced; the balance remaining on each account shows the value of the stock at the end of the month.

• For simplicity, control accounts have not been used. An example of a wages control account is shown in Chapter 3, page 55.

OVERHEADS: UNDER-ABSORPTION AND OVER-ABSORPTION

In Chapter 5, we saw that businesses often set pre-determined overhead rates for production overheads. However differences occur between the pre-determined rate and the actual amount of overhead absorbed into the cost units because of a combination of:

- actual output differing from expected output
- actual costs incurred differing from expected costs

Thus it is common for overhead to be either under-absorbed, or over-absorbed:

- with under-absorption the overheads absorbed into the cost units are less than the overheads actually incurred
- with over-absorption the overheads absorbed into the cost units are more than the overheads actually incurred

Under-absorbed overhead is debited to profit and loss account, where it adds to costs and reduces profit; over-absorbed overhead is credited to profit and loss account, where it increases profit. Remember that neither excessive under- or over-absorption of overheads is desirable; they are an indication that the product has been costed inaccurately, which is likely to mean that the selling price has been calculated either too low (under-absorption) or too high (over-absorption).

For non-production overheads, there are no under-absorption or over-absorption amounts. This is because non-production overheads are not part of production cost; instead their costs are debited directly to profit and loss account.

CASE STUDY

UNDER-ABSORPTION AND OVER-ABSORPTION OF OVERHEADS – DEPARTMENTS A AND B

DEPARTMENT A

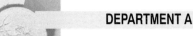

situation

- overhead absorption rate is £2.00 per direct labour hour
- direct labour hours worked in March were 2,000
- actual cost of production overhead in March was £4,500

solution

overhead absorbed by cost units £2.00 x 2,000 hours	=	£4,000
actual cost of production overhead	=	£4,500
under-absorption of overhead	=	£500

The work-in-progress account is charged with production overheads of £4,000; however, this will leave a debit balance of £500 on production overheads account. This amount is transferred to profit and loss account as follows:

- debit profit and loss account

- credit production overheads account

Production overheads account appears as follows:

Dr		**Production Overheads Account: Department A**	Cr
	£		£
Bank	4,500	Work-in-progress	4,000
		Profit and loss (under-absorption)	500
	4,500		4,500

The amount of under-absorbed overhead adds to the total costs of the business, and so reduces profits.

DEPARTMENT B

situation

- overhead absorption rate is £5.00 per machine hour
- machine hours worked in March were 5,000
- actual cost of production overhead in March was £23,000

solution

- overhead absorbed by cost units £5.00 x 5,000 hours = £25,000
- actual cost of production overhead   = £23,000
- over-absorption of overhead   = £ 2,000

The work-in-progress account is charged with production overheads of £25,000; however, this will leave a credit balance of £2,000 on production overheads account. This amount is transferred to profit and loss account as follows:

- debit production overheads account

- credit profit and loss account

Production overheads account appears as follows:

Dr		**Production Overheads Account: Department B**	Cr
	£		£
Bank	23,000	Work-in-progress	25,000
Profit and loss (over-absorption)	2,000		
	25,000		25,000

The amount of over-absorbed overhead adds to profits; however, it should be remembered that the overhead recovery rate may have been set too high and, as a consequence, sales might have been lost because the selling price has been set too high.

VARIANCES

In the book-keeping system for costing, variances are divided into two groups:

1 variances that relate to costs

- – materials price variance
- – labour rate variance
- – fixed production overhead expenditure variance
- – variable production overhead expenditure variance

2 variances that relate to usage and efficiency

- – materials usage variance
- – labour efficiency variance
- – idle time variance
- – fixed production overhead capacity variance
- – fixed production overhead efficiency variance
- – variable production overhead efficiency variance

The first group of variances, because the variances relate to changes in costs, is recorded in the appropriate expenses account, eg materials account, labour costs account. The second group of variances, because the variances relate to the efficiency of production, is recorded in the work-in-progress account. As we will see, for all variances:

- • a favourable variance is debited
- • an adverse variance is credited

The opposite book-keeping entry for these is recorded in a *variance account* which stores up details of the variances. The balance of this account, ie the difference between favourable and adverse variances, is transferred to profit and loss account as follows:

- • if adverse variances exceed favourable variances, the difference is *debited* to profit and loss account
- • if favourable variances exceed adverse variances, the difference is *credited* to profit and loss account

Note that the alternative accounting treatment is to maintain separate variance accounts for each variance, eg materials price variance account, materials usage variance account, etc. Each variance – favourable or adverse – is then transferred to profit and loss account where it can be identified by managers.

This flow of book-keeping for variances is shown in the diagram below.

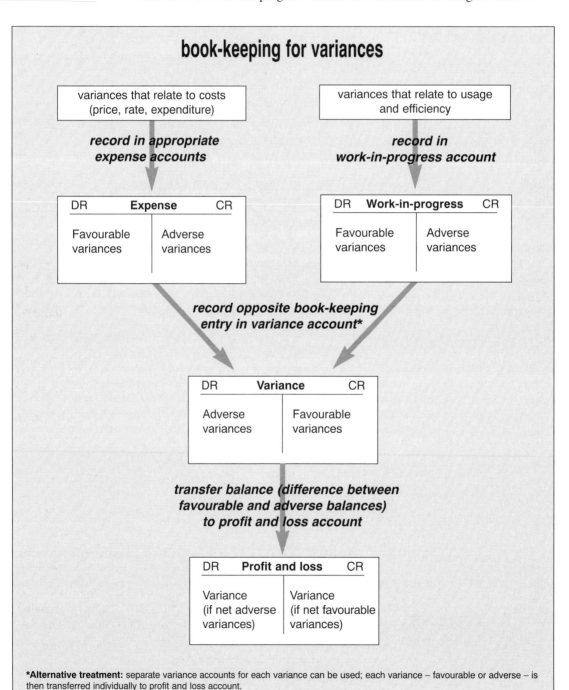

book-keeping for variances

variances that relate to costs (price, rate, expenditure)	variances that relate to usage and efficiency

record in appropriate expense accounts   *record in work-in-progress account*

DR	Expense	CR		DR	Work-in-progress	CR
Favourable variances	Adverse variances			Favourable variances	Adverse variances	

record opposite book-keeping entry in variance account*

DR	Variance	CR
Adverse variances	Favourable variances	

transfer balance (difference between favourable and adverse balances) to profit and loss account

DR	Profit and loss	CR
Variance (if net adverse variances)	Variance (if net favourable variances)	

*Alternative treatment: separate variance accounts for each variance can be used; each variance – favourable or adverse – is then transferred individually to profit and loss account.

MARTLEY MANUFACTURING: BOOK-KEEPING FOR VARIANCES

situation

The accountant of Martley Manufacturing is in the process of completing the month-end cost accounts in respect of materials and labour. She has calculated the materials usage variance at £3,000 favourable, and the labour efficiency variance at £4,000 adverse. These, together with the materials price variance and the labour rate variance, have not yet been recorded in the accounts which are as follows:

Dr		**Materials Account**		Cr
	£			£
Balance b/d	25,000	Work-in-progress		175,000
Creditors	175,000	Balance c/d		20,000

Dr		**Labour Costs Account**		Cr
	£			£
Bank	106,000	Work-in-progress		108,000

Dr		**Work-in-Progress Account**		Cr
	£			£
Balance b/d	15,000	Finished goods		277,000
Materials	175,000	Balance c/d		20,000
Labour	108,000			

Dr		**Variance Account**		Cr
	£			£

Show how these accounts will be completed to show the variances at the month-end.

solution

- On materials account, as the work-in-progress transfer and the balance of materials at the month-end have been completed, the remaining entry to record is materials price variance; this is £200,000 – £195,000 = £5,000 *adverse*.
- For labour, the rate variance is £2,000 *favourable*.
- The materials usage variance and the labour efficiency variance will be recorded in work-in-progress account.

Dr		Materials Account		Cr
	£			£
Balance b/d	25,000	Work-in-progress		175,000
Creditors	175,000	Balance c/d		20,000
		Variance account (materials price variance)		5,000
	200,000			200,000

Dr		Labour Costs Account		Cr
	£			£
Bank	106,000	Work-in-progress		108,000
Variance account (labour rate variance)	2,000			
	108,000			108,000

Dr		Work-in-Progress Account		Cr
	£			£
Balance b/d	15,000	Finished goods		277,000
Materials	175,000	Balance c/d		20,000
Labour	108,000			
Variance account (materials usage variance)	3,000	Variance account (labour efficiency variance)		4,000
	301,000			301,000

Dr		Variance Account*		Cr
	£			£
Materials price variance	5,000	Labour rate variance		2,000
Labour efficiency variance	4,000	Materials usage variance		3,000
		Profit and loss account		4,000
	9,000			9,000

* As noted earlier (page 169), separate accounts for each variance could be used.

Note that, in the variance account, adverse variances exceed favourable variances by £4,000; thus profit and loss account is debited with net adverse variances of £4,000. This reduces profit by £4,000, and the cause of the variances will need to be investigated.

CHAPTER SUMMARY

- A manufacturing account shows prime cost and production cost.

- Profit and loss account shows non-production overheads and the net profit of the business.

- Correct identification and coding of costs is important in the preparation of accurate final accounts.

- An integrated book-keeping system incorporates the accounts of the business for both costing and financial accounting.

- Under- or over-absorption of overheads affects profit:
  - under-absorbed overhead is debited to profit and loss account, so reducing profit
  - over-absorbed overhead is credited to profit and loss account, so increasing profit

- Variances that relate to costs are recorded in the appropriate expenses account.

- Variances that relate to the efficiency of production are recorded in work-in-progress account.

- Adverse variances are debited to variance account; favourable variances are credited to variance account.

- The balance of variance account is transferred to profit and loss account:
  - if net adverse variance, it is debited, so reducing profit
  - if net favourable variance, it is credited, so increasing profit

KEY TERMS

manufacturing account	double-entry account which brings together all the elements of cost that make up production cost
integrated book-keeping	combines the accounts for costing and financial accounting
under-absorption of overheads	where overheads absorbed into the cost units are less than the overheads actually incurred; profit is reduced
over-absorption of overheads	where overheads absorbed into the cost units are more than the overheads actually incurred; profit is increased
variance account	account which is - debited with adverse variances - credited with favourable variances the difference is transferred to profit and loss account

8.1 Which one of the following does not appear in a manufacturing account?

(a) depreciation of factory machinery

(b) indirect labour

(c) depreciation of office equipment

(d) factory light and heat

Answer (a) or (b) or (c) or (d)

8.2 For a manufacturing business, which type of stock is recorded in the profit and loss account?

(a) raw materials

(b) work-in-progress

(c) partly manufactured goods

(d) finished goods

Answer (a) or (b) or (c) or (d)

8.3 Allocate the following costs to:

• manufacturing account

• profit and loss account

(a) factory rent

(b) production supervisors' wages

(c) insurance of factory buildings

(d) depreciation of office equipment

(e) sales commission

(f) raw materials purchased

(g) advertising

8.4   The following figures relate to Crown Heath Manufacturing Company for the year ended 31 December 1998:

	£
Stocks at 1 January 1998:	
Raw materials	10,500
Finished goods	4,300
Stocks at 31 December 1998:	
Raw materials	10,200
Finished goods	3,200
Expenditure during year:	
Purchases of raw materials	27,200
Factory wages – direct	12,600
Factory wages – indirect	3,900
Factory rent and rates	1,200
Factory power	2,000
Depreciation of factory machinery	900
Repairs to factory buildings	300
Sundry factory expenses	900
Non-production overheads	6,500
Sales during year	60,400

You are to prepare the year end:
- manufacturing account
- profit and loss account

8.5   The following figures relate to the accounts of Barbara Francis, who runs a furniture manufacturing business, for the year ended 31 December 1998:

	£
Stocks of raw materials at 1 January 1998	31,860
Stocks of raw materials, 31 December 1998	44,790
Stocks of finished goods, 1 January 1998	42,640
Stocks of finished goods, 31 December 1998	96,510
Purchases of raw materials	237,660
Sale of finished goods	796,950
Rent and rates	32,920
Manufacturing wages	234,630
Manufacturing power	7,650
Manufacturing heat and light	2,370
Manufacturing expenses and maintenance	8,190
Salaries	138,700
Advertising	22,170
Office expenses	7,860
Depreciation of plant and machinery	7,450

Three-quarters of the rent and rates are to be treated as a manufacturing charge.

You are to prepare the year end:
• manufacturing account
• profit and loss account

8.6   P & A Manufacturing started in business on 1 July 1999. During July the following transactions took place:

	£
Opening capital paid into bank	50,000
Bought machinery, paying by cheque	20,000
Direct materials bought on credit	7,500

Direct labour costs paid by cheque	10,000
Production overheads paid by cheque	5,000
Non-production overheads paid by cheque	4,000
Credit sales	37,000
Receipts from debtors	25,000
Paid to creditors	7,000
Direct materials transferred to work-in-progress	6,000
Work-in-progress transferred to finished goods	19,000
Finished goods transferred to cost of sales	16,000

You are to:

(a) Record the above transactions in the integrated book-keeping system of P & A Manufacturing and show the net profit for the month. (Note that the full cost of direct labour and production overheads is to be transferred to work-in-progress.)

(b) Show the the trial balance at 31 July 1999, *after* preparing the profit and loss account.

8.7 A company's wages account for last week had two credit entries:

- work-in-progress account   £16,500
- production overheads account   £5,900

Explain the purpose of these two entries.

8.8 Production overheads of £125 have been under-absorbed in the machining department of Mereford Limited. Identify the double-entry book-keeping to record this in the accounts.

8.9 Last month the overheads of the finishing department of Eveshore Packers were over-absorbed.

- What is the accounting treatment for this?
- What will be the effect on profit for the period?

8.10 The following information is available about two departments of Mac Manufacturing for the month of April 1999:

DEPARTMENT A

- overhead absorption rate is £3.00 per direct labour hour
- direct labour hours work in April were 1,240
- actual cost of production overhead in April was £3,800

DEPARTMENT B

- overhead absorption rate is £6.00 per machine hour
- machine hours worked in April were 1,660
- actual cost of production overhead in April was £9,040

You are to show for each department:

- the under- or over-absorption of overhead
- the production overheads account, including any transfer to profit and loss account

8.11 An adverse materials usage variance has been identified. Which is the correct book-keeping entry to record this?

(a)   debit materials account; credit variance account

(b)   debit work-in-progress account; credit variance account

(c)   debit variance account; credit materials account

(d)   debit variance account; credit work-in-progress account

Note: assume that a variance account is in use.

Answer (a) or (b) or (c) or (d)

8.12 The following variances of Rowcester Manufacturing have been calculated for the four weeks ended 19 February 1999:

- materials price variance, £95 favourable
- materials usage variance, £40 adverse
- labour rate variance, £102 adverse
- labour efficiency variance, £55 favourable
- variable production overhead expenditure variance, £35 adverse
- variable production overhead efficiency variance, £47 favourable

You are to show how these will be recorded in:

- materials account
- labour costs account
- production overheads account
- work-in-progress account
- variance account, including any transfer to profit and loss account

preparing reports & returns

NVQ competences covered

UNIT 6: PREPARING REPORTS AND RETURNS

element 1

prepare and present periodic performance reports	chapter
❏ information derived from different units of the organisation is consolidated into the appropriate form	9,10
❏ information derived from different information systems within the organisation is correctly reconciled	9
❏ when comparing results over time an appropriate method, which allows for changing price levels, is used	12
❏ transactions between separate units of the organisation are accounted for in accordance with the organisation's procedures	10
❏ ratios and performance indicators are accurately calculated in accordance with the organisation's procedures	10
❏ reports are prepared in the appropriate form and presented to management within required timescales	11,12

element 2

prepare reports and returns for outside agencies	chapter
❏ relevant information is identified, collated and presented in accordance with the conventions and definitions used by outside agencies	13
❏ calculations of ratios and performance indicators are accurate	13
❏ authorisation for the despatch of completed reports and returns is sought from the appropriate person	13
❏ reports and returns are presented in accordance with outside agencies' requirements and deadlines	13

element 3

prepare VAT returns	chapter
❏ VAT returns are correctly completed using data from the appropriate recording systems and are submitted within the statutory time limits	14,15
❏ relevant inputs and outputs are correctly identified and calculated	14,15
❏ submissions are made in accordance with current legislation	14,15
❏ guidance is sought from the VAT office when required, in a professional manner	14,15

9 REPORTING INFORMATION

this chapter covers . . .

In this chapter we take a practical look at the types of financial and non-financial information used by management. We look at:

- external information, such as government statistics
- the different types of internal financial information – related to costs and revenue – that will be recorded
- non-financial internal information such as the number of units of output
- the different types of organisations and their structure
- the need for financial information at different levels within the organisation

In the next chapter we examine the way in which performance – eg profitability – can be measured by the use of performance indicators.

NVQ PERFORMANCE CRITERIA COVERED

unit 6: PREPARING REPORTS AND RETURNS

element 1

prepare and present periodic performance reports

❏ information derived from different units of the organisation is consolidated into the appropriate form

❏ information derived from different information systems within the organisation is correctly reconciled

THE NEED FOR INFORMATION

There are many different types of organisation that an accountant may deal with, ranging from the sole trader business to the public limited company or major charity. People who run organisations need a wide variety of information – financial data and other forms of information – in order to make management decisions. Information can either be *external* or *internal*.

EXTERNAL INFORMATION

External information includes:

• the way individual competitors are performing
• the way the industry is performing
• the way the economy is performing
• what is required by legislation

This type of information can be gathered by studying Government statistics (economic reports), trade and Chamber of Commerce publications and by subscribing to commercially available industry and company reports.

government statistics

Government statistical publications, available in reference libraries and in certain cases on-line, can be very useful to businesses in the planning process, showing patterns of change in population, income, and economic well-being in the UK. These publications include:

Social Trends   This book of statistics presents a interesting picture of the UK's social make-up, providing details about population, income, transport and leisure interests.

Economic Trends   This provides data about the economic performance within the UK

Censuses   The government regularly publishes data relating to population and production in the regions.

Other useful publications include the *Annual Abstract of Statistics, Monthly Digest of Statistics, Business Monitor, National Income Statistics, Import and Export Statistics.*

commercial organisations and Trade Associations

Much useful information can be gathered from organisations which cater for the needs of businesses and particular trades and professions. These include the Confederation of British Industry (CBI), Chambers of Commerce – local and national, Business Clubs and Trade Associations.

the relevance of external statistics

You may well ask what relevance these publications have for Accounting Technicians. Your studies do not require you to be familiar with the details of all these sources, but their relevance is the point that no business can afford to 'bury its head in the sand' – an awareness of external information will enable it to make sensible decisions. For example, the fact that people have more leisure time than previously and that there are more retired people with money to spend than ever before means that a business developing up-market holidays is likely to be profitable – because the statistics are in its favour.

Another area in which these statistics are relevant is in their compilation. As we will see in Chapter 13 you may be required to provide financial and other information to government agencies and other bodies that are collecting data.

INTERNAL INFORMATION

Internal information can be financial or non-financial.

Financial internal information required by an organisation includes:

* *costs* – eg wages, the price of supplies, overheads, and
* *revenues* – the sales of products and services

Non-financial information includes items such as units of output, the numbers of employees and the number of items in stock.

The information collected may well cover a wide time period:

* *past* performance – eg previous years' costs and revenues
* *present* performance – up-to-date reports
* *future* performance – eg what is forecast to happen in the next 12 months

The way this information is gathered and presented forms the material for the remainder of this book. An organisation which successfully gathers and summarises this information is in a position to make informed decisions.

The problem is that some organisations are in a better position to carry out this process than others. Organisations with 'flat' structures (these are often the smaller organisations) have fewer problems with communication than the 'hierarchical' organisations which have more levels through which the information has to pass.

ORGANISATIONAL STRUCTURES

flat organisational structure

The sole trader business will have a 'flat' organisational structure. The example shown below shows the simple structure of a sole trader shop which employs four assistants: three in the shop and one in the stock room.

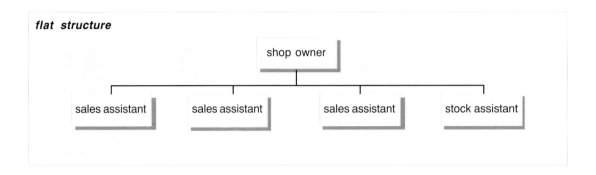

flat **structure**

The information that the owner needs will be simple and readily available: sales figures from the shop tills and stock levels from the stockroom. Financial control is straightforward: sales can be monitored easily and decisions about what to stock and what not to stock taken on a day-to-day basis. Flat structures are also typical of modern larger organisations which have had layers of middle management 'stripped out'.

hierarchical organisational structure

Many organisations, however, are far more complex in structure, and reporting has to take place through a series of different levels. Such an organisation has a *hierarchical* structure such as the one illustrated on the next page. This is a traditional structure, typified by a limited company business. It is also known as a *pyramid* or *tall* structure. The main features of this type of structure are:

- a hierarchy – a series of levels, each responsible to and controlled by the level above

- as you move up the levels, the number of people or units decreases – hence the 'pyramid' effect

- at the top of the pyramid is the managing director (or equivalent) who is ultimately responsible for all decision-making, including financial decisions based on information passed up through the company

hierarchical structure

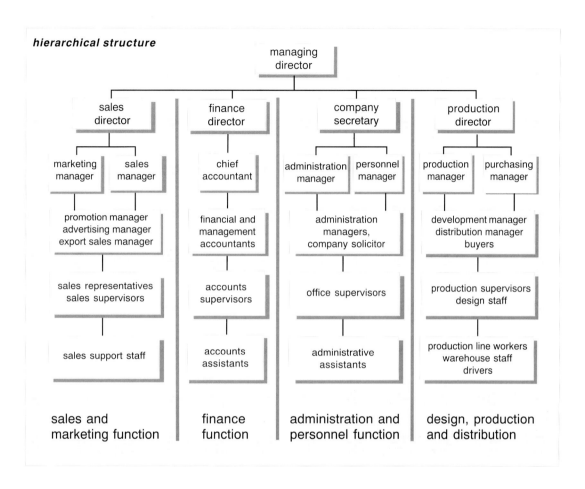

REPORTING INFORMATION

reporting at different levels

It should be noted at this point that the *amount* of detail reported at each level varies according to the *needs* of the person for whom the report is prepared. This is best understood by looking at a working example.

Labour cost is often a significant item for any organisation. What type of reporting is necessary at the different levels of a manufacturing business?

- *production-line workers* will complete time sheets or clock cards
- *payroll clerks* will prepare a payroll analysis showing what each employee has earned and will be paid each time the payroll is run
- *line management* will obtain labour costings for various product areas and compare against budget and take decisions relating to efficiency and work practices

- *senior management* will obtain an overall report of the labour cost of all the areas of the business and take strategic decisions – what products to develop, what products to scrap, which departments to expand and where to look for redundancies

In other words, as the reporting process goes up through the hierarchy (the management levels), there is *less depth of detail at each level* but more of an overall picture of what is going on in the organisation.

what is recorded and reported?

So far we have referred to labour hours in a manufacturing business, but it is important to appreciate that the recording and reporting process is common to all organisations and covers a wide variety of *costs* and *revenues* and other statistics. The table on the next page shows in more detail what might be recorded and used in the reporting process in manufacturing and service industries. You will see that in addition to costs and revenues other factors such as floor area and occupancy rates are recorded in order to provide information about the efficiency and profitability of the organisation.

quality reporting

It is obvious that if the reporting process is to be valid and efficient, the data brought together must be in a *appropriate* format. It must:

- *be consistent* – the same forms and counting systems must be used throughout the organisation; for example there is no point in comparing Shop A and Shop B if floor areas are measured in square metres and square feet respectively
- *relate to the same time period* – if the reporting period is a week, it must be the same week and all data must cover the same hours
- *be reported promptly* – if data is late in coming in, it may miss the deadline for a report; this may invalidate the whole process
- *be accurate* – if inaccurate information is provided, not only will the reporting process be flawed but a wrong decision may result; as an extreme example management might decide to discontinue a product

reconciling information from different sources

The internal checking procedures within an organisation should ensure that information collected centrally for reporting purposes should be reconciled. For example:

- the total labour hours recorded for all employees on the payroll analysis should agree with the total of the hours charged out to the departments
- the total unit sales of a chain of shops – normally recorded on the shops' electronic tills – should agree with the records of stock movements

A MANUFACTURER	- sales revenue from each product
	- the cost of producing each product
	- administration and finance costs
	- the number of units of each product manufactured

These statistics enable the management to calculate the cost and the profitability of manufacturing each product.

A SUPERMARKET CHAIN	- the sales of each shop
	- the staffing and overhead cost of each shop
	- the selling area of each shop (square metres)
	- the number of customers per shop

These statistics enable the management to calculate how busy each shop is, how much customers spend and how profitable each shop is per square metre.

A GROUP OF HOTELS	- the revenue from each hotel
	- the running costs of each hotel
	- the number of rooms per hotel
	- the number of rooms occupied each night

These statistics enable the management to calculate how full each hotel is, and how profitable it is.

A HEALTH SERVICE TRUST	- the revenue from each hospital
	- the running costs of each hospital
	- the number of beds per hospital
	- the number of patients treated

These statistics enable the management to calculate the efficiency and profitability of each hospital.

manufacturing and service industries: reporting of information

- Organisations need accurate information to help them make management decisions. This information can be internal or externally sourced. It can relate to past, present or future time periods.

- Externally-sourced information includes data from government published statistics, Chambers of Commerce and Trade Associations.

- Internal financial information that will be particularly useful involves both revenues and costs – money in and money out.

- Non-financial information which will be used includes items such as: units produced, hours worked, number of employees, floor areas.

- The ability for information to pass within an organisation will depend to some extent on its structure; traditionally, communication has been better in a 'flat' structure than in a hierarchical structure with a number of management levels.

- The amount of detail in reporting will vary according to the level for which the report is prepared: a senior management report will comprise an overall picture with summarised information; a lower level report will contain more operational detail and less of a 'global' picture.

- Valid reported information must be consistent, prompt, accurate and relate to a specific time period.

- Information gathered within an organisation must be reconciled with the internal records of the organisation in order to ensure that it is accurate and consistent.

financial information	information which is measured in money terms, eg revenues and costs
non-financial information	information which is not measured in money terms but relates to other areas of business activity such as the level of output and the number of employees
flat structure	an organisational structure which has few 'layers' of management – it is typical of a small business or a modern organisation which has had its middle layers 'stripped out'
hierarchical structure	an organisational structure which has a number of different layers of management through which communication and information has to pass

9.1 (a)   State four reasons why an organisation needs external information.

(b)   What are the main *sources* of external statistics?

(c)   Why should *Social Trends* prove useful?

9.2 What are the *two* main types of internal financial data used in the information gathering process of an organisation?

9.3 The flow of information through a hierarchical structure is likely to be more efficient than the flow through a flat structure.

True or false? Give reasons for your answer.

9.4 What data is likely to be included in

(a)   a labour performance report for a supervisor?

(b)   a labour performance report presented to a managing director?

Explain the reasons why the two reports are likely to be different.

9.5 What types of internal information are likely to be used in performance reports for the following organisations:

(a)   a hospital

(b)   a firm of accountants

(c)   a manufacturer of computer games

(d)   a company owning a gym in three different towns

10 MEASURING PERFORMANCE

this chapter covers . . .

In this chapter we take a more detailed look at the financial information recorded within organisations and used by management. We look at the way the information is reported in the form of:

- performance indicators relating to productivity, cost per unit, the utilisation of resources and profitability
- specific ratios and percentages: gross profit margin, net profit margin and the return on capital employed
- the recording of transactions between separate units of an organisation

In the next chapter we examine the way in which this type of information is presented in report format.

NVQ PERFORMANCE CRITERIA COVERED

unit 6: PREPARING REPORTS AND RETURNS

element 1

prepare and present periodic performance reports

❑ information derived from different units of the organisation is consolidated in the appropriate form

❑ ratios and performance indicators are accurately calculated in accordance with the organisation's procedures

❑ transactions between separate units of the organisation are accounted for in accordance with the organisation's procedures

PERFORMANCE INDICATORS

In simple terms a *performance indicator* is a method of expressing by way of a formula how well a business is performing in certain areas:

- *productivity* – how well it is using its available resources
- *cost per unit* – how much it costs to produce each item it makes
- *resource utilisation* – how well it is making use of its workforce and equipment
- *profitability* – how great a return it is making on its sales and capital employed

Remember that more businesses are now in the service sector than in manufacturing: the terms 'product' or 'item sold' apply equally to holidays, audits carried out, sessions in the gym, as to manufactured goods such as cars and packets of crisps.

We will deal with each of these performance indicators in turn.

PRODUCTIVITY

If you say that you have had a 'productive' day you mean that you have achieved a great deal despite all the circumstances. For a business or organisation which manufactures a product or provides a service 'productivity' measures

the level of output (goods manufactured or services provided) in relation to the cost of producing the product or service

labour productivity

Labour productivity is normally measured by dividing the output (the number of items produced or services provided) over a given period (eg week, year) by the number of employees. Take, for example, a travel agency business which employs 4 staff and aims to arrange 500 holidays in a week.

The productivity (the output per employee per week) is calculated as follows:

$$\text{output per employee} = \frac{\text{output (500 holidays)}}{\text{number of employees (4)}} = \frac{500}{4} = 125$$

It is common practice to compare *actual* output against the benchmark of *expected* (standard) output. For example, the travel agency may have set 125 holidays per week as the standard level of productivity per employee, but over a four week period with 4 staff it achieves the results shown below. The right-hand column shows productivity per employee.

period	holidays booked	productivity
Week 1	520	130
Week 2	600	150
Week 3	440	110
Week 4	580	145

A further method of measuring labour productivity, which is useful when there is a variety of products and a fluctuating number of employees is to compare output in money terms (eg the sales figure) and the number of hours worked over a given period:

$$\text{labour productivity (sales per hour)} = \frac{\text{output (£) over a given period}}{\text{hours worked over a given period}}$$

efficiency

The efficiency of an organisation – expressed as a percentage – is calculated by comparing actual output (in units) with expected (standard) output:

$$\text{efficiency \%} = \frac{\text{actual output (units)} \times 100}{\text{expected/standard output (units)}}$$

In the case of the travel agency on the previous page, the efficiency percentage in week 1 in which 520 holidays have been booked (against the expected 500) is:

$$\text{efficiency \%} = \frac{520 \text{ (actual output)} \times 100}{500 \text{ (expected output)}} = 104\%$$

It is then a simple calculator operation (dividing actual output by expected output) to see that the efficiency in the other weeks was: 120% in week 2, 88% in week 3 and 116% in week 4.

other productivity measures

Organisations often find it useful to compare output over a given period with factors other than labour. Examples in the manufacturing sector include:

machine productivity   = $\dfrac{\text{sales (£) over a given period}}{\text{machine hours for the period}}$

capital productivity   = $\dfrac{\text{sales (£) over a given period}}{\text{capital employed (see page 199)}}$

Examples in the services industries include:

in a supermarket (sales per employee): $\dfrac{\text{sales (£) over a given period}}{\text{employees}}$

at a college (contact hours per lecturer): $\dfrac{\text{total student contact hours}}{\text{lecturers employed}}$

cost per unit

Another performance indicator is the cost per unit.

cost per unit is the cost of producing each unit

This is calculated using the formula

cost per unit   = $\dfrac{\text{cost of production over a given period}}{\text{number of units produced over a given period}}$

This performance indicator provides useful information because costs can be compared over different time periods. It must be remembered that the 'unit' ('cost unit') referred to can be produced by a service industry as well as in a manufacturing process. Costs can be worked out for:

'producer'	unit
BMW	car produced
Kelloggs	packet of cereal produced
police force	offence dealt with
fire service	incident dealt with

Further detail can be extracted by relating the number of units produced to different cost classifications of cost, eg advertising cost per unit, labour cost per unit, distribution cost per unit. These all assist management in monitoring performance and identifying problem areas.

resource utilisation

The major resources of any organisation – whether in the manufacturing or in the services sector – are *labour* and *equipment.* The ideally efficient organisation will ensure that its employees and its equipment are working 'flat out' all the time. Resource utilisation in this case will obviously be 100% and there is no *idle time* or *slack time*:

- *idle time* – hours in the working day spent by employees *not* working, not through any fault of their own, but because of factors such as computer/machine breakdown, power cuts, or simply because the work in hand is finished and no other task has been allocated

- *slack time* – hours in the working day during which machinery and equipment is not in productive use, eg a printing press switched off because there are no books or catalogues to print

Resource utilisation – for labour and for equipment – can be measured as a percentage. Clearly the higher the percentage, the better:

$$\text{resource utilisation \%} \quad = \quad \frac{\text{actual hours worked} \quad \times \quad 100}{\text{hours available for working}}$$

Monitoring of resource utilisation will highlight any problem areas and enable management to take decisions, eg to reduce the contracted hours of the workforce, to lay off staff, to sell or replace machinery. Of course the management also has a major responsibility in operations management to plan for efficient working of staff and machine utilisation.

profitability

One of the principal objectives of any business is to make a profit which will benefit the owners, employees and customers. This objective also extends to other organisations such as charities and public sector services, but the motives are different – a charity helps a good cause and a public service aims to be efficient, given the resources that are available.

There are a number of ways of measuring profit performance, normally expressed as *percentages,* but traditionally and perhaps misleadingly called *ratios.* We will deal with some of these in the next section. Before examining the ways in which profit is measured it is important to appreciate the way in which profit is *calculated.* As you will know from your studies, a business (or its accountants) will normally draw up a *profit and loss account* from the accounting records. Now study the notes and refer to the profit and loss account illustrated on the next page.

sales	this figure represents the sales for the period (often a year); it may be sales of a product or it may be sales of a service (eg fees for a management consultant)
cost of sales	this figure is what it has cost the business to acquire what has *actually been sold* during the period, eg raw materials for a manufacturer or stock bought from wholesalers in the case of a shop
gross profit	*sales minus cost of sales* – this gives an indicator of the 'mark-up' of a business, eg a shop buying jeans in at £15 a pair and selling them at £35 – the gross profit on the jeans will be £20, ie £35 minus £15
overheads	these are expenses which have to be paid, such as insurance, advertising, rates, power bills; they are not normally directly related to the level of sales; they are deducted from gross profit
net profit	*gross profit minus overheads* – this is essentially sales minus all costs, and represents the final profit figure the business has achieved for the period

PROFIT AND LOSS ACCOUNT

		£	£
	Sales		600,000
less	**Cost of sales**		360,000
equals	**Gross profit**		240,000
less	**Overheads**:		
	Administration/labour	85,000	
	Selling and distribution	50,000	
	Finance costs	15,000	
			150,000
equals	**Net profit**		90,000

Note: for further details of the workings of profit and loss accounts, please see the Appendix of Osborne Books' *Financial Accounting Tutorial*.

RATIO ANALYSIS

We will now explain the performance indicators relating to profitability:

- gross profit margin
- net profit margin
- return on capital employed

As noted earlier, these indicators are often known as accounting *ratios:* although they express a relationship between two figures, they are often quoted as *percentages.*

gross profit margin

$$\text{gross profit margin \%} \quad = \quad \frac{\text{gross profit} \times 100}{\text{sales}}$$

This percentage relates gross profit (sales less cost of sales) to the sales figure for the period. In the example profit and loss account shown on the previous page the calculation is:

$$\text{gross profit margin \%} \quad = \quad \frac{£240,000 \times 100}{£600,000} = 40\%$$

In other words, for every £100 of sales, gross profit is £40. An organisation should expect to see this percentage stay fairly constant from year-to-year, and to be similar to the gross profit margin of other organisations in the same line of business. Gross profit margins in different types of business will vary widely: a jeweller will have a high margin and a food supermarket a low margin, reflecting the length of time it takes to sell the stock.

a note on mark-up and margin

In your study of incomplete records (Osborne Books' *Financial Accounting Tutorial,* page 199) you will encounter the use of *mark-up* and *margin* – these sometimes cause confusion. It is the *margin* which is generally used in ratio analysis. Using the profit and loss account on page 195:

the *margin* is based (as seen above) on the selling price:

$$\frac{\text{gross profit} \times 100}{\text{sales}} \quad = \quad \frac{£240,000 \times 100}{£600,000} \quad = \quad 40\%$$

the *mark-up* is based on cost price (cost of sales):

$$\frac{\text{gross profit} \times 100}{\text{cost of sales}} \quad = \quad \frac{£240,000 \times 100}{£360,000} \quad = \quad 67\%$$

net profit margin

In the same way, *net profit margin* relates net profit to sales.

net profit margin % = $\dfrac{\text{net profit} \times 100}{\text{sales}}$

This percentage relates net profit (gross profit less overheads) to the sales figure for the period. In the example profit and loss account shown on the previous page the calculation is:

net profit margin % = $\dfrac{£90,000 \times 100}{£600,000}$ = 15%

The business is making £15 overall profit on every £100 of sales. Ideally an organisation would hope to see this percentage increase from year-to-year, as this profit figure represents funds which can be used in expanding the business. If the percentage falls over time the management will be concerned: sales may be falling or expenses may be increasing (or both).

return on capital employed (ROCE)

return on capital employed % = $\dfrac{\text{net profit} \times 100}{\text{capital}}$

Here 'capital' is the investment in the business made by the owner(s) plus profits. Capital is not found in the profit and loss account but at the bottom of the balance sheet – the statement of what the business owns and owes. The return on capital employed is exactly what it says it is – it is the percentage return made on the owner's investment.

This ratio involves a closer look at the balance sheet of a business. An example of a sole trader balance sheet is shown on the next page. It is essentially an equation based on a 'snapshot' of a business at a particular moment in time:

assets (items owned by the business) – shown in the top half

minus

liabilities (items owed by the business) – shown half-way down

equals

capital (capital and profit) – shown at the bottom

Net assets are total assets less total liabilities. They are equal to the owner's stake or investment in the business.

SOLE TRADER BALANCE SHEET

Fixed assets

Premises		250,000
Machinery		18,000
Vehicle		15,000
		283,000

Current assets

Stock	24,000	
Debtors	15,000	
Bank	13,500	
	52,500	

Less **Current liabilities**

Creditors	25,500	
Working capital		27,000
		310,000

Less **Long-term liabilities**

Bank loan		10,000
NET ASSETS		300,000

FINANCED BY

Capital		240,000
Add Profit		90,000
Less drawings		30,000
		300,000

assets

less

liabilities

equals

capital

balance sheet format

Note: for further details of balance sheets see the Appendix of Osborne Books' *Financial Accounting Tutorial*..

definitions of return on capital employed

It must be stressed that the *return on capital employed* formula already quoted (and shown below) is not the only way of calculating return on capital employed. The terms 'return' and 'capital employed' may mean different things to different types of business. For example, in some circumstances, the term 'capital employed' can include long-term liabilities such as fixed bank loans (see the balance sheet illustrated on the previous page).

The sole trader business shown here is the simplest form of business; a limited company, on the other hand, may have a complex capital structure made up of different types of shares and other forms of funding; the profit and loss account, too, will be more complex. These, however, are subject areas covered in NVQ Level 4 Accounting, and you do not need to study them at this stage.

In this text we will adopt the formula:

return on capital employed %   = $\dfrac{\text{net profit} \times 100}{\text{capital}}$

If we then apply this to the balance sheet shown on the previous page:

return on capital employed %   = $\dfrac{£90,000 \times 100}{£300,000}$ =   30%

This sole trader is clearly running a very profitable enterprise: he or she is achieving a 30% return on the money tied up in the business – better than any bank account. Note, however, that profit does *not* equal cash which can be drawn out of the business. The profit earned will have been ploughed back into the business and will be represented by the assets on the balance sheet, eg the bank balance, stocks, machinery and so on.

PERFORMANCE INDICATORS AND PERFORMANCE REPORTING

The performance indicators and ratios explained so far are commonly used in periodic performance reports prepared by businesses. They enable the owner(s) of the business and other interested parties such as lenders and the Inland Revenue to monitor the financial 'health' of the business. A lender, for example, will want to know if the business is profitable because the profits will provide the repayments; the Inland Revenue will be interested in the level of profits because they are taxable!

In the Case Study which follows we analyse the performance of Citro Plc, a soft drinks manufacturer, and provide comments which can be used in the reporting process (which will be explained in the next chapter).

CITRO PLC: PERFORMANCE INDICATORS

situation

Citro Plc is a company which manufactures soft drinks. It operates three separate production divisions in the UK: Citro North, Citro South and Citro West. Performance figures for the last three months have just been made available. What do they say about the performance of the company's three divisions and about the company as a whole?

	CITRO NORTH	CITRO SOUTH	CITRO WEST	TOTAL
	£000s	£000s	£000s	£000s
profit and loss data				
Sales	400	600	500	1,500
Cost of sales	250	375	375	1,000
Gross profit	150	225	125	500
Overheads	85	150	100	335
Net profit	65	75	25	165
balance sheet data				
Capital employed	1,300	1,250	1,250	3,800
other data				
Employees	120	130	135	385
Total labour hours available	55,200	63,000	75,000	193,200
Total hours worked	54,720	62,400	69,660	186,780
Units produced and sold	320,000	400,000	325,000	1,045,000
Target unit production	300,000	360,000	375,000	1,035,000

You have been asked to calculate performance indicators and ratios for the three month period (as far as the data allows) and to comment on your findings. The areas you are looking at are:

- **productivity** – how well Citro is using its available resources
- **cost per unit** – how much it costs to produce each item sold
- **resource utilisation** – how well Citro is making use of resources, eg its workforce
- **profitability** – what return Citro is making on its sales and its capital employed

You first draw up the table of results shown on the next page, and then you add your comments under the four headings listed above.

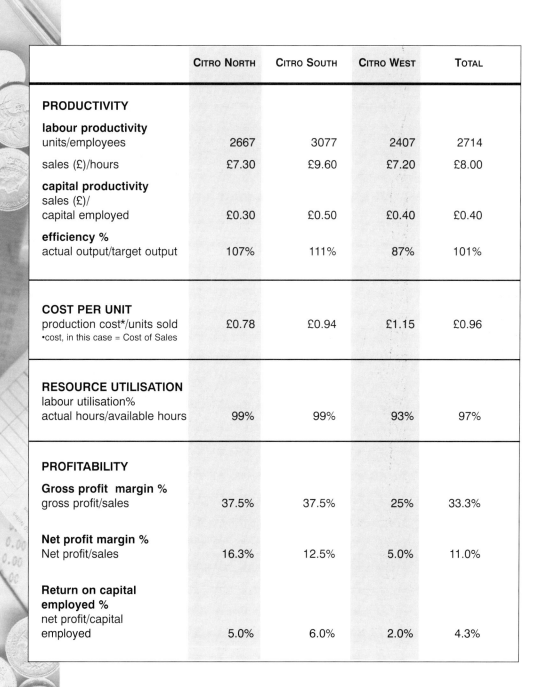

	CITRO NORTH	CITRO SOUTH	CITRO WEST	TOTAL
PRODUCTIVITY				
labour productivity				
units/employees	2667	3077	2407	2714
sales (£)/hours	£7.30	£9.60	£7.20	£8.00
capital productivity				
sales (£)/				
capital employed	£0.30	£0.50	£0.40	£0.40
efficiency %				
actual output/target output	107%	111%	87%	101%
COST PER UNIT				
production cost*/units sold	£0.78	£0.94	£1.15	£0.96
•cost, in this case = Cost of Sales				
RESOURCE UTILISATION				
labour utilisation%				
actual hours/available hours	99%	99%	93%	97%
PROFITABILITY				
Gross profit margin %				
gross profit/sales	37.5%	37.5%	25%	33.3%
Net profit margin %				
Net profit/sales	16.3%	12.5%	5.0%	11.0%
Return on capital employed %				
net profit/capital employed	5.0%	6.0%	2.0%	4.3%

comments on productivity

There are two measures of *labour productivity*. They link

- the number of employees to units produced
- hours worked to the sales income from the units sold

The *labour productivity* of the three divisions follows the same pattern over the three month period: Citro North and Citro South have higher labour productivity (2,667 and 3,077 units per employee, whereas Citro West is the least productive (2,407 units per employee).

Citro West is also the least *efficient:* 87% against 107% (Citro North) and 111% (Citro South). The *capital productivity* of the three divisions is reasonably consistent.

The overall conclusion is that the productivity of Citro West needs investigating.

comments on cost per unit

These figures are not strictly comparable because each division manufactures a different range of products, each of which will have different levels of cost. The figures that will need to be compared are the three-monthly results for *each division* over a period of time to pick up any trend.

comments on resource utilisation

Citro North and Citro South are performing very well with 99% of available hours worked. Again Citro West is the weakest division with labour utilisition of only 93%. This will need investigating.

comments on profitability

Gross profit margin is consistent at 37.5% at Citro North and Citro South; Citro West is less profitable at 25%. This pattern is repeated for net profit margin and return on capital employed. Citro West's overheads need investigating.

overall conclusion

All companies are profitable and achieving a reasonable level of productivity. Citro West is the weakest performer. Management may need to investigate this division, and look particularly at:

- working practices – to improve productivity
- containing costs – to improve profitability

Management will also need to look at the figures for the other financial periods so that trends over time can be established and analysed.

a note on formal reports . . .

As this case study shows, once the figures have been extracted, some skill is needed in reporting the information and in presenting it in a meaningful way. The case study is only a 'halfway house' in this respect – in the next chapter we look at the format of the report and the ways in which information can be presented in the form of graphs and charts.

TRANSACTIONS WITHIN A BUSINESS – TRANSFER PRICING

There are situations where a business will sell products to itself. A manufacturing business which is divided into different divisions may well use the products of one division in the manufacturing process of another division. Take, for example, a company manufacturing computer disk drives. It sells the bulk of its production to other computer manufacturers for use in their machines, but it also has a division manufacturing its own computers, 'buying in' the company's own disk drives.

The division manufacturing the drives will 'sell' the drives to the computer division at an agreed *transfer price*. This should normally be below the market price, otherwise the division manufacturing the computers will turn to outside sources for the drives. Calculation of the transfer price is simple:

cost of product   +   agreed percentage margin   =   transfer price

The 'percentage margin' will be agreed between the divisions. It may, of course, change if market prices change. In the reporting process this 'margin' will appear as an addition to the profit of the division and will reflect positively on its performance. It must be stressed, however, that the transfer price is purely *on paper* – the overall performance of the group is unchanged.

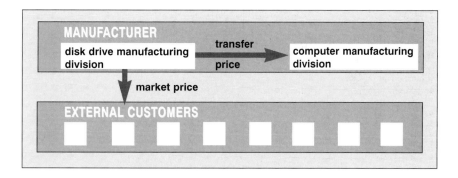

Further examples of transfer pricing are manufacturing companies using subsidiary companies in countries where the cost of labour is low. The subsidiary companies' products are then 'sold on' at a substantial profit to the parent company which will sell them for as much as the local market will bear. Transfer pricing can also occur in an organisation that provides a *service*. A large marketing company, for example, may provide its own advertising services. The advertising division will charge out its services appropriately.

The accounting aspects of transfer pricing are covered in Osborne Books' *Financial Accounting Tutorial*, page 237.

CHAPTER SUMMARY

KEY TERMS

- Performance within a business is measured by means of formulas, percentages and ratios – known as performance indicators. These cover:
  - productivity – how well the business is using its available resources
  - cost per unit – how much it costs the business to produce each item it makes
  - resource utilisation – how well the business is making use of its workforce and equipment
  - profitability – how great a return the business is making on its sales

  These performance indicators are covered in the Key Terms section set out below.

- An important skill, once the performance indicators have been extracted, is to comment and report on them. The reporting process is covered in detail in the next chapter.

- Transfer pricing shows how one division of an organisation can fix a price on products provided to another division – normally at a fixed percentage over cost.

productivity	the level of output (goods manufactured or services provided) in relation to the cost of producing the product or service
labour productivity	$\dfrac{\text{output (units)}}{\text{number of employees}}$ *or* . . .
	$\dfrac{\text{output (sales £)}}{\text{hours worked}}$
capital productivity	$\dfrac{\text{output (sales £)}}{\text{capital employed}}$
efficiency %	$\dfrac{\text{output (units) x 100}}{\text{expected (standard) units}}$
cost per unit	$\dfrac{\text{cost of production over a given period}}{\text{number of units produced over a given period}}$
resource utilisation %	$\dfrac{\text{actual hours worked x 100}}{\text{hours available for working}}$ note: this can apply to both labour hours and machine hours
gross profit margin %	$\dfrac{\text{gross profit x 100}}{\text{sales}}$
net profit margin %	$\dfrac{\text{net profit x 100}}{\text{sales}}$
return on capital employed %	$\dfrac{\text{net profit x 100}}{\text{capital employed}}$
transfer price	cost of product + agreed percentage margin

STUDENT ACTIVITIES

10.1 Severn Car Insurance Brokers employ five sales staff. They record between them the following number of new policies arranged each month of the year:

January	600	July	890
February	545	August	675
March	655	September	465
April	680	October	750
May	550	November	670
June	615	December	560

The expected average monthly number of policies is 625.

You are to calculate:

(a)   the monthly labour productivity (output per employee)

(b)   the monthly efficiency percentage (to the nearest %)

(c)   the average monthly labour productivity (a) and average efficiency (b) over the year

Set out your results in a table and comment on the figures.

10.2 Sentinel Security installs domestic alarm systems. During the year it records the following figures for systems installed and total costs incurred:

month	units	costs	month	units	costs
January	20	£4,000	July	20	£4,000
February	25	£4,800	August	21	£4,200
March	22	£4,400	September	26	£4,900
April	30	£5,500	October	28	£5,000
May	32	£5,600	November	30	£5,600
June	28	£5,200	December	26	£5,000

You are to calculate

(a)   the monthly cost per unit (to the nearest £)

(b)   the average annual cost per unit

Set out your results in a table comparing units sold, costs and unit costs. Comment on the figures.

10.3 Cool Designs provides a computer graphic design service. The business employs eight staff who all work a seven hour day, five days a week. During the course of a week their timesheets record the total daily hours worked: Monday 56, Tuesday 50, Wednesday 28, Thursday 56, Friday 48.

You are to calculate:

(a)   the labour utilisation percentage for each day (to the nearest %)

(b)   the labour utilisation percentage for the week

State why you think idle time may have occurred and how it might reflect on working practices.

10.4 Trend Toys plc is a UK manufacturer planning to capture the Christmas market with its new 'RoboZapper' toy which has been heavily advertised in the pre-Christmas period. In the month of November the marketing campaign proves very successful, demand takes off and orders flood in. In order to cope with this increased demand, extra staff are taken on and overtime is worked in the factory and in the despatch department. Extra raw materials have to be purchased from new suppliers, and the price negotiated for these materials is higher than Trend Toys normally pays.

The following figures are reported for the four weeks of November.

Production figures for the Trend RoboZapper:				
	Week 1	*Week 2*	*Week 3*	*Week 4*
Sales (£)	240,000	300,000	330,000	360,000
Units produced and sold	16,000	20,000	22,000	24,000
Expected output (units)	15,500	19,000	20,000	21,000
Cost of production (£)	120,000	150,000	190,000	210,000
Hours worked	4,000	4,700	4,850	5,150
Capital employed (£)	1,500,000	1,500,000	1,500,000	1,500,000

You are to calculate for each week:

(a)   labour productivity (sales [£] per hour worked) – to the nearest £
(b)   capital productivity (sales per £1 of capital employed) – to the nearest p
(c)   efficiency percentage – to the nearest %
(d)   cost per unit

Set out your results in the form of a table and comment on the trends shown.

10.5 The accounts office of Witley Agricultural Machines Limited has brought together the sales and costs figures for the four quarters of the financial year (which ends on 31 December):

	Jan-March	April-June	July-Sept	Oct-Dec
Sales	280,000	350,000	375,000	210,000
Cost of sales	168,000	217,000	221,250	128,100
Overheads	70,000	77,000	80,000	65,000

You are to calculate for each quarter *and* for the whole financial year:

(a)   the gross profit and the gross profit percentage (to the nearest %)
(b)   the net profit and the net profit percentage (to the nearest %)

and for the financial *year* only:

(c)   return on capital employed of £1.25 million

Set out your results in the form of a table and comment on them.

10.6 Wyvale Cycles is a well-established manufacturer of cycle parts and has built up a strong reputation for cycle frames which it supplies to a wide range of European cycle manufacturers.

In recent years, however, competition from manufacturers in the Far East, who benefit from low labour costs, has resulted in a decline in demand for quality UK-sourced frames. Wyvale therefore – for reasons of profit maximisation – has taken the decision to build its own complete cycle and six months ago launched a range of competitively priced machines branded as the 'Gemini' range manufactured by a separate operating division – Sprint Cycles Limited.

You work in the Accounts Department and have been handed production data from the frame manufacturing division for the last six months in the form of a table. The production and sales figures have already been entered on a form, and it is your job to complete it.

	Jan £	Feb £	March £	April £	May £	June £
Raw materials	40,000	42,000	45,000	46,500	52,100	53,950
Direct costs	15,000	16,500	17,554	18,100	19,925	18,200
Production overheads	5,000	5,000	5,300	7,450	8,300	8,350
Production cost						
plus 20% profit						
Transfer cost						
Cost per unit to Sprint						
Units sold	1,200	1,250	1,290	1,310	1,350	1,400
Production cost per unit						

You are to calculate for each month (and fill in the gaps on the form):

(a)   the production cost
(b)   the profit amount (20% of production cost)
(c)   the total transfer cost to Sprint Cycles
(d)   the cost per unit to Sprint Cycles
(e)   the production cost per unit to Wyvale Cycles

10.7   Discussion point following on from Activity 10.6

You are studying a trade journal to analyse the prices of your competitors' products. Because of a rise in the pound sterling the cost of similarly specified cycle frames has fallen substantially. What would you recommend if the price per frame imported from the Far East was: (a) £47.50 (b) £60.00?

11 REPORT WRITING

this chapter covers . . .

In this chapter we examine written reports:

- the context in which reports are written
- the report format
- interpreting data for use in reports
- techniques used in report writing
- the importance of keeping to deadlines

NVQ PERFORMANCE CRITERIA COVERED

unit 6: PREPARING REPORTS AND RETURNS

element 1

prepare periodic performance reports

❑ reports are prepared in a clear and understandable form and presented to management within required timescales

REPORT WRITING

the report in context

Reports are written in a wide variety of contexts; they may be very long or they may be very short. Examples of extended reports include the report to shareholders produced by quoted public limited companies, or Government reports on areas such as Higher Education or Prisons. The shortest reports are probably school reports! They are all essentially the same: performance is reported, commented on and recommendations normally made. The important point about a report is that it should set out information clearly and concisely and come to a firm conclusion. It should also be submitted within the given timescale.

In the context of your accounting studies a report is often a relatively short document – maybe one or two pages – setting out financial data and analysis, normally for the benefit of management, and suggesting a specific course of action or investigation. This type of report is often known as the 'short formal report'.

report format

Report writing may sound difficult and complex, but it is in fact a very straightforward process.

Reports normally fall into a series of sections. These sections can be given a formal heading, eg 'introduction', or they can be left as a series of self-contained paragraphs. For the purposes of your studies, it is suggested that you use the headings – they help to concentrate the mind and they do make the document look clearer and more structured. The sections commonly found in a report are shown below. These can, of course, be varied to suit the situation. There is no 'right' or 'wrong' format.

decimal numbering systems

Some reports which have a complex structure of headings, subheadings and sub-subheadings, use a decimal numbering system for the various sections. Although you are unlikely to get involved in such complexities in the presentation of short formal reports, you should be aware of the system used as you may encounter it when reading longer reports.

Each section is given a number (eg 1.0) and any subsection within that section is given a number after a decimal point (ie 1.1, 1.2, 1.3), and subdivisions of that are given a further decimal point and a number (eg 1.1.1, 1.1.2). As you will see in the illustration on the next page, each section is indented from the left margin.

2.0   **Procedure**

    2.1   Source material

          2.1.1   Sales budget

          2.1.2   Production budget

CONTENTS OF A REPORT

When reading this section, refer to the report format shown opposite.

title and preliminaries

A report is always given a title. It is also common practice for a report, like a memorandum, to be addressed from one person to another. Job titles are normally added to these names. The report should also be dated.

introduction

This section, sometimes called 'Terms of Reference' will set out the circumstances and scope of the report:

- the person who requested it
- the ground it has to cover
- the date by which it has to be submitted
- whether it has to make any recommendations

For example: "This report, requested by the Finance Director, will analyse the revenues and costs for the three divisions of Sphere Paints for the last three financial years and will make recommendations for improving future performance. The report is due for completion by March 30."

procedure

This section will set out the methods used, eg "Data produced by the Accounts Department was used for this report. A table of financial data is included in the body of this report."

findings

This will set out the main findings and trends, highlighting figures and commenting on performance indicators; these can be set out in the form of tables, graphs and charts (see the next chapter).

This section can also be used to point out any *limitations* of the data, eg "this was an exceptional year because the accounting policies changed" or "the factory was burnt down" or "the business was taken over" . . . and so on.

---

report to ....(name + job title)   report date ....

report from ....(name + job title)

REPORT TITLE (in capitals)..

introduction/terms of reference
Circumstances and scope of the report – what it covers, why it is being written, for whom, and when.

procedure
Where the data comes from and how it is used.

findings
The data is set out and analysed. Any limitations of the findings will be highlighted.

conclusions
A summary of the findings – with comments.

recommendations
Recommendations made on the basis of the conclusions reached.

appendices
Extra data included here if there is not room for it in the findings.

---

short formal report format

conclusions

This section summarises and makes comments on the findings so that recommendations may follow if required.

recommendations

If required by the report, recommendations should be made based on the conclusions reached.

appendices

Although it is unlikely that you will deal with appendices in your studies, you should be aware that if some of the data is too bulky to go in the main 'findings' section, it can be included in an appendix – eg three years' profit and loss statements and balance sheets, stock reports or budget reports.

HINTS ON REPORT WRITING

Writing a successful report is an exercise in communication. You have to get a message across clearly, accurately and on time.

Before starting the actual report, make sure that:

- you have all the facts and figures needed – you may need to construct or complete a table which sets out performance indicators
- you have checked all the calculations
- you have planned out the report – you may need to 'rough out' a series of points on a separate piece of paper, a process which will help you come to a reasoned conclusion
- you know what format of report is to be used

When putting pen to paper (or fingers to keyboard), bear in mind the following points:

be clear   Avoid using complex words and phrases when simple ones will do – for example:

'Sales have improved at Citro North'

is far preferable to:

'The recorded level of turnover has seen a significant uplift at the Citro North operating division.'

be brief   Remember that the person reading the report will not have hours to spare. Keep the text brief – for example:

'The stock level will need examining.'

is preferable to:

'It is my view that the levels of stock maintained should become the subject of a thorough investigation.'

be objective   Avoid using 'I' and 'We' which are *subjective*, but instead be *objective* – for example:

'Citro West's low liquidity is likely to be the result of a high stock level.'

is far preferable to

'In my view, Citro West's poor liquidity may be a result of their having too much stock.'

Giving opinions is a form of subjectivity and should be avoided. Statements beginning 'In my view. . .' or 'I think that . . .' should be avoided as they suggest that what follows is based on guesswork rather than on fact.

avoid slang

Using slang is lazy and should be avoided at all costs.

For example:

'It is recommended that management should take measures to improve profitability'

is far better than

'I think that these results are total rubbish – they really could be improved a lot.'

Do not write 'don't' – which is the spoken version – but 'do not' and similarly 'could not' rather than 'couldn't'.

be accurate

Always *check that* figures quoted in the text tally with the data provided. If you are calculating ratios and percentages, always carry out the calculation twice and make sure you are using the right figures. An incorrectly calculated ratio could throw your conclusions completely !

PRODUCING THE REPORT

If you refer to the Case Study in the last chapter (it starts on page 200) you will see that all the performance indicators have been set out in a table (reproduced on the next page) and 'comments' have been added. These comments are a rough and ready form of report to management: they highlight the main trends and pinpoint weaknesses. They conclude with recommendations relating to the weakest performing division of the business.

These comments could be rewritten in the form of a structured report, as shown on the pages which follow the table of results.

CASE STUDY

CITRO PLC: PERIODIC PERFORMANCE REPORT

situation

The table below shows the performance of Citro PLC's three sales divisions for the three months ended 31 March 1998. You have been asked to prepare a performance report for the Finance Director, Brian Cousins.

	CITRO NORTH	CITRO SOUTH	CITRO WEST	TOTAL
PRODUCTIVITY				
labour productivity units/employees	2667	3077	2407	2714
sales (£)/hours	£7.30	£9.60	£7.20	£8.00
capital productivity sales (£)/ capital employed	£0.30	£0.50	£0.40	£0.40
efficiency % actual output/target output	107%	111%	87%	101%
COST PER UNIT production cost*/units sold •cost, in this case = Cost of Sales	£0.78	£0.94	£1.15	£0.96
RESOURCE UTILISATION labour utilisation% actual hours/available hours	99%	99%	93%	97%
PROFITABILITY				
Gross profit margin % gross profit/sales	37.5%	37.5%	25.0%	33.3%
Net profit margin % Net profit/sales	16.3%	12.5%	5.0%	11.0%
Return on capital employed % net profit/capital employed	5.0%	6.0%	2.0%	4.3%

solution
You draft the report set out on the next two pages. It will be checked for accuracy within your Department and then sent to the Finance Director. The report may then be referred to the Board of Directors and decisions made at that level.

---

from A S Dent, Accounts Assistant

to Brian Cousins, Finance Director   **date** 10 April 1998

CITRO PLC QUARTERLY PERFORMANCE REPORT
(for the three months ended 31 March 1998)

INTRODUCTION

This report, produced by the Finance Department as part of its normal reporting procedure will set out the performance indicators for the three operating divisions of Citro PLC: Citro North, Citro South and Citro West for the three months ended 31 March 1998. It will compare the performance and make recommendations based on its findings by 15 April 1998.

PROCEDURE

The data for this report has been compiled as part of the monthly management reporting process by the Finance, Production and Sales Departments. A table of financial data is included in the body of this report.

FINDINGS

productivity
The *labour productivity* of the three divisions follows the same pattern over the three month period: Citro North and Citro South have higher labour productivity (2,667 and 3,077 units per employee), whereas Citro West is the least productive (2,407 units per employee).

Citro West is also the least *efficient:* 87% against 107% (Citro North) and 111% (Citro South).

The *capital productivity* of the three divisions is reasonably consistent, averaging 40p of sales per £1 of capital employed.

cost per unit

The figures for cost per unit are not strictly comparable because the three divisions manufacture a different range of products, each of which will has a different level of cost.

labour utilisation

Citro South and Citro North are performing very well with 99% of available hours worked. Again Citro West is the weakest division with labour utilisition of only 93%

profitability

Gross profit margin is consistent at 37.5% at Citro North and Citro South; Citro West is less profitable at 25%. This pattern is repeated for net profit margin and return on capital employed: the margins for Citro North and Citro South are satisfactory, whereas the results for Citro West are less so.

It should be pointed out that the table does not show figures for the other financial quarters; this additional data will enable trends to be established and analysed.

CONCLUSIONS

All divisions are profitable and achieving a reasonable level of productivity. Citro West is the weakest performer in terms of labour productivity, labour utilisiation and profitability. Profitability in particular is weak, pointing to a higher level of costs in this division.

RECOMMENDATIONS

Management may need to investigate areas in Citro West such as:
- working practices – to improve labour productivity
- containing costs – to improve profitability

The results of these investigations will enable management to take measures to improve performance in these areas.

CHAPTER SUMMARY

- Reports are written in a wide variety of contexts and can vary substantially in length.
- Periodic performance reports produced to present accounting data normally take the form of a short formal report.
- The sections of the report normally include:
    - report title and preliminaries (date, sender, recipient)
    - the Introduction (or 'Terms of Reference') – what it is about
    - Procedure – the sources used
    - Findings – presentation and analysis of data
    - Conclusions
    - Recommendations
    - Appendices – data which is too bulky for the 'Findings' section
- Guidelines for report writing state that a report should:
    - be clear
    - be brief
    - be objective rather than subjective
    - avoid slang
    - be accurate
- Reports should be completed within the given deadlines.

KEY TERMS

short formal report	a brief formally structured report (see 'sections' above), often used within an organisation for management purposes
terms of reference	the section of the report which sets out the scope and content, date of submission and intended recipient
procedure	the section of the report which sets out the sources used and the methods used to extract the data
findings	the section of the report which sets out the data, analyses it and comments on it; it also highlights any limitations of the data
conclusions	the section of the report which comes to a firm conclusion about the findings
recommendations	the section of the report which makes recommendations – if required – on the basis of the conclusions reached
appendices	the section of the report which contains data used in the 'Findings', but which is too extensive to be quoted in full in the 'Findings' – eg financial statements

11.1 Refer to Student Activity 10.4 at the end of the last chapter (page 206).

If you have not already done this Activity you should do it now – the text is set out below.

When you have completed your table and drafted your comments

you are to . . .

Produce a short formal report based on your comments. Use today's date, your name (job title – Assistant, Accounts Department) and address the report to the Finance Director (invent a name). The report should be headed up with the section headings (Introduction, Procedure etc) and include a Recommendations section. The table of performance indicators should be included as an Appendix.

Trend Toys plc is a UK manufacturer planning to capture the Christmas market with its new 'RoboZapper' toy which has been heavily advertised in the pre-Christmas period.

In the month of November the marketing campaign proves very successful, demand takes off and orders flood in. In order to cope with this increased demand, extra staff are taken on and overtime is worked in the factory and in the despatch department.

The following figures are reported for the four weeks of November.

Production figures for the Trend RoboZapper:				
	Week 1	*Week 2*	*Week 3*	*Week 4*
Sales (£)	240,000	300,000	330,000	360,000
Units produced and sold	16,000	20,000	22,000	24,000
Expected output (units)	15,500	19,000	20,000	21,000
Cost of production (£)	120,000	150,000	190,000	210,000
Hours worked	4,000	4,700	4,850	5,150
Capital employed (£)	1,500,000	1,500,000	1,500,000	1,500,000

You are to calculate for each week:
(a)   labour productivity (based on output related to hours worked)
(b)   capital productivity (sales per £1 of capital employed)
(c)   efficiency percentage
(d)   cost per unit
Set out your results in the form of a table and comment on the trends shown.

11.2 Oasis Computers sells hardware and software from a chain of shops. It has representation in three towns: Kidderport, Stourminster and Persham. Each shop is self-accounting. The figures for the first six months of the year have just been brought together:

	Kidderport	Stourminster	Persham	Total
	£	£	£	£
financial information				
Sales	120,000	95,000	110,000	325,000
Cost of sales	65,000	55,000	72,000	192,000
Gross profit	55,000	40,000	38,000	133,000
Overheads	40,000	29,000	36,000	105,000
Net profit	15,000	11,000	2,000	28,000
Capital employed	150,000	120,000	135,000	405,000
non-financial information				
Employees	5	4	6	15
Hours worked	4,375	3,600	5,100	13,075
Floor space of shop	500m²	450m²	625m²	1,575m²
Units sold	2,400	1,900	2,200	6,500

You are to

Calculate appropriate ratios and percentages for all three shops and the business as a whole, covering the areas listed below; set out your results in the form of a table.

(a) labour productivity – relating units to employees, and sales to hours worked

(b) capital productivity – sales per £1 of capital employed (to the nearest p)

(c) cost per unit – units sold related to cost of sales plus overheads

(d) resource utilisation – sales per square metre of floorspace

(e) gross profit percentage (to the nearest %)

(f) net profit percentage (to the nearest %)

(g) return on capital employed (to the nearest %)

Then, having discussed your findings within your student group (if this is possible), draft a short formal report to Bill Bates, General Manager of Oasis Computers. Use your own name (job title – Assistant, Accounts Department). The report should be headed up with the section headings (Introduction, Procedure etc) and include a Recommendations section. The table of performance indicators and ratios should be included as an Appendix.

12 USING TABLES AND DIAGRAMS

this chapter covers . . .

In this chapter we examine the techniques used in presenting the performance indicators in the form of tables and diagrams:

- the construction of tables and the use of 'time series' data
- visual presentation of this data in the form of:
  - line graphs
  - bar charts
  - pie charts
- using averages
- calculating moving averages for use in tracking and forecasting trends
- the construction and use of cumulative frequency graphs
- the construction and use of Z charts
- the technique of indexing numbers when comparing figures over a period of time in order to allow for changing price levels

NVQ PERFORMANCE CRITERIA COVERED

unit 6: PREPARING REPORTS AND RETURNS

element 1

prepare periodic performance reports

❏ when comparing results over time an appropriate method, which allows for changing price levels, is used

❏ reports are prepared in the appropriate form and presented to management within required timescales

TIME SERIES ANALYSIS

a definition

Time series analysis is a phrase which means

'comparing figures recorded over a period of time.'

In an accounting context time series analysis can include, for example, annual, quarterly, monthly or weekly comparison of figures for

- sales
- cost of sales
- overhead costs
- gross and net profits

In short, 'time series analysis' is a technical term for the commonly-used technique of comparing the results of different accounting periods.

constructing a time series table

In many of the Assessments and Student Activities that you will be doing, the data is already set out in a table. If you are processing the figures at work you may have to construct a table; alternatively the table may be in 'pro-forma' form (ready made) or it may be output from a computer information system, or be completed as a computer spreadsheet. Look at the example shown below, and read the notes that follow.

Sphere Paints PLC Summary Profit Statement				
	Year 1 *£000s*	**Year 2** *£000s*	**Year 3** *£000s*	**Year 4** *£000s*
Sales	500	970	1,430	1,912
Cost of sales	250	505	750	985
Gross profit	250	465	680	927
Overheads	185	370	548	780
Net profit	65	95	132	147

- the title clearly sets out the subject matter of the data
- each time period is allocated a vertical column
- each time period is clearly headed up (it could be a year, a month or a week)

- the units are stated below the time period – here £000s are chosen to prevent the table being cluttered up with unnecessary zeros
- the variables (ie sales, costs, profits) are set out in the left-hand column
- lines are added to clarify the table – it is not necessary in this case to draw a line under each variable as the columns can easily be read across; if, however, there was a large number of columns, lines would be helpful

presenting a time series – graphs and charts

Figures set out in a table can be interpreted: upward and downward trends can be detected by reading across the rows of figures, in other words by *interpreting the time series*. A much clearer idea of trends can be obtained by presenting the time series in the form of a graph or chart which will provide a very visual concept of each trend. This process can be carried out manually or by using a computer spreadsheet or charting package. The graphs and charts which follow in the next few pages were produced by a simple spreadsheet program into which the figures above had been input.

LINE GRAPH

The simplest form of visual representation of a time series is the *line graph*.

A line graph – which can be in a straight line or a curve – shows the relationship between two variables. One variable will always depend on the other. They are kown as:

- the *independent variable* – the measurement that is at a fixed interval
- the *dependent variable* – the figure that will depend on the independent variable

A common independent variable is time, and a common dependent variable is money but as you will see from the table shown below, it is not the only fixed measurement.

independent variable	dependent variable
time (years)	sales (£)
units produced	costs of production (£)
income level (£)	number of holidays per year
working out in gym (hours)	calories burned up

Now study the diagram shown on the next page and read the notes which follow.

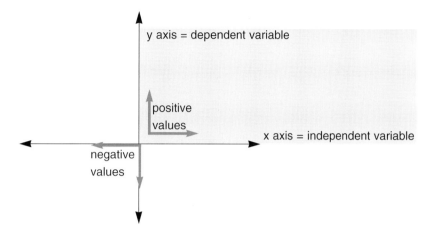

- the *independent variable* (eg years) is set out on the *horizontal* 'x' axis
- the *dependent variable* (eg sales) is set out on the *vertical* 'y' axis
- the line graph can show negative figures as well as positive figures (eg a company showing a loss over a period of years), but the most common format shows the area shaded in grey – ie both variables being positive; it is this format which is illustrated below

Now study the graph shown below and note the points made in grey type.

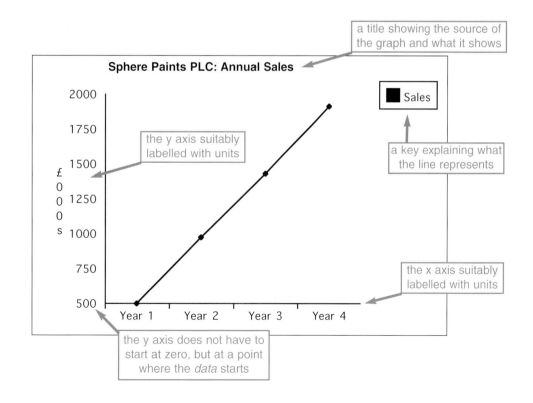

showing trends on line graphs

The graph shown below has added the gross profit and net profit figures for Sphere Paints PLC from the table on page 221. It shows simply and clearly the upward trends in a way that the table of raw data is unable to do.

The graph is also useful in that it shows the *comparative* trends – ie sales are increasing proportionally more than gross profit, and gross profit is increasing proportionally more than net profit – as you would expect. The visual effect is quite dramatic in its impact.

On the technical side, note:

- the scaling has changed on the 'y' axis – it now goes down to zero
- each of the lines is identified by a label (or a key could be used)
- the title has changed

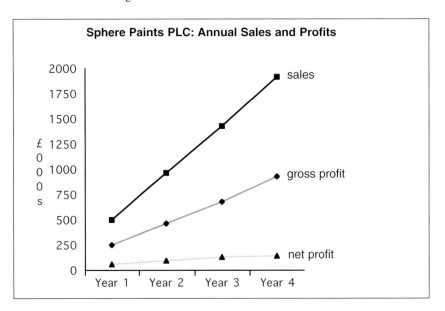

extrapolation of trend lines

Sometimes a trend line on a line graph can be extended beyond the plotted points to *forecast* a future trend. If a sales line, for example, shows that sales have increased by approximately 10% a year for the last five years, it is possible to plot a point for next years's sales 10% above this years figure. This is known as *extrapolation.* It is really no more than an educated guess and should be treated with caution; see page 231 for an example.

In the next section we will look at the way in which these same trends can be illustrated by means of a *bar chart.*

BAR CHARTS

A bar chart is a chart which sets out a series of bars, the height of which indicates the extent of the dependent variable. It is normal to set out a bar chart along the horizontal 'x' axis (so that they look like high-rise buildings) but the practice can be varied so that they stretch left to right from the 'y' axis.

Bar charts can be simple, compound or component, depending on what data comparisons need to be made.

simple bar chart

The simple bar chart is the most common type. It works on the same basis as a line graph and illustrates a trend. Set out below is a simple bar chart which uses the sales figures for Sphere Paints PLC from the table on page 221. Compare it with the line graph on page 223.

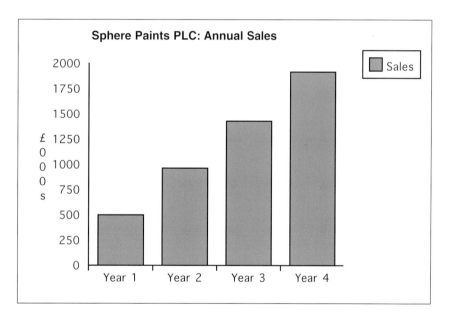

Note that:

- the labelling conventions are the same as for a line graph – here the bars are given a shading identity
- the 'y' axis goes down to zero – the whole length of the bar is needed (this is different from the line graph scaling)
- the bars are separated – this is common, but not essential – they can be drawn so that their sides touch

compound bar chart

Just as it is possible to draw a line graph with more than one line, it is also possible to construct a bar chart with more than one set of data for each independent variable – eg sales and profits for each year. This is known as a *compound bar chart*. An example, constructed from the table of data on page 221 is shown below.

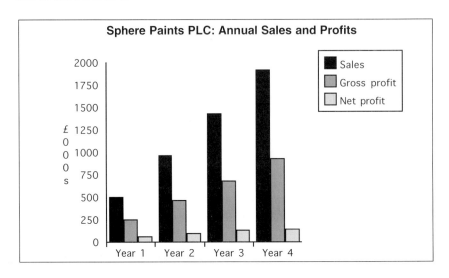

component bar chart

A component bar chart is a bar chart which divides each bar into segments, showing how the total for each bar is made up. For example, if the annual sales totals for Sphere Paints PLC were made up of totals for three sales divisions A, B and C, each bar could be shown as having three segments.

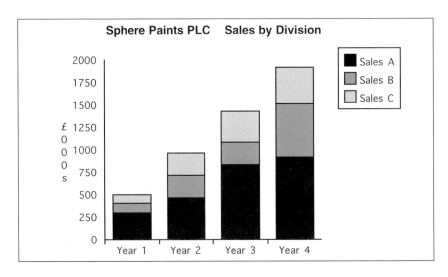

PIE CHARTS

A *pie chart* is a circle divided into sectors to represent in the correct proportions the parts of a whole. It is called a pie chart because, like a meat or fruit pie, it can be cut into 'slices'.

Line graphs and bar charts are suitable for the presentation of *time series* data – data which varies from time period to time period. Pie charts, on the other hand, are useful in showing the breakdown of a whole into its constituent parts at a particular moment in time.

Pie charts can be constructed by hand, or by using a computer spreadsheet or charting package. If you are constructing a pie chart by hand you will need a calculator, accurate drawing equipment and a protractor.

If you take Sphere Paints PLC's sales figures for Year 1 you will equate the total sales of £500,000 with the whole pie circle. This will be divided into segments, each of which will proportionally represent a divisional sales figure. As the angle at the centre of a circle is 360° it is necessary to work out the angle for each segment individually. The formula is as follows:

$$\frac{\text{Divisional sales figure} \times 360°}{\text{Total sales figure}} = \text{the angle at the centre for the segment (°)}$$

Applying the formula to the Year 1 divisional sales figures for Sphere Paints PLC, the calculation is:

Sales Division	Calculation		Angle of segment (°)
Division A	$\frac{£300,000 \times 360°}{£500,000}$	=	216
Division B	$\frac{£110,000 \times 360°}{£500,000}$	=	79.2
Division C	$\frac{£90,000 \times 360°}{£500,000}$	=	64.8

If you then carry out the same procedure for Year 2, you can construct pie charts as set out on the next page. Note the labelling and shading, and the fact that the degrees are not indicated (they are of no interest to the reader). The percentages are of more significance. They can be worked out by dividing the number of degrees for each sector by 360 and multiplying by 100.

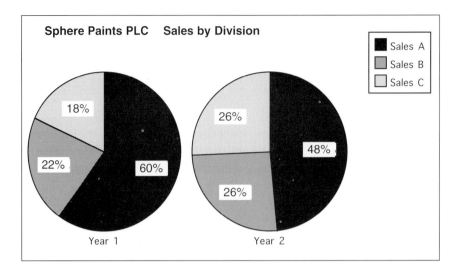

USING AVERAGES

A statistical technique which is useful when reporting on a series of performance figures is the use of *averages*. There are three commonly-used types of average: the mean, the median and the mode

which average?

Suppose the finance manager of a kitchen installation business wanted to know for budgeting purposes the average job completion time in days, from initial enquiry through to final installation. He has just received the figures for the jobs completed last month. The figures are (in days):

20, 25, 35, 35, 35, 36, 37, 55, 60, 65, 65

What is the average job completion time? We will look in turn at the mean, median and mode averages.

the mean

The arithmetic mean is probably the most commonly used and statistically reliable form of average.

The arithmetic mean is the sum of all the figures divided by the number of figures.

The sum of 20, 25, 35, 35, 35, 36, 37, 55, 60, 65, 65 = 468

The arithmetic mean = $\dfrac{468}{11}$ = 42.5 days

This tells the manager that, on average, a job takes approximately 43 days to complete. This will help him in the planning and budgeting process. Note:

- the result is not a whole number of days – rounding up to 43 is necessary
- the result takes into account all values – if there had been an exceptional job taking 165 days instead of 65, the result will have been a mean average of $568 \div 11 = 51.6$ days

the median

The median is the value of the middle figure in a series of figures.

Note that if there is no middle figure, as with an even number of values, the median is the arithmetic mean of the two figures nearest to the middle.

Here the median is 20, 25, 35, 35, 35, **36**, 37, 55, 60, 65, 65 = 36 days.

This will not be as helpful to the manager as the mean in this context; it is useful because it is not distorted by extreme values (eg 165 days) – the mean, however, is more reliable because an equal weighting is given to each value.

the mode

The mode is the value that occurs most often in a series.

In this case the most common period is 35 days (3 jobs), followed closely by 65 days (2 jobs). Note that these two time periods are very widely dispersed. This would suggest that this type of average is not as helpful in the planning process. The mode is more useful in areas such as market research in answering questions such as

"How much do people on average spend on a meal?"

"What is the most commonly occurring size of shirt?"

USING AVERAGES IN FORECASTING

Forecasts in the reporting process are based on information about the way in which trends have established themselves in the past and are showing themselves in the present. It is then assumed that these trends will continue into the future. If one takes a profits trend, for example, established in the past, it is possible to predict a trend for the future by using a number of techniques, including the *moving average*.

The use of moving averages is the technique of repeatedly calculating a series of different arithmetic mean values for a dependent variable along a time series to produce a trend graph.

A moving average will move forward in time (the independent variable), step by step along the trend line, calculating a new average from the given data at each step, removing in the averaging process data which is literally "out of line" with the trend. Some data will be above the line, some below it; in the averaging process these fluctuations will offset each other to produce a smooth line. The following example, assuming the date is now 1998, shows the profit figures of a company, Arco Plc, over 15 years.

Year	annual profit	5 Year Moving Average
	£M	£M
1984	10	
1985	4	
1986	8	64 ÷ 5 =12.8
1987	18	17.6
1988	24	20.8
1989	34	21.6
1990	20	23.2
1991	12	26.4
1992	26	26.8
1993	40	26.4
1994	36	30.4
1995	18	34.0
1996	32	34.0
1997	44	
1998	40	

This table has been produced as follows:

- the profit figures were plotted on a line graph (see opposite page)
- a five-yearly fluctuating cycle was noted
- the profit figures for the first five years were added and divided by five to find the first of the moving averages:

    (10 + 4 + 8 + 18 + 24 = 64; 64 ÷ 5 = 12.8)

- the next arithmetic mean is calculated over the five years 1985 to 1989, ie the average moves forward a year:

    (4 + 8 + 18 + 24 + 34 = 88; 88 ÷ 5 = 17.6)

- the process is repeated for the following years until the data is exhausted
- the moving average line is plotted on the same axes as the annual profit

This line graph shows that the moving average smooths out the fluctuations, plotting a profit trend line which can be extended as a profit forecast.

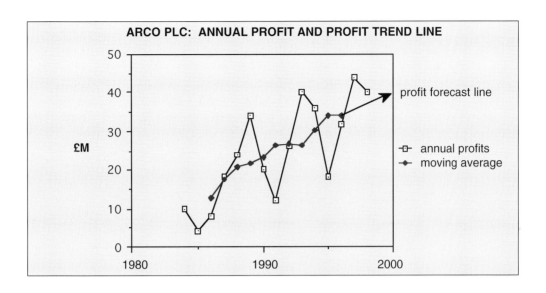

CUMULATIVE FREQUENCY GRAPHS (OGIVES)

Line graphs are sometimes used to show the *frequency* of certain results. This concept is best explained by looking at an example: a car factory will want to know the number of cars produced each week over, say, a year. All this data will be useful for management of any business for planning and costing purposes. It will be particularly useful if the data can be displayed so that management can see for how many weeks of the year production (or sales) will be *below* certain levels.

The starting point for this exercise is a table of data. The first column shows the weekly production levels in 'bands' of 100. The second column sets out the number of weeks each level is achieved; ie the number of times (the 'frequency'). The third column adds up the frequencies from the second column; ie 10 + 12 = 22 then 22 + 18 = 40 then 40 + 8 = 48, and so on.

weekly production of cars	number of weeks with production at this level (frequency)	cumulative frequency
0 to 1,000	10	10
1,001 to 1,100	12	22
1,101 to 1,200	18	40
1,201 to 1,300	8	48
1,301 to 1,400	4	52

constructing the graph (ogive)

The cumulative frequency graph, also known as the *ogive*, is plotted from the table on the previous page. The units are shown on the x axis and are plotted at the upper end of each band, eg the 0–1000 band is plotted at the 1000 point.

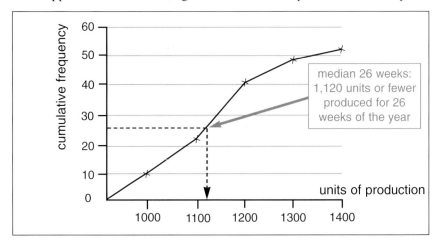

interpreting the graph

The cumulative frequency graph (ogive) can be used to estimate the number of frequencies that lie below any chosen value. The ogive is associated with values such as the median (the value of the middle ranked item): 26 weeks in the case of the graph shown here. Ogives are sometimes described as 'less than' curves: they can show for how many weeks of the year production fell *below* any particular level. This can be very useful in the costing process.

Z CHARTS

The Z chart is so-called because it combines three separate lines in the shape of the letter Z. The lines are:

1 any variable such as sales figures plotted over a time period (eg a year)

2 the cumulative total of that variable, plotted over the same period

3 the annual total to date of that variable (usually incorporating data from the previous year)

Z charts are useful to business because they show:

- *present trends* – monthly totals
- *cumulative totals* – performance to date can be compared with budgeted performance
- *a moving annual total* indicating performance compared with last year

A simplified Z chart for sales figures looks like this:

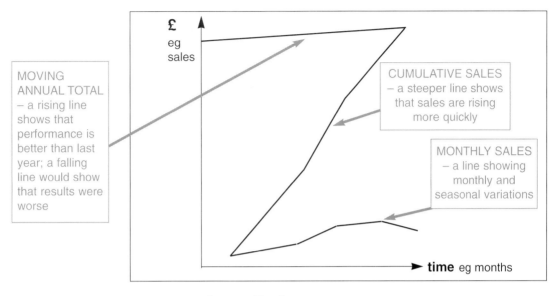

constructing a Z chart

The first step is to construct a *table* for the data. The example below is based on the sales of a business and sets out:

- monthly sales figures for this year (B) and a cumulative total (C)
- monthly sales figures for the previous time period (A) – ie last year – required for calculating the moving annual total (D)

The calculations on the table are explained on the next page.

month	sales (£000) A year 1	sales (£000) B year 2	cumulative sales (£000) C year 2	moving annual D total (£000)
January	10	11	11	163
February	11	12	23	164
March	12	13	36	165
April	12	14	50	167
May	15	16	66	168
June	15	17	83	170
July	15	18	101	173
August	16	18	119	175
September	15	18	137	178
October	15	16	153	179
November	14	16	169	181
December	12	15	184	184
	162	184		

calculations for the Z chart table

The monthly sales figures for years 1 and 2 are taken from the sales records of the business.

The calculation for the *cumulative sales* (column C) is that of the ogive (see page 231) – they are a running total of the monthly figures in column B: ie 11 + 12 = 23, 23 + 13 = 36, 36 + 14 = 50 and so on to 184 in December. A useful cross check is that this total (184) equals the total of column B.

The *moving annual total* for any month (column D) is the sales total for the last twelve months, including the figure for that month. To calculate the moving annual total you start at month 1 (January):

total sales for previous year <u>less</u> sales for month 1 in the previous year <u>plus</u> sales for month 1 in the current year

The calculation here is £162,000 (total sales for Year 1) less £10,000 (sales for January, Year 1) plus £11,000 (sales for January Year 2) = £163,000

The calculation for the next month takes this total of £163,000 as the starting point and performs the same process with the February sales figures in columns A and B: £163,000 – £11,000 + £12,000 = £164,000.

This process continues until December when the moving annual total is, of course, the sales total for Year 2, ie £184,000. If it is not, you will need to check your arithmetic!

Once the table is complete you can then chart the graph (shown below):

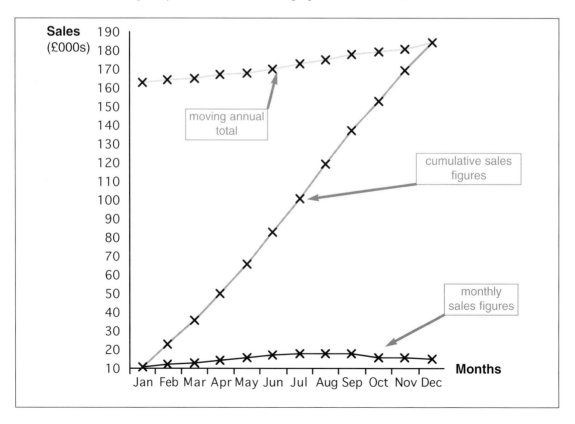

ALLOWING FOR CHANGES IN PRICES: INDEX NUMBERS

performance figures as index numbers

A further method of presenting a numeric trend over a time series is converting the figures in question into a series of *index numbers.*

An index is a sequence of values where one base value is equated to 100 and the other values are proportionally related to 100.

The object of using an index system is to simplify comparison of complex values by replacing the complicated figures with simple ones, all related to a base of 100.

It is therefore possible to convert periodic performance figures such as sales and profits to index numbers in order to analyse trends much more easily. The procedure for doing this is explained at the bottom of the page.

RPI: price levels as index numbers

Another form of index is the Retail Price Index (RPI) which regularly looks at the price of a defined 'shopping basket' of products in the UK economy and gives them an index number related to a base year. This index charts the rise in the level of prices. This is important to businesses because if prices are rising sharply, a true comparison of performance figures becomes difficult. There is no point in saying that sales in money terms have increased by 10% when the level of prices has risen by 15% – in this case the volume of sales may have gone down.

calculating index numbers

The procedure for creating an index series is as follows:

■ Take a series of values, for example the total sales for Osborne PLC over four years:

Year 1	£500,000
Year 2	£520,000
Year 3	£525,000
Year 4	£535,000

■ Equate the first figure (the base year) with 100, ie say £500,000 = 100
■ Convert each of the subsequent years' figures to index numbers by applying the formula:

$$\frac{\text{other year's figure} \times 100}{\text{base year figure}} = \text{index number of other year}$$

The calculation for the index for the sales of Osborne PLC is therefore:

Year 1	£500,000 (base year figure)	=	100
Year 2	$\frac{£520,000}{£500,000}$ × 100	=	104
Year 3	$\frac{£525,000}{£500,000}$ × 100	=	105
Year 4	$\frac{£535,000}{£500,000}$ × 100	=	107

The indices (index numbers) for the four years are therefore: 100, 104, 105 and 107. There would seem to be a modest upward trend in sales. Or is there? Suppose that for the four years in question the prices of goods and services in the economy had been rising sharply – in other words in real terms the value of money had been declining. It follows that sales *in real terms* may also have been declining. Using index numbers it is possible to compare the sales trend with inflation. The table below shows the RPI (Retail Price Index) as quoted for the four years in question:

	RPI index	Osborne sales index
Year 1	150	100
Year 2	160	104
Year 3	170	105
Year 4	182	107

It is clear from this exercise that sales are increasing at a slower rate than the level of prices: the RPI index figures are increasing at a higher rate. In the next section we will see how these sales figures can be adjusted to *sales in real terms* by using the RPI index figures.

converting figures to adjust for price changes

The following formula is used to present the sales trend in the light of the rise in the price level as shown by the RPI:

$\frac{\text{Sales figure for year in question x RPI index for Year 1}}{\text{RPI index for year in question}}$ = Adjusted sales figure

For Year 2, therefore, the calculation is:

$\frac{£520,000 \times 150}{160}$ = Adjusted sales figure of £487,500

For Year 3 the calculation is:

$$\frac{£525,000 \times 150}{170} = \text{Adjusted sales figure of } £463,235$$

For Year 4, therefore, the calculation is:

$$\frac{£535,000 \times 150}{182} = \text{Adjusted sales figure of } £440,934$$

The sales figures can then be presented in a table as follows:

Year	Actual sales figures £	Sales figures adjusted by RPI index £
Year 1	500,000	500,000
Year 2	520,000	487,500
Year 3	525,000	463,235
Year 4	535,000	440,934

It is clear from these adjusted figures that sales *in real terms* are on a serious decline: although the actual figure for Year 4 is £535,00, when adjusted for the change in price levels as measured by the RPI, it is only £440,934.

CHAPTER SUMMARY

- Performance reports contain the presentation of figures – money amounts, units produced hours – over a period of time. This is known as *time series analysis*.

- Time series analysis normally starts with the presentation of the figures in a table; these are the raw data from which can be constructed a variety of graphs and charts, either on paper or on a computer.

- A line graph is a simple and effective way of showing trends over time. More than one line can be displayed on a line graph.

- A bar chart also illustrates trends and can be in simple form (one variable charted) or compound (a number of variables charted separately) or component (showing the make-up of a figure in a single bar).

- A pie chart – a circular 'pie' divided into slices – shows the proportional make-up of a single figure. A pie chart is not so helpful in showing trends as it is limited to a single time period.

- When analysing periodic performance figures it is important to be able to use averages. There are three types of average: the mean (the most common), the median (the middle figure in a series) and the mode (the most common figure). All types have their particular uses (see Key Terms below).

- The use of moving averages enables a trend to be established when the figures in the time series vary widely; this technique also enables a future trend to be forecast.

- A cumulative frequency graph shows how frequently a range of results is achieved.

- A Z chart is a graph showing three separate lines: a set of variables , the cumulative total of that data and the moving annual total of that data. The lines form a shape like the letter Z.

- A series of index numbers enables a set of complex time series values (eg sales over five years) to be related to a base figure of 100. This makes comparison of the values much simpler.

- The Retail Price Index (RPI) charts changes in price levels in the UK economy over time. It is useful – particularly when prices are rising rapidly – to adjust a set of time series figures (eg sales) to the RPI index. This will show the *actual* trend of the time series figures.

KEY TERMS

time series analysis	the comparison of a set of figures recorded over a period of time
line graph	a visual representation of a time series
independent variable	the measurement on a line graph which is set at fixed intervals – this is often time, eg months, years
dependent variable	the measurement on a line graph which *depends* on the independent variable, eg sales, profit, over time
simple bar chart	a chart which sets out a series of bars, the height of which indicates the extent of the independent variable
compound bar chart	a bar chart which displays more than one set of data (and more than one bar) for each independent variable
component bar chart	a bar chart which divides each bar into segments which shows how the total for each bar is made up
pie chart	a circle divided into sectors to represent in the correct proportion the parts of a whole – like a pie divided into 'slices'
arithmetic mean	an average worked out as the sum of all the figures in a series divided by the number of figures
median	an average which is the value of a middle figure in a series of figures
mode	an average which is the value that occurs most often in a series

moving average

the technique of repeatedly calculating a series of different arithmetic mean values for a dependent variable along a time series to produce a trend graph

cumulative frequency graph

a graph showing the frequency of certain results over a time period – it is also known as an *ogive*

Z chart

a chart presenting three line graphs in the shape of a letter Z. The three lines show

– a set of dependent variables

– a cumulative total of those figures

– an annual moving total

index

a sequence of values where one base value is equated to 100 and the other values are proportionally related to 100

Retail Price Index (RPI)

an index which represents the price of a 'shopping basket' of products in the UK economy over time – it measures the price level and is an indicator of inflation

STUDENT ACTIVITIES

The answers to these Student Activities are printed in the back of this book. Further questions and more fully extended Student Activities and Assessments are to be found in the accompanying Osborne Books' text *Costing, Reports & Returns Workbook*.

Note: graphs and charts may be drawn by hand (pencil and graph paper are recommended) or produced using a computer package. If a computer is used, care must be taken with specification of labels, keys, axes, etc.

12.1 A colleague hands you the following table which is to be used in a performance report. What is wrong with it? Redraft it as you think it should appear and construct a line graph to illustrate sales and profitability. Note: the figures for sales, cost of sales and overheads are known to be correct.

Gemini PLC				
	Year 1	**Year 2**	**Year 3**	**Year 3**
Sales	1,000	1,250	1,300	1,450
Cost of sales	500	650	650	700
Gross profit	500	600	640	750
Overheads	350	350	380	400
Net profit	250	300	260	350

12.2 The table below shows the divisional sales figures for Newbury Products PLC.

Newbury Products PLC Sales by Division				
	Year 1 £000s	Year 2 £000s	Year 3 £000s	Year 4 £000s
Sales Division A	400	500	550	600
Sales Division B	100	250	350	400
Sales Division C	350	300	250	300
Total Sales	850	1,050	1,150	1,300

You are to:

(a) Construct a compound bar chart showing the sales for all three divisions over the four years. Make brief comments on the trends shown. Is this the best form of chart to use to show these trends?

(b) Construct a component bar chart using the same data. Comment on the differences between the charts in (a) and (b) and state in what circumstances you would use them.

(c) Construct pie charts for Year 1 and Year 4 and comment on what they do and do not show.

12.3 Calculate the average (mean, median and mode) hourly rate of shopfloor workers pay from the following figures:

£5.50, £5.75, £5.80, £5.85, £5.90, £8.00, £10.00, £10.00, £35.00.

Which average figure are you likely to use if you are compiling a report on wage costs, and why?

12.4 The following figures represent the number of unit sales (measured in thousands) of a new product over the last 15 weeks, following the placing of a newspaper advert promoting the product.

2, 5, 10, 7, 4, 9, 12, 10, 6, 12,14,11,7,13,18

Work out a moving average on these figures, using as a base for the average the number of figures which you think appropriate.

Plot the original figures and the moving average figures on a line graph.

What general trend do you predict on the basis of these figures?

12.5 Oakwood Limited manufactures sets of dining tables and chairs. The factory has compiled production figures for the last year:

weekly production of dining sets	number of weeks at this level of production
0 to 100	4
101 to 110	12
111 to 120	21
121 to 130	12
131 to 140	3

You are to:

(a)   calculate the cumulative frequency of the data

(b)   draw up a cumulative frequency graph

(c)   identify where the graph is at its steepest and explain what this indicates

12.6   The comparative sales figures for the first six months of this year and last year for Monarch Products are shown below.

month	sales (£M) year 1	sales (£M) year 2
January	6	8
February	7	9
March	9	10
April	10	12
May	11	12
June	10	11

You are to:

(a)   Draw up a table in the format used on page 233, but showing only six months' figures.

(b)   Calculate the six-monthly total for both years.

(c)   Calculate the monthly cumulative sales figure for Year 2 (third column of figures). Check that the June cumulative total is the same as the total in the second column of figures.

(d)   Calculate the moving half-year total for Year 2 (the calculation is carried out on the same basis as an annual moving total). Check that the June moving total is the same as June cumulative total.

(e)   Draw up a Z chart using the data from your table. What trends does it show?

12.7   The following table shows the sales and net profit figures for Pilot Design Consultancy for the last five years, together with the Retail Price Index for those years.

Pilot Design Consultancy: sales and profitability			
	Sales (£)	Net profit (£)	RPI
Year 1	350,000	45,000	155
Year 2	355,000	46,000	163
Year 3	365,000	48,000	169
Year 4	380,000	48,500	176
Year 5	390,000	49,000	189

You are to:

(a)   Convert the sales and net profit figures into index numbers, using year one as the base. Comment on the trends shown.

(b)   Adjust (to the nearest £) the sales and net profit figures for the changing price levels shown by the RPI indices. Comment on the trends shown.

13 REPORTS AND RETURNS TO OUTSIDE AGENCIES

this chapter covers . . .

In this chapter we examine a range of reports that organisations may have to complete and send to external bodies. These are required from time-to-time by a variety of external agencies:

- regulatory bodies such as the Inland Revenue and HM Customs & Excise
- organisations that award grants and provide finance, eg the Department of Trade and Industry and banks
- information-collecting organisations, eg Chambers of Commerce
- trade associations

We also stress the need to make sure that reports being sent off are:

- authorised by the appropriate person
- checked carefully for accuracy
- sent off on time and as required by the outside body

NVQ PERFORMANCE CRITERIA COVERED

unit 6: PREPARING REPORTS AND RETURNS

element 2

prepare reports and returns for outside agencies

❑ relevant information is identified, collated and presented in accordance with the conventions and definitions used by outside agencies

❑ calculations of ratios and performance indicators are accurate

❑ authorisation for the despatch of completed reports and returns is sought from the appropriate person

❑ reports and returns are presented in accordance with outside agencies' requirements and deadlines

WHO NEEDS REPORTS?

As well as the requirement for internal reporting seen so far in this book, organisations will need from time-to-time to complete returns to external agencies. As you will see, some of these returns are covered elsewhere in your studies, eg a VAT Return. In this chapter we will present a series of Case Studies covering all the main types of return, showing how information held by the organisation is entered onto the form.

Most returns are on 'pro-forma' forms – ie the information is entered in boxes or on defined lines on pre-printed pages. This makes the information easier to identify and to collect by the organisation completing the return, and easier to process by the body asking for it. Occasionally a return may require a written report – eg part of a business plan submitted for a grant application – but the majority of returns will be straightforward forms, and these will be illustrated in detail in the Case Studies.

grant awarding bodies

If an organisation needs to raise money there are banks and other financial companies which will provide loans and public sector (government owned or controlled) bodies which will provide grants, and, in some cases, loans. Details of these sources of finance are available through Chambers of Commerce and Business Link offices. Any application for finance or a grant will invariably involve sending the organisation financial and non-financial details, as we will see in the Case Studies. Examples of finance and grant-awarding bodies include:

- banks
- local authorities
- the Department of Trade and Industry
- the European Commission

statistical information collectors

Organisations may from time-to-time be asked to complete questionnaires sent them by government agencies or Chambers of Commerce. These will cover areas such as economic trends, employment trends, skills shortages, transport, information technology, and so on. These are not like the regulatory returns which *have to be* returned, but many organisations do complete them. Although much of the required detail is not 'accounting' data as such, these returns may well involve financial aspects such as sales trends and wage rates which will involve input from the accounting function.

trade associations

A trade association is basically a membership 'club' for businesses in a particular trade, eg ABTA (Association of British Travel Agents) and the Publishers Association. As well as safeguarding and promoting the interests of businesses in those sectors, trade associations collect data from their individual members for statistical purposes and in some cases to produce directories. This data, for a retailing organisation might include details such as the level of annual sales (within certain bands), terms of trade (discounts given) and the number of employees. The accounting function of a retailer – whether it be a small shop or a major retail chain – may well have to send in these details on a regular basis.

regulatory bodies

Organisations are subject by law to a variety of external regulations and need periodically to provide returns to the bodies that administer those regulations. Examples include:

- the *Inland Revenue* which requires details of payroll (employer's P35 annual return), tax liabilities (self-assessment form for sole traders, accounts for larger businesses)
- *HM Customs & Excise* which requires regular completion of a VAT 100 (VAT return) by VAT-registered businesses (see page 255)
- *Companies House* which regulates the running of limited companies and requires an annual return from companies and the filing of accounts for larger companies

authorisation of returns

All reports and returns sent to external agencies should go through a rigorous checking and authorisation procedure. There should be no short cuts in the process. Checks should ensure that all the information required is present and in the correct format. External reports and returns should also be sent off on time; most organisations will set up a diary system to ensure that this happens. Some returns will require an authorised signature; this should not be overlooked.

This aspect of reports and returns cannot be stressed too highly: there are fines for late company returns and also for errors on VAT returns, even if the error was accidental. Late submission of VAT returns can sometimes trigger off a VAT inspection. No more need be said!

CASE STUDIES

The remainder of this chapter is made up of Case Studies which explain what reports and returns are likely to be encountered and how they will be completed. They are:

- Trading figures for a bank – Design Furniture Limited
- Application for an Export Award – Helios Vision
- Chamber of Commerce Questionnaire – Villas of Italy
- Trade Association return – Microwise Publications
- VAT Return – Pomona Garden Supplies

It must be stressed that the businesses on which the Case Studies are based are entirely fictitious. The bodies to which the returns are sent are real. Osborne Books is grateful to these bodies for permission to reproduce material which they have supplied.

CASE STUDY

TRADING FIGURES FOR THE BANK: DESIGN FURNITURE LIMITED

situation

Design Furniture Limited is a small shop selling quality design furniture to a wide range of commercial and private customers. Much of the furniture is imported; many of the customers pay on credit.

Two years ago Design Furniture Limited took out a long-term loan of £50,000 from the bank to help set up its present premises.

As part of the financing arrangements Design Furniture Limited undertook to provide trading figures for the bank on a monthly basis so that the bank could monitor the progress of the company. Clearly if the company was running into any difficulties, the bank could pick up the warning signs from the trading figures.

The trading figures show:

        Current assets (money due to the company in the short term)

less   **Current liabilities** (money owed by the business in the short term)

The bank would want to know that current assets were greater than current liabilities. The difference between the two (the 'working capital' of the business) enables the business to pay bills as they fall due.

source of the trading figures

The figures for the return (shown opposite) will be found in the accounting records of the company.

Trade debtors are listed in the Aged Debtor Summary, an extract from which is shown below. The summary – often produced as a monthly report on a computer accounting program – lists all customers to whom the business sells on credit. It is essentially the Sales Ledger summarised to show who owes what, and when. Its balance total will equal the total of debtors' control account. It lists in columns:

- customer names
- credit limits
- balances
- amounts not yet due – ie 'current' – assuming the company gives 30 days' credit
- amounts outstanding over 30 days
- amounts outstanding over 60 days

An extract from this schedule, with some sample entries, is shown below. It is the total line which will be used to complete the return

AGED DEBTOR SCHEDULE (extract)				date:	31 March 1999
Customer	limit	balance	current	over 30 days	over 60 days
	£	£	£	£	£
Adams Trading	2,000	1,457.67	1,457.67		
Braswell Ltd	2,000	1,590.50	1,000.00	590.50	
Duff Limited	1,000	1,300.00			1,300.00
TOTAL		75,060.00	35,431.00	23,906.00	15,723.00

The remaining figures are provided by the accounts office:

- the stock figure will be taken from the total of the Stores Ledger Records.
- the following figures will be taken from the monthly trial balance (list of account balances): cash account, creditors control, VAT due
- creditors figures will be taken from an aged creditor summary – constructed on the same principle as the aged debtor summary shown above
- prepayments and accruals will be noted in the records
- PAYE – income tax and National Insurance due to the Inland Revenue by the 19th of the following month – the figures will be known by the payroll office

solution

These figures are inserted on the form shown opposite and are then checked carefully. When all is in order and authorised, the form will be sent to the bank within the stipulated deadline – early in the next month. A copy will be taken for the records.

Statement of Current Trading Position
("Quick Figures")

Business Name	*DESIGN FURNITURE LTD*
As at (date)	*31 MARCH 1999*

Current Assets

a. Total Trade Debtors (ie. funds owed to you by your customers) £ *75,060*

Please give a breakdown of your trade debtors according to how long they have been outstanding:

Up to 30 days	£	*35,431*
31 to 60 days	£	*23,906*
Over 60 days	£	*15,723*

b. Stock and Work in Progress £ *36,107*

c. Cash Held and Total of all Bank and Building Society Credit Balances in your books £ *5,920*

d. Other Current Assets (please specify, eg. prepayments) *PHONE RENTAL PREPAID*

£ *120*

Total Current Assets	**(a)+(b)+(c)+(d)** £	*117,207*

Current Liabilities

e. Trade Creditors (ie. funds you owe your suppliers) £ *59,235*

Please give a breakdown of your trade creditors according to how long they have been outstanding:

Up to 30 days	£	*45,165*
31 to 60 days	£	*12,107*
Over 60 days	£	*1,963*

f. Total of all Overdrawn Bank Balances in your books £ *NIL*

g. Pay As You Earn (PAYE) Owed by the Business £ *1,483*

h. Value Added Tax (VAT) Owed by the Business £ *6,270*

i. Other Current Liabilities (please specify, eg. accruals) *AUDIT FEE ACCRUED*

£ *1,500*

Total Current Liabilities	**(e)+(f)+(g)+(h)+(i)** £	*68,488*

© Barclays Bank PLC

**CASE
STUDY**

APPLICATION FOR AN EXPORT AWARD:
HELIOS VISION

situation

Helios Vision Plc is a fast-growing UK manufacturer of fashion sunglasses. This company has been particularly successful in exporting to the USA and Australia. One of its success stories is the distinctive 'Cool Shade' brand which was adopted by Brad Street, star of the American TV soap 'Sunrise Park'.

The Board of Directors has decided to apply for a Government-backed Export Award for smaller businesses – over £50,000 worth of cash and professional services are available. Applications for awards are competitive. Eligible businesses must be: independent UK-based businesses, manufacturers or providers of services, employers of no more than 250 people and not a previous award winner.

On the financial side, applicants must:

• show growth in export earnings over the last 3 years

• achieve at least £100,000 in export earnings over the most recent year

The application involves:

• an entry form signed by the Managing Director (see opposite)

• a Statement of Export Achievement on one side of A4 paper

John Brandon, the MD, has asked the Sales Department to provide the written statement. It is your job to complete the figures in Part 2b of the form shown opposite.

solution

You research the accounting records and extract the following figures, which you set out in a table ready for checking and transferring to the form. You also contact the payroll supervisor for employee numbers over the last three years.

HELIOS VISION PLC			
Year to:	31.12.98	31.12.99	31.12.00
	£	£	£
UK Sales	487,612	542,373	680,063
Export Sales	105,961	189,731	249,500
Total Sales	593,573	732,104	929,563
Net profit (after tax)	71,725	93,763	121,811

When the figures have been checked and authorised, the form should be completed and passed to the MD's office for signature by John Brandon and submission by 20 May – the stipulated deadline.

ENTRY FORM
(Please type or print clearly using a ball point pen)

PART 1   Full name and address

Chairman/Managing Director	JOHN BRANDON
Company Name	HELIOS VISION
Company Address	UNIT 17 HARTBURY ESTATE
	MEREFORD

County & Postcode MRL 5HN   Tel: 01902 743193   Fax: 01902 743748

Parent Company (if any) —

Subsidiaries (if any) —

Total number of employees in Group (incl. Directors & employees of parent & subsidiary companies)   120

Type of Company: Manufacturing ✓   Service ◇   *(Please tick)*

Description of products or services exported from the UK: SUNGLASSES

PART 2   Figures   *(Please tick one box to show which Award you are applying for)*

2a   Entry for Regional Award ✓
The Best Exporting Company of the Year will be selected from the Regional Winners. Figures must be provided for the latest three complete financial years, ending no later than 28th February 1998.

2b   Entry for Best Newcomer Award ◇
Figures must be provided for the first full year of exporting (the financial year must either start or finish in 1997, but must end no later than 28th February 1998). Turnover and profit figures must also be provided for the previous two years if the company was trading.

Full financial years ended MONTH | YEAR	Number of employees (Applicant firm only)	Export earnings	Whole annual turnover	Net profit after tax
DEC 1998	98	£105,961	£593,573	£71,725
DEC 1999	107	£189,731	£732,104	£93,763
DEC 2000	120	£249,500	£929,563	£121,811

PART 3   Statement of Export Achievement

A Statement of Export Achievement (not exceeding one side of A4 paper) must be submitted with this entry. Its scope is at the discretion of the entrant company but should include a short resume of the business, a description of its products/services and most importantly, details of how current export success has been achieved. Points of particular interest are sales and marketing methods, market research methods and export management.

Statement attached *(Please tick)* ✓

PART 4   Certification

◆ We submit this entry and attach a TYPED ONE-PAGE statement of export achievement. We undertake to submit immediately our latest audited Report and Accounts and an Auditor's Certificate supporting the figures in Part 2 above, in the event of our company being included on the preliminary shortlist.

◆ We hereby certify that all the particulars supplied by us in our entry are correct to the best of our knowledge and belief and comply with definitions set out and that no material information has been withheld.

◆ We accept the rules and conditions of entry A to D and agree to abide by the decisions of the Panel of Judges and the sponsors on all matters relating to these Awards.

Date 11 April 2001   Signature (of Chairman or Managing Director)

The Award Administrator will acknowledge receipt of your entry and will advise you whether or not you have been included on the preliminary shortlist in due course. You will be provided with a reference number which you should quote in any correspondence concerning this application.

CHAMBER OF COMMERCE QUESTIONNAIRE: VILLAS OF ITALY

the business

You work as an accounts assistant for Villas of Italy, a Bristol-based agency which arranges Italian villa holidays for UK clients. The business is owned and managed by Luigi Ferrini. The typical holiday is two weeks spent in a luxury Tuscan hilltop villa with swimming pool and maid service. Villas of Italy hires the properties from Italian landowners and their agents, arranges charter flights to local airports and car hire and insurance as required.

Villas of Italy employs nine staff, most of them based at its Bristol headquarters. They have just been given a well-deserved pay rise. Although business performance has been steady for the last year, the fall in value of the pound against the Italian Lira has resulted in a rise in costs.

the questionnaire

Villas of Italy is a member of the local Chamber of Commerce, which Luigi finds useful, not only for its discounts on business services, but also for the opportunity he has to meet up with other business owners.

He has recently received a questionnaire from the Chamber of Commerce asking for a wide range of business information, including details of:

- market trends
- the labour market
- business investment plans
- business cash flow
- business sales and profitability
- details of influences on prices and costs

The text of the questionnaire is set out on the next three pages.

Although no financial figures are requested in the questionnaire, he asks you as accounts assistant to extract figures which provide evidence for the trends enquired about in the questionnaire. In particular you find out details of:

- sales and profit performance (Questions 2 and 7)
- cash flow (Question 5)
- investment plans (Question 6)
- sales budgets (Question 7)
- cost budgets (Question 9)

It is likely that Luigi will then complete the form with your help. The office will ensure that the form is sent off on time, to the correct person at the correct address.

BRITISH CHAMBERS OF COMMERCE

QUARTERLY ECONOMIC SURVEY

All responses are treated in the strictest confidence

1) Your Business

a) How many people do you currently employ? 9

b) Please state your postcode (this is so we can break results down by area) MR1 2JF

c) What is your main activity ?   VILLA   LETTINGS

Manufacturing		Services	
Energy and Water Supply		Distribution, Hotels/Catering, repairs	✓
Minerals and Chemicals		Transport and Communication	
Metal Goods and Engineering		Financial and Business Services	
Other Manufacturing		Other Services	
Construction		Agriculture	
Don't Know (please describe)		Don't Know (please describe)	

2) For Businesses involved in the UK market, excluding seasonal variations, over the past 3 months

a) Sales / Custom / Bookings have ...

increased ✓
remained constant
decreased

b) Orders / Advance Custom / Bookings have ...

increased ✓
remained constant
decreased

3) For Businesses involved in Overseas Markets, excluding seasonal variations, over the past 3 months   N/A

a) Overseas Sales / Custom / Bookings have ...

increased
remained constant
decreased

b) Overseas Orders / Advance Custom / Bookings have..

increased
remained constant
decreased

4) The Labour Force

a) Over the past 3 months, has your workforce:

increased ☑
remained constant ☐
decreased ☐

b) Over the next 3 months do you expect your workforce to:

increase ☐
remain constant ☑
decrease ☐

c) Have you attempted to recruit staff over the past 3 months?

Yes ☑
No ☐

d) If YES, were they for: (please tick all that apply)

part-time jobs? ☑
full-time jobs? ☐
temporary jobs? ☐
permanent jobs? ☐

e) Did you experience any difficulties finding suitable staff?

Yes ☐
No ☑

f) If YES, for which of the following categories of employment?

Skilled manual/technical ☐
Professional/managerial ☐
Clerical ☐
Un and semi skilled ☐

5) Cashflow

During the last 3 months has your cashflow:

improved ☑
remained the same ☐
worsened ☐

6) Investment

Over the past 3 months, what changes have you made to your investment plans:

a) For plant / machinery / equipment?

revised upwards ☐
no change ☑
revised downwards ☐

b) For training?

revised upwards ☐
no change ☑
revised downwards ☐

7) Business Confidence

Do you believe that over the next 12 months:

Turnover		
will improve		
remain the same	✓	
worsen	·	

Profitability		
will improve		
remain the same	✓	
worsen		

8) Capacity

Are you currently operating at :

full capacity ?	✓
below full capacity ?	

9) Prices / Costs

a) Over the next 3 months, do you expect the price of your goods / services to

increase		
remain the same	✓	
decrease		

b) Is your business currently suffering pressures to raise its prices from any of the following ?

pay settlements	✓
raw material prices	
finance costs	
other overheads	

10) External Factors

Please indicate which of these following factors are more of a concern to your business than 3 months ago. (please tick all that apply)

Interest rates			Competition	
Exchange rates	✓		Corporate taxation	
Business rates			Better Industrial Relations	
Inflation			Improved cash availability	

CASE STUDY

TRADE ASSOCIATION RETURNS: MICROWISE PUBLICATIONS

Microwise is the trade name of Microwise Publications Limited, a small company which publishes books and manuals explaining how to operate computers and use computer programs.

Microwise supplies wholesalers and bookshops and also operates a mail order department which advertises in computer magazines and sells direct to the general public.

Microwise has dealings with two Trade Associations:

- it is a member of the Independent Publishers Guild which looks after the interests of small publishers
- it provides information to the Booksellers Association, which looks after the interests of bookshops and wholesalers

The returns it has to make contain basic statistics which are important for trading. The data will be readily available in the accounts and sales departments of the company. An extract from the annual return to the Independent Publishers Guild is shown below.

INDEPENDENT PUBLISHERS GUILD ANNUAL RETURN

```
Microwise Publications Limited
Laurel House
Heathcote
Lincs
PE14 6TR
```

COMPANY DETAILS

Year Started Trading:	1987
Number Titles in Print:	153
Turnover Range*:	D

NUMBER OF STAFF

Working Owners
No. Full Time:	2
No. Part Time:	1

Other Staff
No. Full Time:	8
No. Part Time:	3
No. Freelances Used:	6

---

*TURNOVER RANGES
A: Under £25,000
B: £25,000 to £100,000
C: £100,000 to £500,000
D: £500,000 to £1,000,000
E: £1,000,000 to £5,000,000
F: £5,000,000 +

CASE STUDY

VAT REGULATION: POMONA GARDEN SUPPLIES

Note: you should already have encountered VAT in your studies and will study it in greater detail in the two chapters which follow. This Case Study helps to put the VAT Return into context as a return required by an external agency, HM Customs & Excise.

Pomona Garden Supplies, based in the East Midlands, grows shrubs and trees which it sells to garden centres throughout the region. The business is VAT-registered, which means that it has to charge VAT on goods which it sells, and can reclaim VAT which it has to pay when it purchases goods and services. Every three months it has to complete a VAT Return on Form VAT 100. This provides details of sales and purchases for the period and totals of VAT charged and paid. The object of the exercise is to calculate how much VAT is due to be paid by the business to HM Customs & Excise for the three months January to March.

The details entered on the form from the accounting records of the business are:

- Sales of £102,901 and VAT of £18,007.67 charged on these sales.

- Purchases of £63,726 and VAT of £10,748.23 charged on most of these (a few transactions are zero-rated – no VAT is payable).

- VAT due to HM Customs & Excise of £7,259.44; a cheque for this amount will be sent with the tax return (note that the box in the bottom left-hand side is ticked).

The illustration below shows the bottom half of the VAT 100 form completed by the business. The signature is that of an authorised employee – very probably the Finance Director. The form, which covers the three months January to March, must be checked carefully and sent off by the end of April.

Before you fill in this form please read the notes on the back and the VAT leaflet *"Filling in your VAT return"*. Fill in all boxes clearl in ink, and write 'none' where necessary. Don't put a dash or leave any box blank. If there are no pence write **"00"** in the pence column. **Do not** enter more than one amount in any box.

	£	p
VAT due in this period on **sales** and other outputs **1**	18,007	67
VAT due in this period on **acquisitions** from other **EC Member States** **2**	–	
Total VAT due **(the sum of boxes 1 and 2)** **3**	18,007	67
VAT reclaimed in this period on **purchases** and other inputs (including acquisitions from the EC) **4**	10,748	23
Net VAT to be paid to Customs or reclaimed by you **(Difference between boxes 3 and 4)** **5**	7,259	44
Total value of **sales** and all other outputs excluding any VAT. **Include your box 8 figure** **6**	102,901	00
Total value of **purchases** and all other inputs excluding any VAT. **Include your box 9 figure** **7**	63,726	00
Total value of all **supplies** of goods and related services, excluding any VAT, to other **EC Member States** **8**	–	00
Total value of all **acquisitions** of goods and related services, excluding any VAT, from other **EC Member States** **9**	–	00

Retail schemes. If you have used any of the schemes in the period covered by this return, enter the relevant letter(s) in this box. –

DECLARATION: You, or someone on your behalf, must sign below.

I, ARTHUR JAMES HENSON declare that the (Full name of signatory in BLOCK LETTERS) information given above is true and complete.

If you are enclosing a payment please tick this box. ✓

Signature .... Date 8 APRIL 19 99
A false declaration can result in prosecution.

CHAPTER SUMMARY

- Organisations may from time-to-time need to make returns to outside bodies.

- The returns are normally on pre-printed forms, but occasionally an additional written text may be required.

- The types of bodies requiring returns are

  - grant awarding bodies and providers of finance, eg banks

  - collectors of statistical information

  - trade associations

  - regulatory bodies such as the Inland Revenue and HM Customs & Excise

- The returns should be completed in the format and manner in which they are requested by the outside agency.

- It is essential that all completed returns are carefully checked, authorised and sent off within the stipulated deadline.

KEY TERMS

pro-forma	a form that has a defined format
public sector bodies	organisations which are government-owned or government controlled
Department of Trade & Industry	the DTI is the UK government agency responsible for administering business incentive schemes
European Commission	the Brussels-based body which is responsible for administering the law and regulations of the European Union
trade association	a membership 'club' for a particular trade, responsible for safeguarding interests and, in some cases, regulation
Inland Revenue	the body responsible for the regulation administration and collection of tax (but not VAT)
HM Customs & Excise	the government body responsible for the regulation and administration of import and export duties and Value Added Tax

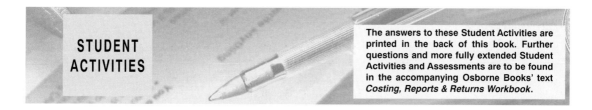

13.1 Romona Smith is the owner/manager of a franchised gift shop in Stourford. The business is called 'Cute Ideas' and is supplied from the franchisor in Kettering.

The franchisor in Kettering requires a regular return of information from its franchisees (shops). Each shop is set an agreed quarterly sales target. Sales are divided into:

•   Category A (books and cards)

•   Category B (novelties)

Each quarter a form (see next page) is sent to shop owners requesting

•   sales figures

•   variances from targets (amounts)

•   variances from target in the form of percentage deviation from the targets

A box is also supplied for comments by the shop owner.

The franchisor takes as commission 10% of the sales figure each quarter as part of the franchise agreement, and a box is included on the form for calculation of this payment.

When the form is completed it is returned to the franchisor together with a commission cheque within fifteen days of the end of the quarter.

It is the first week in April. Romona has just reached the end of her January - March trading quarter and has to fill in the form from the accounting information she has printed out from her computer:

	Target (£)	Actual (£)
Sales A	15,000	13,500
Sales B	21,000	18,000

Romona tells you that the last three months have not been good for a number of reasons – bad weather keeping customers away, a similar shop opening up two doors away, road works and customers being short of cash after Christmas.

You are to:

(a)   Enter the sales figures on the form

(b)   Calculate the variances (amounts and percentages – to the nearest £ and %)

(c)   Calculate the commission due

(d)   Provide comments in the space

(e)   Sign and date the form in Romona's name (assume the current year, first quarter)

<table>
<tr><td colspan="2">CUTE IDEAS   Trading Report</td><td>Quarter ended ..../......../.......</td><td></td><td></td></tr>
<tr><td>£</td><td></td><td>£</td><td>£
variance</td><td>%
variance</td></tr>
<tr><td>Sales A (actual)</td><td>Sales Target A</td><td></td><td></td><td></td></tr>
<tr><td>Sales B (actual)</td><td>Sales Target B</td><td></td><td></td><td></td></tr>
<tr><td>Total Sales (actual)</td><td>Total Sales Target</td><td></td><td></td><td></td></tr>
<tr><td colspan="5">10% Commission on sales £   (cheque enclosed)</td></tr>
<tr><td colspan="5">Comments</td></tr>
<tr><td colspan="2">signature</td><td colspan="3">date</td></tr>
</table>

13.2 Heather Springer runs 'Just Desserts' a pudding and dessert manufacturing company which supplies local pubs and restuarants. She has recently borrowed £45,000 from the bank to extend her baking facilities and has just been sent a 'Statement of Current Trading Position' (shown opposite) to complete and return to the bank. The date is today's date.

You are to:

(a) Complete the form for her. She provides you with the following information:

AGED DEBTOR SCHEDULE (extract)				
Customer	balance £	current £	over 30 days £	over 60 days £
TOTALS	29,216.00	21,075.00	4,629.00	3,512.00

- Stock held is valued at £8,760; there is £5,631 in the bank business account.
- She is due to pay £8,920 corporation (company) tax shortly.
- She owes £1,720 to the Inland Revenue from a recent payroll run.
- No VAT is due because her goods are zero-rated. She is due a refund of £890.
- She owes £7,329 to suppliers (up to 30 days) and £8,160 (31 to 60 days).

(b) State whether you think the bank will be happy with her return.

Statement of Current Trading Position
("Quick Figures")

Business Name

As at (date)

Current Assets

a. Total Trade Debtors (ie. funds owed to you by your customers)   £

Please give a breakdown of your trade debtors according to how long they have been outstanding:

Up to 30 days   £

31 to 60 days   £

Over 60 days   £

b. Stock and Work in Progress   £

c. Cash Held and Total of all Bank and Building Society Credit Balances in your books £

d. Other Current Assets (please specify, eg. prepayments)

£

Total Current Assets   **(a)+(b)+(c)+(d)**   **£**

Current Liabilities

e. Trade Creditors (ie. funds you owe your suppliers)   £

Please give a breakdown of your trade creditors according to how long they have been outstanding:

Up to 30 days   £

31 to 60 days   £

Over 60 days   £

f. Total of all Overdrawn Bank Balances in your books   £

g. Pay As You Earn (PAYE) Owed by the Business   £

h. Value Added Tax (VAT) Owed by the Business   £

i. Other Current Liabilities (please specify, eg. accruals)

£

Total Current Liabilities   **(e)+(f)+(g)+(h)+(i)**   **£**

14 THE PRINCIPLES OF VAT

this chapter covers . . .

In this chapter we explain what Value Added Tax (VAT) is and how it works in practice. We cover the following areas:

- a definition of Value Added Tax
- the law that regulates VAT
- the various rates of VAT
- registration for VAT
- VAT on sales (ouput tax) and VAT on purchases (input VAT)
- the timing of VAT – the 'tax point'
- VAT invoices – the different types and what they involve
- VAT on imports and exports

In the next chapter we will examine the accounting records that need to be kept for VAT and how they provide the information for the VAT return.

Note: you will still often see references to 'EC' (European Community) in publications; in this chapter we will use the more recent term 'EU' (European Union).

NVQ PERFORMANCE CRITERIA COVERED

unit 6: PREPARING REPORTS AND RETURNS
element 3
prepare VAT returns

❏ VAT returns are correctly completed using data from the appropriate sources and are submitted within the statutory time limits

❏ relevant inputs and outputs are correctly identified and calculated

❏ submissions are made in accordance with current legislation

❏ guidance is sought from the VAT office when required, in a professional manner

VAT AND REGULATION OF VAT

a definition

Value Added Tax (VAT) is a tax on the sale of goods and services

VAT is not only charged in the UK: many countries charge VAT (or a similar sales tax), and at varying rates. VAT – essentially a tax on spending – is an important source of revenue for any government. In the UK, VAT is also a tax on *imports* into the country. VAT is charged at a standard percentage rate (currently 17.5% in the UK) on *business* transactions.

VAT regulation and sources of information

The body which regulates and collects VAT in the UK is HM Customs & Excise – familiarly (if not politically correctly) known as the 'VAT man'.

VAT law in the European Union is governed by Directives which are brought into effect in the UK by statute law: the Value Added Tax Act (1994), the annual Finance Acts, and other regulations issued by the government, including sections of the 'The VAT Guide' issued by HM Customs & Excise which explains and interprets the VAT regulations. The 'VAT Guide' is available free of charge from local VAT offices and is *essential reading*. HM Customs & Excise also publishes a series of supplementary leaflets and booklets which are useful reference material. Much of this material, together with updating material, is also available on the HM Customs & Excise website – www.HMCE.gov.uk – which is an invaluable source of information for keeping up-to-date with the changes in VAT regulations.

You will not be expected in your studies to know all the 'ins and outs' of the VAT regulations, but you will be required to know *where* to find the required information, as would any practising accountant.

It should also be mentioned that the accounting treatment of VAT is set out in Statement of Standard Accounting Practice (SSAP) 5 'Accounting for Value Added Tax'. This is covered elsewhere in your Level 3 studies – see Osborne Books' *Financial Accounting Tutorial* (pages 121 to 122). The unit covered by this book concentrates on the administration of VAT and the VAT records needed for the VAT return.

an overview of VAT

Before explaining VAT in detail we will first take a brief look at the whole VAT process.

Most suppliers of goods and services charge VAT, unless, of course, there is no VAT payable, as in the case of the sale of food and young childrens' clothes (see page 264 for zero-rated and exempt supplies). There is a registration threshold set by the government each year, normally in the Budget. From 1 April 2001 the threshold was set at £54,000. If at the end of any month a supplier's total sales (turnover) for the past *year* exceeds this figure, or is *likely to exceed this figure during the next 30 days*, that supplier must by law register with HM Customs & Excise to become what is known as a *taxable person.*

The effect of this registration means that the supplier (taxable person)

• *must* charge VAT on chargeable supplies (ie goods and services)
    – this is known as *output tax*

• can *reclaim* VAT paid on most supplies received
    – this is known as *input tax*

As most businesses are run to make a profit – ie more money will be received from sales than is spent on supplies – most businesses will charge more VAT (output tax) than they pay (input tax). The difference between these two must be paid to HM Customs & Excise.

If a business trades in goods or services on which no VAT is payable (eg books or sewerage services) the business will pay more VAT than it will charge, so it can reclaim the difference from HM Customs & Excise.

The business owner will have to fill in a VAT Return (Form VAT 100) on a regular basis (normally quarterly) to account to HM Customs & Excise for the amount of VAT due or refundable. This is covered in the next chapter.

VAT – a tax on the final consumer

VAT is a tax which is paid by the final consumer of the goods.

If we take, for, example, a member of the public buying a computer for £705, the amount paid includes VAT of £105 (ie 17.5% of £600). The buyer stands the cost of the VAT, but the VAT is actually *paid* to HM Customs & Excise by all those involved in the manufacturing and selling process.

This procedure is illustrated by the flow chart shown on the opposite page. You will see that the right hand column shows the amount of VAT paid to HM Customs & Excise at each stage in the process. The supplier of raw materials, the manufacturer and the shop all pay over to HM Customs & Excise the difference between VAT on sales (outputs) and VAT on purchases (inputs), but this amount is collected from the next person in the process. It is the *consumer* who foots the VAT bill at the end of the day. The VAT is paid to the shop, but as you can see from the diagram, the tax has already been paid (or will soon be paid) to HM Customs & Excise.

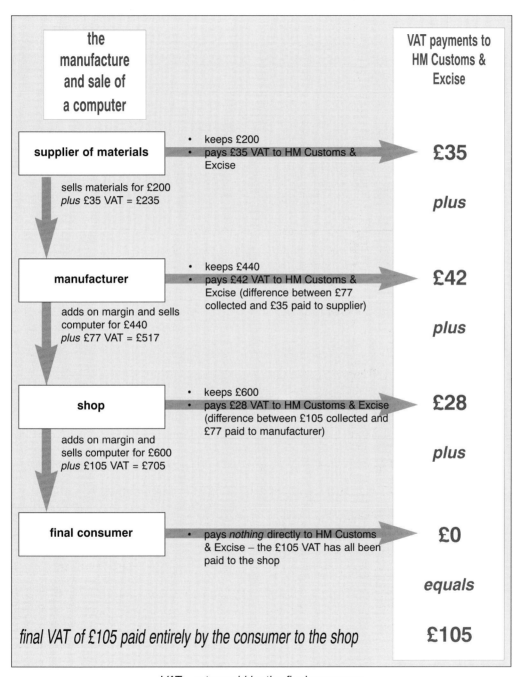

VAT – a tax paid by the final consumer

RATES OF VAT

There are currently three rates of VAT in the UK:

- standard rate   17.5%

- reduced rate (eg on domestic fuel and child car seats)   5%

- zero rate   0%

Zero-rated supplies are *not* the same as exempt supplies, although the result is the same – no VAT is charged. We will now look at these types of supply.

zero-rated supplies

Zero-rated supplies are goods and services taxed at 0%. This may sound odd, but all it means is that the supplies are taxable, but the government has decided that no tax should be charged, normally because the goods are an essential part of spending and to tax them would place a burden on the less well-off. Examples of zero-rated supplies are:

- food bought in shops, but not in restuarants

- young childrens' clothes and shoes (this was extended in 2001)

- transport – eg bus and train fares

- newpapers, magazines and books

- pedal cycle helmets

An important point here is that businesses that sell zero-rated goods *can reclaim the VAT charged* (the input tax) on supplies that they have bought. For example, there was no VAT charged on this book, but the publisher was able to reclaim the VAT paid on the cost of the book, eg the paper used, the marketing costs and so on. The situation with *exempt supplies* is quite different.

exempt supplies

Whereas zero-rated supplies are chargeable – at 0% – exempt supplies are not chargeable at all. Also, *a supplier who supplies only VAT-exempt goods or services cannot reclaim any input VAT.* Examples of supplies that are exempt include:

- insurance

- postal services from the Post Office

- education and healthcare

- betting and gambling, burials and cremations

You should read Appendix A of the 'VAT Guide' which illustrates these points further.

REGISTRATION FOR VAT

who should register?

A person in business selling goods and services on which VAT is chargeable must apply to Customs & Excise on Form VAT 1 to become VAT registered:

- when the value of the taxable supplies (the *taxable turnover*) over a twelve month period *has exceeded* a registration limit set annually by the Government (£54,000 from 1 April 2001) – the person must apply within 30 days of the end of the 12 months

- when the value of the taxable supplies (before VAT is added on) *is likely within the next thirty days* to exceed the annual registration limit

In short, a person must apply to the local VAT Office to register (within 30 days) if taxable supplies have exceeded, or are likely to exceed the annual limit. If this registration is not carried out within the 30 day time limit the person can be fined – the reason being that the supplier will be failing to collect tax due to HM Customs & Excise.

Suppliers of zero-rated goods and services are included in these regulations, although they *may* apply for exemption from registration. It is unlikely that they will do so, however, because then they will lose the right to reclaim any VAT on goods and services they have purchased, and will be out of pocket!

It is critical that a person should register for VAT if the supplies are chargeable. There have been cases of profitable businesses which have not registered and have been 'discovered' by HM Customs and Excise after a period of years: they have had to pay *from their own resources* all the VAT they should have charged and have been bankrupted in the process.

a business or not a business?

A business is defined by the VAT authorities as an activity which involves selling goods or a service for money over a period of time. Note that:

- it is only a *business* activity which can be VAT-registered – hobbies cannot normally be registered and business owners are *not* able to reclaim VAT on private expenses

- it is the person running the business who applies for registration – this term 'person' is fairly wide ranging and includes:

  - sole proprietors

  - partnerships

  - limited companies or groups of companies

  - clubs and associations

  - charities

non-registered businesses

Businesses that have a turnover below the annual limit do not have to register for VAT. This can be useful for a business owner, for example, because he or she can in effect become more competitive and charge less for goods and services, although there is the downside that the trader cannot reclaim VAT paid on supplies he or she has bought. This is *not* the same as the practice adopted by some 'shady' VAT-registered businesses saying to their customers "If you pay me cash in hand you won't have to pay the VAT". This is illegal and an attempt to defraud HM Customs & Excise of VAT due.

voluntary registration

A supplier whose taxable turnover falls below the annual limit may register for VAT. This is normally because he or she will benefit from claiming back input tax on purchases, eg if the business deals in zero-rated goods.

deregistration

If a business finds that annual turnover falls – or is likely to fall – below a certain limit (normally slightly less than the registration limit) that business can apply to HM Customs & Excise and *deregister,* if it seems advantageous to do so.

practicalities of registration

• When a person has been registered for VAT a registration certificate will be issued giving full details of registration, including the *VAT number* which must be quoted on all VAT invoices.

• VAT paid by the person on expenses in setting up the business may normally be reclaimed.

• VAT must be charged on sales as soon as registration takes place.

OUTPUT TAX AND INPUT TAX - FURTHER POINTS

output tax value

The *tax value* of a supply is the value on which the VAT percentage rate is calculated. This seems a fairly obvious point, but there are situations where this value is not clear.

• *cash discounts* – as you may have seen in your previous studies, if a supplier offers a percentage discount for prompt payment (eg within 7 days), the VAT will be calculated on the *discounted* amount, even if the purchaser does take up the offer and takes 30 days or more to pay

- *foreign currency values* – importers of goods and services into the UK invoiced in a foreign currency must always work out the VAT on the *sterling equivalent* of the foreign currency converted using a consistent method (the rates used can be the newspaper rates or the rates published by HM Customs & Excise)

input tax exceptions

A VAT-registered business will obviously try to claim back input tax on as many expenses as it legitimately can. There are however a number of items on which VAT *cannot* be reclaimed. These include:

- purchase of a car for a business
- business entertainment expenses
- goods and services purchased, but *not* used in the business

It is quite common for a business owner to have the benefit of goods and services which are used *partly* for the business and *partly* for personal domestic use, eg home telephone, heating and lighting in a home office. In these instances, the business owner can *apportion* the tax, ie split the input VAT between business and private use and claim back only the input tax relating to business use.

TAX POINTS

The *tax point* of a taxable supply is the date on which it is recorded as taking place for the purposes of the tax return.

For *goods* the *basic tax point* is normally when the goods are sent to the customer or taken away by the customer. For *services* the basic tax point is normally when the service is performed.

It is usual practice for the tax point to be *fixed:*

- if a VAT invoice (see page 269) is issued or payment is received *before* the basic tax point (the supply of the goods or service) then the date of the invoice or payment – whichever happens first – becomes the *actual tax point*
- if a VAT invoice is issued *up to 14 days* after the basic tax point (date of supply) the date of issue of the invoice becomes the tax point

The 14 day rule may be varied – with the written approval of the local VAT Office. For example, a supplier may issue monthly invoices on a regular basis for goods or services supplied during the whole of the month. The date of the invoice or the last day of the month – consistently applied – can then become the *actual tax point*.

The principle of the tax point is important to the VAT-registered business:

• it results in a consistent and accurate method of recording VAT transactions

• it can help cash flow in a business – an early tax point helps a business purchasing goods because the input tax can be reclaimed earlier; for example if a VAT-registered business bought a computer in the last week of the VAT quarter and the computer was invoiced *in that week*, the input tax claimed back could be included in that quarter rather than in the next

VAT INVOICES

When a VAT-registered supplier sells standard-rated goods or services to another VAT-registered person, the supplier must give or send to the purchaser within 30 days of the supply a VAT invoice (see opposite page) which contains information about the goods or services supplied. A copy should be kept on file by the supplier. The information includes:

• an invoice number

• the name, address and VAT number of the supplier

• the date of supply and date of issue (if different)

• the purchaser's name and address

• the nature of the supply – eg a sale, sale or return, hire

• a description of the goods or services

For each item the following details are needed (these are usually found on the bottom half of the invoice):

• the quantity of goods (eg 4 items) or the extent of the service (eg 2 hours)

• the charge made before any VAT is added

• the rate(s) of VAT charged and the amount of VAT charged at each rate (shown in £ sterling)

• the total charge made, excluding VAT

• the total charge made, including VAT

• the rate of cash discount offered – an increasingly rare feature nowadays

• the total amount of VAT charged

Study the invoices shown on the next two pages and see how they differ.

SALES INVOICE

Trend Designs
Unit 40 Elgar Estate, Broadfield, BR7 4ER
Tel 01908 765365 Fax 01908 7659507 Email lisa@trend.u-net.com
VAT Reg GB 0745 4172 20

invoice to

Crispins Fashion Store
34 The Arcade
Broadfield
BR1 4GH

invoice no	787906
account	3993
your reference	1956
date/tax point	21 04 98

deliver to

as above

details	quantity	price	amount (excl VAT)	VAT rate %	VAT amount £
Schwarz 'T' shirts (black)	20	5.50	110.00	17.5	19.25
Snugtight leggings (black)	15	12.50	187.50	17.5	32.81

terms
Net monthly
Carriage paid
E & OE

Total (excl VAT)	297.50
VAT	52.06
TOTAL	349.56

This invoice has been issued by a supplier of fashion clothes, Trend Designs, to Crispins Fashion Store on 21 April (the tax point). Note that all the requirements of a VAT invoice are met: both items sold are charged at the standard rate of tax; the VAT rates and amounts are indicated for each item and the totals shown at the bottom of the invoice. The VAT total of £52.06 will recorded as output tax for Trend Designs and as input tax for Crispins Fashion Store. There is no cash discount offered and the buyer has to settle the full £349.56 a month after the invoice date, at the end of May.

───── SALES INVOICE ─────

Paragon Printers

Partners: Edwin Parry, George Dragon
Unit 43 Elgar Estate, Broadfield, BR7 4ER
Tel 01908 765312 Fax 01908 7659551 Email Ed@paragon.u-net.com VAT Reg GB 0745 4672 71

invoice to

Prime Publicity Ltd 4 Friar Street Broadfield BR1 3RG	

invoice no	787923
account	3993
your reference	47609
date/tax point	07 05 98

deliver to

as above

details	price	amount (excl VAT)	VAT rate %	VAT amount £
Printing 2,000 A4 leaflets	189.00	189.00	zero	00.00
Supplying 2,000 C4 envelopes	75.00	75.00	17.5	13.12

terms
Net monthly
Carriage paid
E & OE

Total (excl VAT)	264.00
VAT	13.12
TOTAL	277.12

This invoice has been issued by a commercial printer, Paragon Printers, to Prime Publicity Limited on 7 May (the tax point) for goods delivered. Note that in this case there are two rates of VAT involved: printing is zero-rated and stationery is standard rated. The VAT rates and amounts are indicated for both items and the totals shown at the bottom of the invoice. The VAT total of £13.12 will be recorded as output tax for Paragon Printers and as input tax for Prime Publicity Ltd. There is no cash discount offered and the buyer has to settle the full £277.12 a month after the invoice date, at the beginning of June.

calculations on VAT invoices

VAT is calculated as a percentage of the cost of the goods. If invoiced goods cost £100, the VAT (at the standard rate of 17.5%) is calculated as:

$$\frac{£100 \times 17.5}{100} \quad = \quad £17.50$$

If the amount of VAT calculated comes out at more than 2 decimal places, you should round *down* to the nearest penny. On the invoice opposite:

$$\frac{£75 \times 17.5}{100} \quad = \quad £13.125 \text{ (rounded down to £13.12)}$$

Guidance relating to rounding may be found in the 'VAT Invoices' section of the 'VAT Guide'. For example, there are rules relating to complex rounding methods when calculating VAT on individual items or 'lines' on a VAT invoice.

The important factor is that any rounding is *consistently applied*. The method of rounding down shown here is simple, and tried and tested.

zero-rated and exempt supplies

If you supply goods which are zero-rated or exempt, the invoices must clearly show this fact and also that no VAT amount is payable. The invoice on the opposite page is an example of the use of mixed rates. Some suppliers use separate invoices for zero-rated and exempt supplies.

situations where VAT invoices are not needed

There are a number of situations where VAT invoices are not needed:

- where the purchaser is not registered for VAT
- if the purchaser is on a *self-billing* system (ie the *purchaser* issues the invoice and sends it with the payment)

The first point mentioned above is sometimes ignored: businesses cannot realistically be expected to enquire if every buyer is VAT-registered, so they will issue a VAT invoice for all routine sales.

There are also situations where invoices may just show the VAT-inclusive amount. These are

- where the transaction total is less than £100
- where the buyer agrees to a modified format – any amount

less detailed invoices – amounts under £100

If the amount charged for the supply is £100 or less (including VAT) a less detailed invoice may be issued. This type of invoice must show:

- the name, address and VAT number of the supplier
- the date of supply
- a description of the goods or services
- each VAT rate used
- the total for each rate payable, *including* VAT

To work out the VAT element in a VAT inclusive price the buyer should use the *VAT fraction*.

If you are given a figure which includes VAT and you need to work out the VAT amount you multiply the amount by the VAT fraction – which for 17.5% is $7/47$. For a total of £117.50 the calculation is:

$$\frac{£117.50 \times 7}{47} = £17.50 \text{ VAT included in the } £117.50$$

This is particularly useful if you receive a less detailed invoice or a receipt, eg for petrol, which includes VAT but does not state the amount.

modified invoices – any amount

If a buyer agrees to the arrangement, a business supplying standard-rated goods or services may issue a modified invoice showing only the VAT-inclusive amount (the charge for the supply plus the VAT amount) *for each item sold*. This type of invoice must, however, show separately – at the bottom of the document:

- the VAT-inclusive total of the supplies – ie the overall total
- the total amount of VAT charged (included in the overall total)
- the total value of the supplies before VAT is added on
- the total value of any zero-rated and exempt supplies on the invoice

This type of invoice will be useful for a supplier that includes a large number of items on each invoice, eg a wholesaler supplying a shop.

other types of invoice – pro-forma invoice

The 'VAT Guide' explains a number of different type of invoice which you would only find in specialised business situations, eg large purchases (over £100) of petrol or diesel, and cash-and-carry wholesalers. If you encounter these you should refer to the 'VAT Guide'.

A further type of invoice, which is more common, is the *pro-forma invoice*. This is a document issued by a seller offering goods at a certain price and inviting the buyer to send a payment in return for which the goods will then be supplied. This is a common arrangement when a seller receives an order from a new customer, but does not want to sell on credit – because there may well be a credit risk – and so needs payment up front.

A proforma invoice (see illustration below) may well look exactly like an invoice, but because it does not relate to a firm sale, *cannot be used as evidence to reclaim input tax.* Pro-forma invoices should be clearly marked 'THIS IS NOT A VAT INVOICE'. Should a sale result from a pro-forma invoice a separate invoice (the VAT invoice) should then be issued.

PRO-FORMA INVOICE

SPICER STATIONERY
45 High Street
Mereford MR1 3TR
Tel 010903 443851
VAT Reg 422 8371 78

R U Dodgy Limited
56 Prison Walk
Mereford MR5 8UH

13 May 1999

Your ref Purchase Order 2934234

45 x A4 Box files (burgundy) @ £4.99 each	£224.55
VAT @ 17.5%	£39.29
TOTAL PAYABLE	£263.84

This is not a VAT invoice.
A VAT invoice will be issued on receipt of the amount in full.

VAT ERRORS ON INVOICES

With the increasing use of computer accounting systems (which automatically calculate the VAT) errors on invoices should become less common. If a VAT invoice is issued by hand, mistakes can occur:

- the wrong rate of VAT could be used
- the calculation of the VAT amount could be wrong

Whatever happens, the invoice should never be altered and sent out to the customer in its amended state. Instead a debit note or credit note should be issued, showing full details of the error and a numerical reference to the faulty invoice.

If the amount of VAT calculated is too high . . .

Issue an adjusting credit note to the customer, or accept an adjusting debit note from the customer. If this is not done, the higher amount must go through the VAT records of the business and be accounted for accordingly.

If the amount of VAT calculated is too low . . .

Issue an adjusting invoice to the customer, billing him/her for the underpaid VAT. If this is not done the supplier must still account for the higher and correct amount to HM Customs & Excise, ie stand the loss. This could be the case if the supplier is too embarrassed to admit the mistake to the customer!

IMPORTS AND EXPORTS

So far we have dealt with VAT as it affects business dealings within the UK. VAT must also be accounted for in dealings with overseas states, both within the EU (European Union, formerly European Community) and also outside the EU (formerly EC).

The basic principle, which applies to exports and imports, is that VAT is a tax on imported goods and some services – it is paid where appropriate by the importer and is treated as an input tax.

VAT and countries outside the EU

- when goods are *imported* into the UK from countries outside the EU, VAT is normally due at the same rate that would apply to a supply of those goods within the UK – it is treated in the same way as input tax

- when goods are *exported* from the UK to countries outside the EU, the goods are normally zero-rated, as long as documentary evidence of export is obtained and retained by the supplier within 3 months of the date of supply

VAT and the Single Market (the EU)

The Single Market is the phrase used to describe trading within the states that make up the European Union (EU). Since the beginning of 1993 the EU has become an area in which movements of goods are no longer called 'imports' and 'exports' but 'acquisitions'. VAT is no longer collected at the frontiers but from the *buyer:*

- *if the buyer is VAT registered* – the goods are zero-rated on despatch and VAT is collected from the buyer at the rate which applies in the buyer's country and accounted for on the buyer's VAT Return as input tax

- *if the buyer is not VAT registered* – the goods will normally be charged by the supplier at the VAT rate which applies in the country of the supplier

the conditions for zero-rating of EU supplies

In the first case above – the supply of goods from one EU state to another between two VAT registered businesses or individuals – the goods can only be zero-rated by a UK supplier if certain conditions are met:

- the buyer's valid VAT registration number must be obtained by the supplier and quoted on the VAT invoice – the number must include the two letter country prefix (eg DE for Germany, GB for Great Britain)

- the goods are sent to a destination in another EU state

- the supplier holds documentary evidence that the goods have been sent (the evidence must be obtained within 3 months of despatch)

tax points for goods supplied to the EU

The tax point for goods despatched by a UK supplier to another EU state is the earlier of:

- the date on the invoice covering the goods

- the 15th of the month following the month of supply

tax treatment for goods sent to UK buyers

When a UK buyer receives goods from another EU state:

- the tax point follows the same rules as above (ie the date of the invoice received or the 15th of the month following supply)

- VAT is payable at the rate applicable to those goods within the UK (eg books will be zero-rated, adult clothes will be standard rated) – the amount will be entered on the VAT Return (see next chapter)

free zones and warehousing

Mention must be made of warehousing and free zones. These are storage facilities for goods, normally at or near ports and airports; they can be used for storage of goods received from overseas.

No VAT is due on these goods until the goods are released from storage to the UK buyer. Goods received from EU states, as mentioned above, are not *imports* but *acquisitions* and are not subject to the import requirements imposed on non-EU goods.

Single Market documentation – sales lists

UK VAT-registered traders who supply other EU states with goods are required to send lists of their EU supplies to HM Customs & Excise, normally on a quarterly basis. The standard form VAT 101 is shown below. Traders with low volumes of EU sales may be exempted from completing these forms.

Form VAT 101 – Sales List

Single Market statistics – Intrastat

Intrastat has replaced customs declarations as a means of supplying statistics on EU trade. It applies only to goods and not to services. The figures are gathered from suppliers' figures entered in boxes on VAT Returns (see the next chapter). Suppliers whose EU trade in goods exceeds a certain threshold (£233,000 from 1 April 2001) have to provide further information in returns known as *Supplementary Declarations* (see below).

Instrastat – Supplementary Declaration Form

- Value Added Tax (VAT) is a sales tax on most goods and services imposed by governments in a number of different countries to raise revenue.

- VAT is regulated in the UK by the Value Added Tax Act (1994) and other regulations, in the EU generally it is governed by Directives.

- VAT is administered and collected in the UK by HM Customs & Excise.

- VAT is paid by the final consumer but is collected and paid to HM Customs & Excise by the businesses involved in the selling and manufacturing processes.

- VAT is charged at different rates: standard, reduced (domestic fuel) and zero. These (except for zero rate) may be changed from time-to-time.

- A person must register for VAT if annual sales liable to VAT exceed (or are likely to exceed within 30 days) an annual threshold.

- A VAT-registered person must pay to HM Customs & Excise the VAT charged on sales (output tax) less tax on purchases (input tax). If input tax exceeds output tax a refund is due. The payment or refund is calculated on the regular VAT return (VAT 100).

- The recording of the date of the sales and purchases is important in this calculation – the date of payment is the tax point.

- A VAT-registered supplier must in most circumstances issue a VAT invoice to the buyer. The VAT invoice must contain defined items of information relating to the transaction.

- VAT is also a tax on the import or acquisition of goods and services from overseas states.

- Exports to EU and non-EU countries are normally zero-rated.

- Acquisitions and imports are normally subject to VAT at the rate applicable in the country to which the goods are sent.

- VAT registered businesses sending significant quantities of goods within the EU record the sales statistics on sales lists and Intrastat returns.

Value Added Tax	a tax on the sale of goods and services
VAT Guide	the book published by HM Customs & Excise which explains the workings of VAT
supplier	a person who sells goods and services
taxable person	a supplier who has been registered for VAT; a person can be a sole trader, a partnership, a limited company, a group of companies, a club or association, a charity

output tax	VAT on sales of goods and services
input tax	VAT on purchases of goods and services
VAT 100	the HM Customs & Excise VAT Return, which calculates VAT to be paid or refunded by off setting input tax and output tax
standard rate	the basic percentage rate at which VAT is calculated – currently 17.5% in the UK
reduced rate	a reduced rate allowed for domestic fuel – currently 5% in the UK
zero-rated goods	supplies which are liable to VAT, but at zero %
exempt goods	supplies which are not liable to VAT
basic tax point	the date on which the supply is made
actual tax point	the date on which the supply is recorded for the purposes of the VAT Return – normally the date of the invoice
VAT invoice	an invoice recording the taxable supply (the sale) containing specific required details; for lower value transactions (under £100) the invoice may be less detailed
pro-forma invoice	a document issued by a supplier, inviting a buyer to pay for goods before they are supplied – this document is not a VAT invoice
VAT fraction	the fraction used to work out the VAT content of an amount which contains VAT: the procedure is to multiply the amount by the fraction. For the 17.5% rate the fraction is $^7/_{47}$.
Single Market	trading within the states of the European Union (EU)
acquisitions	imports within the Single Market
free zone	a defined area within a country into which goods can be imported and stored, VAT only being due when the goods are taken out of that area
sales lists	lists of sales made by UK VAT-registered suppliers of goods to other EU states, sent on a regular basis to HM Customs & Excise
Intrastat	periodic figures relating to supplies to other EU states supplied by completing boxes on the VAT Return, or in the case of larger traders on Supplementary Declaration forms

The answers to these Student Activities are printed in the back of this book. Further questions and more fully extended Student Activities and Assessments are to be found in the accompanying Osborne Books' text *Costing, Reports & Returns Workbook*.

STUDENT ACTIVITIES

14.1 What does VAT tax?

14.2 State three sources of VAT regulation in the UK.

14.3 Define a 'taxable person'.

14.4 What is the difference between input tax and output tax?

14.5 In what circumstances may a supplier reclaim VAT from HM Customs & Excise?

14.6 Why does the final consumer pay all the VAT on chargeable goods and services, but pay nothing personally to HM Customs & Excise?

14.7 What are the three rates of VAT currently charged in the UK?

14.8 Explain the difference between the terms 'zero-rated' and 'VAT-exempt'. Give three examples of each.

14.9 State two circumstances in which a person must register for VAT.

14.10 Which of the following are likely to be registered for VAT?

    (a)   a sole proprietor with an annual sales turnover of £35,000

    (b)   a partnership with an annual turnover of £150,000

    (c)   a public limited company with a sales turnover of £1.5 million

    (d)   a local sports club with an annual bar turnover of £95,000

    (e)   a national charity which raises money for cancer research and has an annual income from commercial fundraising activities of £1.2 million

14.11 A VAT invoice offers 2.5% cash discount for early settlement. If the total invoice amount before VAT is £100, the VAT charged (at 17.5%) should be:

    (a)   £17.06

    (b)   £17.07

    (c)   £17.50

    (d)   £17.05

14.12 On which of the following purchases (all paid through the business bank account of a VAT-registered company) can VAT be reclaimed?

(a)   a new computer for use in the business

(b)   a new company car for the managing director

(c)   business entertainment expenses

(d)   the managing director's home telephone bill – the home telephone is often used for business calls in the evenings and at weekends

14.13 The invoice below has been issued as a VAT invoice. What is wrong with it?

SALES INVOICE

Trend Designs
Unit 40 Elgar Estate, Broadfield, BR7 4ER
Tel 01908 765365 Fax 01908 7659507 Email lisa@trend.u-net.com

invoice to

Persephone Fashion
45 The Broads
Broadfield
BR1 8UH

details	quantity	price	amount (excl VAT)	VAT rate %	VAT amount £
Bianca 'T' shirts	42	4.99	209.58	17.5	36.68

terms
Net monthly
Carriage paid
E & OE

Total (excl VAT)	209.58
VAT	36.68
TOTAL	273.26

14.14 When is the tax point in the following circumstances?

(a) a tax invoice is issued before the delivery of the goods sold; payment is made 30 days later

(b) a pro-forma invoice is issued and payment is made before the delivery of the goods and issue of the VAT invoice

(c) a VAT invoice is issued and dated 7 days after the date of the supply of goods

(d) a supplier issues regular monthly invoices to cover supplies made during the month; the invoices are dated the last day of the month

14.15 Your business receives five invoices from a VAT registered trader. The amounts are:

£87.50, £41.12, £47.00, £55.75, £99.05

Your colleague notes that

• none of the invoices has the VAT amount listed separately – there is just a total on each which includes the amount for the goods and VAT combined (ie the figures quoted above)

• the invoices have all the other details you would expect to see on a VAT invoice

You are to:

(a) state whether the invoices are valid VAT invoices

(b) calculate the VAT on each invoice so that you can enter up the purchases day book

14.16 A trader running a plant nursery business has just registered for VAT. He supplies garden centres with bedding plants, shrubs and small trees. Often his invoices to the garden centre purchasing departments are long - running to over thirty items and totalling thousands of pounds. He asks if he has to show the VAT on every single invoice line, as his computer stationery is set up for showing just the overall VAT total for each rate of VAT charged at the bottom of the invoice. What would be your advice?

14.17 You work as Accounts Supervisor at ABC Wholesalers, Unit 3 Severn Estate, Mereford MR4 7AS. Your invoicing clerk had rather a bad day recently and exactly seven days ago two invoices went out to customers showing incorrect VAT amounts – the wrong rates had been used in the calculations. The rate that should have been used was 17.5% standard rate. The details are:

(1) Invoice 4562 issued to Bradley Supplies, 41 Stroud Road, Bagley MR3 6YH, for £250 net shows VAT of £46.25. The contact there is Miss Sharon Pitts, Purchasing Manager.

(2) Invoice 4566 issued to J Simpson, 56 Cathedral View, Mereford MR1 2JF, for £400 net shows VAT of £60. The contact there is Ms Janice Simpson.

You are to:

(a) work out the correct amounts (VAT and invoice totals) and the differences for each invoice

(b) state what ABC Wholesalers should do with the errors to comply with VAT regulations

(c) draft appropriate letters to the customers, using your own name and the current date; if you decide not to send a letter to a customer you should write a memo to the Accounts Manager (John Penny) explaining your reasons

14.18 Fabricius Furniture of Farnham, UK, plans to sell its range of luxury hand-made furniture to a VAT-registered dealer in Leipzig, Germany. The UK Sales Manager has a number of questions:

(a)   What happens to the payment of VAT on the goods? Furniture is standard-rated in the UK.

(b)   What conditions (relating to VAT) have to be complied with by the supplier on the supply of the goods?

(c)   When is the tax point for the supply of the goods?

(d)   Would it make any difference if the dealer in Leipzig was not VAT registered?

14.19 Biblios Books is a VAT-registered specialist bookshop which imports books from Spanish-speaking Ruritania. Books in the UK are zero-rated, but in Ruritania they attract a VAT rate of 10%.

(a)   Will VAT be payable on the books imported into the UK from Ruritania?

(b)   Will VAT be payable on the books sold in the UK?

14.20 (a)   What form has to be completed by a business that supplies goods within the EU and needs to provide Sales Lists?

(b)   What figures and returns have to be made by a VAT-registered business in respect of Instrastat?

15 VAT RECORDS AND THE VAT RETURN

this chapter covers . . .

In this chapter we explain:

* the records a VAT-registered business needs to keep to satisfy the requirements of HM Customs & Excise

* the treatment of VAT in manual accounts and computer accounts

* the way the figures are collected from the accounting records to supply information for the VAT Return

* the need for a VAT control account

* the completion of the VAT Return Form VAT 100

* how to deal with errors in the VAT records and how to avoid default situations

* the implications of special schemes – annual accounting, cash accounting, bad debt relief, retail schemes

* dealings with the local VAT office

Note: you will still often see references to 'EC' (European Community) in publications; in this chapter we will use the more recent term 'EU' (European Union).

NVQ PERFORMANCE CRITERIA COVERED

unit 6: PREPARING REPORTS AND RETURNS

element 3

prepare VAT returns

❏ VAT returns are correctly completed using data from the appropriate sources and are submitted within the statutory time limits

❏ relevant inputs and outputs are correctly identified and calculated

❏ submissions are made in accordance with current legislation

❏ guidance is sought from the VAT office when required, in a professional manner

KEEPING VAT RECORDS

VAT and the accounting system

The accounting system of a VAT-registered business should record:

- input tax on purchases and expenses
- output tax on sales

It must be appreciated that accounting systems vary substantially from business to business, but the basic *principles* will remain the same: data has to be collected periodically (normally quarterly) so that input tax can be set off against output tax for the completion of the VAT Return.

VAT records

It is important to have a working knowledge of the records that have to be maintained by a VAT-registered business. They are set out in the 'Records and accounts' section of the 'VAT Guide' and also in the shorter 'VAT: Keeping records and accounts' published by HM Customs & Excise. The basic records that relate specifically to VAT include:

- *copies of sales invoices* (ideally in numerical/date order) – these are the tax invoices which set out the output tax charged (if it is charged)
- *originals of purchase invoices* (ideally given a consecutive reference number) – these are the tax invoices which set out the input tax which the business can reclaim
- *credit notes* and *debit notes* relating to adjustments made to tax invoices
- documentation relating to *imports and exports* – eg proof of despatch
- a *VAT control account* – which records or summarises all items of input and output tax and acts as the source of data for the VAT Return

It should be noted that proposals have now been made for a 'flat rate' scheme which will allow businesses with an annual turnover of less than £100,000 to base their VAT liability solely on taxable turnover, thus avoiding the need to record VAT in so much detail. Check www.HMCE.gov.uk for developments.

other business records

VAT-registered businesses may be visited by VAT officers from time-to-time for *VAT inspections* to ensure that the records are being correctly maintained and administered. Businesses may also be investigated by the Inland Revenue, by the Department of Social Security, and, depending on the level of sales turnover, they may require an audit of their accounts. Accurate business record keeping is therefore critically important if the owner wants to avoid accountants' fees for the reconstruction of incomplete records. The business records that should be kept – in addition to those listed above – include:

- bank statements, paying-in slips and cheque book stubs
- purchase orders and delivery notes
- cash books and petty cash books
- purchases and sales day books
- ledger accounts
- payroll records
- computer printouts and reports
- annual accounts

We will now look in more detail at the records needed for sales (output tax) and purchases and expenses (input tax). For the purposes of your studies we will initially look at a business that buys and sells on credit and maintains a manual accounting system. You should always bear in mind that there are other businesses that trade on cash terms (immediate payment) and which have computer accounting programs which automate many of the processes that we will be describing. We will cover these later in the chapter.

records for output tax (sales)

Records for output tax include:

sales day book

This lists all sales made on credit and has an analysis column for VAT which is totalled periodically.

credit notes issued and debit notes received

Any credit given (eg for returned goods, adjustments for overcharges) may involve VAT and deduction should be made from output tax. Sometimes a separate sales returns day book, with a VAT analysis column, will be kept by the business.

cash book

This includes a VAT analysis column and records details of other receipts *not on credit* which involve output tax, eg cash sales. Receipts for credit sales should be ignored.

records for input tax (purchases and expenses)

Records for input tax include:

purchases day book

This lists all purchases made on credit and has an analysis column for VAT which is totalled periodically.

credit notes received and debit notes issued

Any credit received (eg for returned goods, adjustments for overcharges) may involve VAT and deduction should be made from input tax. Sometimes a separate purchases returns day book, with a VAT analysis column, will be kept by the business.

cash book

This lists all the expenses paid by the business; VAT *for non-credit items* should be taken from the cash book analysis column. VAT on payments for credit purchases should be ignored. A petty cash book with a VAT column may also be used to list small expenses and will need to be accounted for.

VAT control account

The central record for any VAT-registered business book-keeping system is the VAT control account into which all input and output tax is entered. The balance of VAT control account represents the amount owing to (or due from) HM Customs & Excise. The diagram below is based on the layout recommended by HM Customs & Excise in the 'VAT Guide'. It shows entries for a supplier who normally has a surplus of output tax over input tax, ie the supplier pays VAT every quarter to HM Customs & Excise.

VAT control account – summary of entries

VAT deductible (input tax)	VAT payable (output tax)
Purchases Day Book VAT monthly totals, *less* any credit notes received/debit notes issued	Sales Day Book VAT monthly totals, *less* any credit notes issued/debit notes received
Cash Book – items not in Purchases Day Book	Cash Book – items not in Sales Day Book
Petty Cash Book – VAT on small expenses	
Acquisitions from EU states	Acquisitions from EU states
Corrections of errors from previous periods (not exceeding £2,000 net)	Corrections of errors from previous periods (not exceeding £2,000 net)
Adjustments from special schemes*	Adjustments from special schemes*
= TOTAL TAX DEDUCTIBLE	= TOTAL TAX PAYABLE
	less TOTAL TAX DEDUCTIBLE
	equals TAX PAYABLE ON VAT RETURN

* special schemes are discussed on pages 297 to 299.

You should note that the control account shown is not a double-entry account in the strict sense, for example, items such as credit notes are deducted on each side rather than being entered on the opposite side. In practice the VAT control account will be maintained in whatever way the accounting system – manual or computerised – requires. The important point is that the entries used for the VAT Return are *all accounted for in a consistent way*.

treatment of VAT paid and reclaimed

One omission from the diagram on the previous page is the VAT actually paid or reclaimed *for the previous VAT period*. Most businesses which sell standard-rated supplies will pay the VAT surplus to HM Customs & Excise; other businesses – eg bookshops – which sell zero-rated supplies, will end up paying more VAT on inputs than they charge on outputs, and so will *reclaim* VAT from HM Customs & Excise each VAT period.

The reason the entries are not shown in the control account is that they cancel each other out and so have *no effect on the VAT due or owing* at the end of the period.

At the beginning of each VAT period the VAT Control account will have an opening balance, *either*

• VAT due to be paid to Customs & Excise – shown on the right-hand side of the account as a credit balance brought forward (this is the figure at the bottom of the diagram on the previous page), *or*

• VAT reclaimable from Customs & Excise – shown on the left-hand side as a debit balance brought forward

When the VAT payment is made by the supplier (or received, if VAT is reclaimable) during the VAT period, the opening balance will be cancelled out. The net effect of the two entries on the account balance will be nil. The examples below show how VAT paid and reclaimed is treated:

VAT CONTROL ACCOUNT (extract) – VAT payable by supplier

VAT deductible (input tax)	£	VAT payable (output tax)	£
Bank (VAT paid by supplier)	12,400	Balance brought forward (previous period's VAT due to be paid by supplier)	12,400

VAT CONTROL ACCOUNT (extract) – VAT recaimable by supplier

VAT deductible (input tax)	£	VAT payable (output tax)	£
Balance brought forward (previous period's VAT reclaimable by supplier)	10,000	Bank (VAT received by supplier from Customs & Excise)	10,000

computer accounts – VAT Control Account

The VAT control account shown on page 287 assumes that all the VAT data is transferred manually from the accounting records. If a business operates a computer accounting program, normally *every transaction* that involves VAT will automatically post the VAT element to VAT control account, eg sales, purchases, journal entries, payment or repayment of VAT.

The reports available will vary according to the sophistication of the program. Up-to-date programs will do all the work for the supplier, including the production of a screen and a printout at the end of the VAT period with figures needed for the VAT Return. The business which relies on this system must make sure that the VAT data is correct before VAT Return is processed. A computer VAT Return screen is shown below.

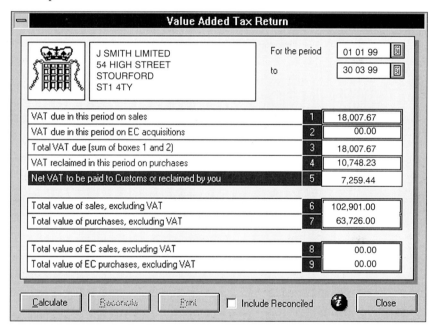

Less sophisticated programs may merely produce summaries of sales and purchases day books and cash books, and a transaction history of VAT Account over the VAT period. If this account history of VAT Account is used for extracting the data for the VAT Return, care must be taken to adjust for payment or repayment of VAT relating to the previous period during the VAT quarter (see the previous page) as this will automatically post to VAT account, but is clearly is not classed as a taxable output or input (you cannot tax tax!). If this is the case,

- payment of VAT to HM Customs & Excise must be deducted from the input tax total

- repayment of VAT received from H M Customs & Excise must be deducted from the output tax total

THE VAT RETURN – FORM VAT 100

When the VAT figures have been transferred to the VAT control account and the amount of VAT due or reclaimable has been calculated, the VAT Return can then be completed. The form is illustrated on the next page, and a Case Study follows. The boxes are completed as follows:

1 The total VAT due on sales and other outputs. This total should be adjusted for any credit notes issued and any underdeclarations (£2,000 net or less) on previous returns.

2 VAT due on acquisitions from other EU states.

3 The total of boxes 1 and 2.

4 The total VAT reclaimed on purchases and other inputs (less any credit notes). This total includes tax on acquisition of goods from other EU states and overdeclarations (£2,000 net or less) on previous returns.

5 Take the figures in boxes 3 and 4, deduct the smaller from the larger and enter the difference in box 5. If the figure in box 3 is more than the figure in box 4, this is the amount payable to HM Customs & Excise. If the figure in box 3 is smaller than the figure in box 4, the amount in box 5 will be repaid to the supplier completing the form.

6 The total of sales and outputs *excluding* any VAT. This will include exempt, standard and zero-rated supplies and supplies to EU member states. Remember to adjust the total for any credit notes/debit notes.

7 The total of purchases (inputs) excluding any VAT. This includes standard, zero and exempt supplies, imports and acquisitions from EU states. Remember to adjust the total for any credit notes/debit notes.

8 The total of supplies of goods and related services, excluding VAT, to EU states (note that 'related services' refers to items such as freight and insurance charges for the goods).

9 The total of acquisition of goods and related services, excluding VAT, from EU states (as above, 'related services' refers to items such as freight and insurance charges for the goods).

notes on completion of VAT 100

- if a VAT payment is being enclosed, the relevant box should be ticked
- the form should be signed by an authorised person
- the form should be returned by the due date shown on the form in the envelope provided (normally one month after the end of the VAT period)
- do not leave any boxes blank – enter 'none' if there is no figure to insert

- always have the arithmetic and figures checked
- mistakes should be crossed through and correct figures inserted; the amendments should be initialled
- for retail schemes, please see page 299

A very useful reference source is the HM Customs & Excise booklet 'Filling in your VAT Return' available from local VAT offices.

		£	p
VAT due in this period on **sales** and other outputs	**1**	31,353	61
VAT due in this period on **acquisitions** from other **EC Member States**	**2**	183	05
Total VAT due (**the sum of boxes 1 and 2**)	**3**	31,536	66
VAT reclaimed in this period on **purchases** and other inputs (including acquisitions from the EC)	**4**	14,826	92
Net VAT to be paid to Customs or reclaimed by you (**Difference between boxes 3 and 4**)	**5**	16,709	74
Total value of **sales** and all other outputs excluding any VAT. **Include your box 8 figure**	**6**	179,163	00
Total value of **purchases** and all other inputs excluding any VAT. **Include your box 9 figure**	**7**	84,725	00
Total value of all **supplies** of goods and related services, excluding any VAT, to other **EC Member States**	**8**	none	00
Total value of all **acquisitions** of goods and related services, excluding any VAT, from other **EC Member States**	**9**	1,046	00

a completed VAT Return Form VAT100

CASE STUDY

FANCY THAT LTD – COMPLETING THE VAT RETURN

situation

Fancy That Limited is a wholesaler of fancy goods – gifts and cards – which are supplied on credit terms to shops in the UK, although a small proportion is sold for cash. Most of the goods are sourced in the UK, but some are imported from Italy and Spain. Fancy That Limited is VAT-registered and its VAT quarters run from January to March, April to June, July to September and October to December. Most of the goods sold are standard-rated, but a few stock lines – mainly books – are zero-rated.

It is now the first week in April. The data for the January-March VAT Return have been compiled. You have been asked to complete the VAT Control Account and prepare the VAT 100 ready for checking and signature by Dan Brookshaw, Finance Director.

The VAT 100 is due back to HM Customs & Excise by 30 April, but the company's practice is to submit it by the middle of the month.

The data is taken from the manual accounting system and summarised as follows:

SALES DAY BOOK SUMMARY

	Zero-rated sales £	Standard-rated sales £	VAT £	Total sales (standard-rated) £
January	2,930.50	15,170.15	2,654.77	17,824.92
February	1,923.81	21,689.03	3,795.58	25,484.61
March	2,706.61	22,729.50	3,977.66	26,707.16
TOTAL	7,560.92	59,588.68	10,428.01	70,016.69

PURCHASES DAY BOOK SUMMARY

	Zero-rated purchases £	Standard-rated purchases £	VAT £	Total purchases (standard-rated) £
January	00.00	8,791.60	1,538.53	10,330.13
February	00.00	12,326.50	2,157.13	14,483.63
March	00.00	9,731.95	1,703.09	11,435.04
TOTAL	00.00	30,850.05	5,398.75	36,248.80

CASH BOOKS – NON CREDIT ITEMS

	NET £	VAT £	GROSS £
from main cash book			
Cash sales (Jan-Mar)	4,926.80	862.19	5,788.99
Cash purchases (Jan-Mar)	3,500.00	612.50	4,112.50
from petty cash book			
Expenses (Jan-Mar)	456.90	79.95	536.85

ADDITIONAL INFORMATION

- Fancy That's purchases and expenses in the period in question are all standard-rated.

- EU acquisitions for the period totalled £17,794.03, VAT due £3,113.95.

- The business has issued the following sales credit notes to its customers:
£491.50 + £86.01 VAT = £577.51

- The business has received the following credit notes from its suppliers:
£579.21 + £101.36 VAT = £680.57

- In January Fancy That paid VAT of £4,106.52 for the last quarter to HM Customs & Excise; as the amount cancelled out the the balance brought down in VAT Control Account, it is ignored for the purposes of the current period VAT calculations.

- The accounts office made an error on a VAT calculation on an invoice during the last VAT quarter: a customer has been undercharged £75.29 output tax. Fortunately he has agreed to accept an invoice for this amount (he can reclaim it as input tax anyway). The problem for you is that the last quarter's VAT Return was £75.29 short on output tax. This error needs correcting on the current VAT Return.

solution

The data will be entered in VAT Control Account in order to calculate the amount of VAT due to HM Customs & Excise. The summary shown at the top of the next page is not the way the ledger account will *actually* appear in the double-entry system of the business, but it is displayed here in summary form to make the entries clearer.

The VAT Control Account Summary shows:

- totals for input tax and output tax – and the source of the figures
- the calculation for the VAT due to HM Customs & Excise for the period

When the VAT Control Account has been checked, the figures can then be used to work out the totals for the VAT 100 form – see the calculations that follow the account summary. The data that will be entered on the VAT 100 are shown here with a grey background. The first five boxes use *VAT amounts* and work out the total amount due to HM Customs & Excise. Note that pence are omitted in boxes 6, 7 and 9.

VAT control account – summary of entries

VAT deductible: input tax		VAT payable: output tax	
	£		£
Purchases Day Book £5,398.75 *less* credit notes £101.36	5,297.39	Sales Day Book £10,428.01 *less* credit notes £86.01	10,342.00
Cash Book	612.50	Cash Book	862.19
Petty Cash Book	79.95		
EU Acquisitions	3,113.95	EU Acquisitions	3,113.95
		Correction of error	75.29
TOTAL INPUT TAX	9,103.79	TOTAL OUTPUT TAX	14,393.43
		less TOTAL INPUT TAX	9,103.79
		equals VAT DUE	5,289.64

data entered in the VAT Return

			£	£
Box 1	Sales Day Book (adjusted for credit notes)		10,342.00	
	Correction of error		75.29	
	Cash sales		862.19	
				11,279.48
Box 2	EU Acquisitions			3,113.95
Box 3	Box 1 plus Box 2			14,393.43
Box 4	Purchases Day Book (less credit notes)		5,297.39	
	Cash book		612.50	
	Petty cash book		79.95	
	EU Acquisitions		3,113.95	
				9,103.79
Box 5	Net VAT due (box 3 less box 4)			5,289.64

Boxes 6 to 9 deal with sales/purchases *before VAT*. Note that pence are omitted.

		£	£
Box 6	Zero-rated credit sales	7,560.92	
	Standard-rated credit sales	59,588.68	
	less credit notes	(491.50)	
	Cash sales	4,926.80	
			71,584.90
Box 7	Purchases on credit	30,850.05	
	less credit notes	(579.21)	
	Cash book	3,500.00	
	Petty cash	456.90	
	EU Acquisitions	17,794.03	
			52,021.77

Box 8   'none'

Box 9   EU Acquisitions: £17,794.03

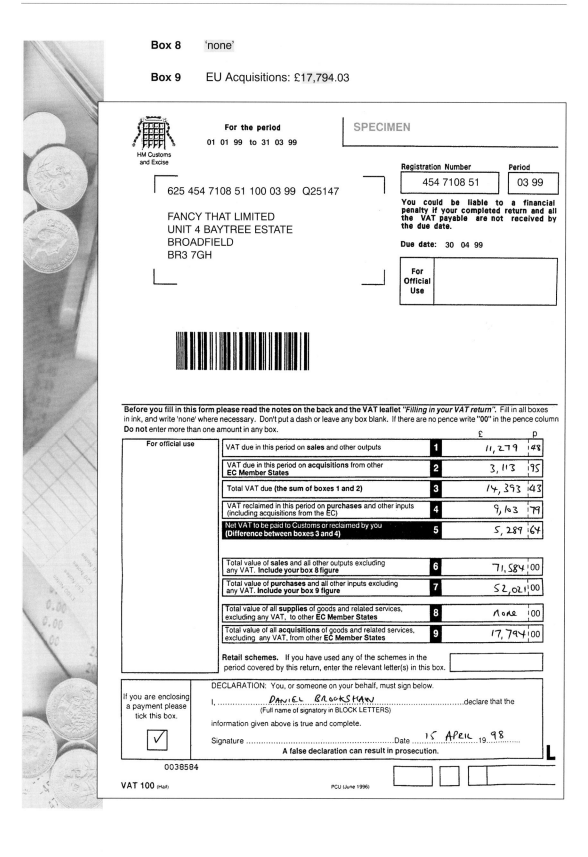

For the period	SPECIMEN
01 01 99 to 31 03 99	

HM Customs
and Excise

625 454 7108 51 100 03 99 Q25147

FANCY THAT LIMITED
UNIT 4 BAYTREE ESTATE
BROADFIELD
BR3 7GH

Registration Number	Period
454 7108 51	03 99

You could be liable to a financial penalty if your completed return and all the VAT payable are not received by the due date.

Due date: 30 04 99

For Official Use

Before you fill in this form please read the notes on the back and the VAT leaflet *"Filling in your VAT return"*. Fill in all boxes in ink, and write 'none' where necessary. Don't put a dash or leave any box blank. If there are no pence write "00" in the pence column **Do not** enter more than one amount in any box.

			£	p
For official use	VAT due in this period on **sales** and other outputs	**1**	11,279	48
	VAT due in this period on **acquisitions** from other **EC Member States**	**2**	3,113	95
	Total VAT due **(the sum of boxes 1 and 2)**	**3**	14,393	43
	VAT reclaimed in this period on **purchases** and other inputs (including acquisitions from the EC)	**4**	9,103	79
	Net VAT to be paid to Customs or reclaimed by you **(Difference between boxes 3 and 4)**	**5**	5,289	64
	Total value of **sales** and all other outputs excluding any VAT. **Include your box 8 figure**	**6**	71,584	00
	Total value of **purchases** and all other inputs excluding any VAT. **Include your box 9 figure**	**7**	52,021	00
	Total value of all **supplies** of goods and related services, excluding any VAT, to other **EC Member States**	**8**	none	00
	Total value of all **acquisitions** of goods and related services, excluding any VAT, from other **EC Member States**	**9**	17,794	00

Retail schemes. If you have used any of the schemes in the period covered by this return, enter the relevant letter(s) in this box.

If you are enclosing a payment please tick this box. ✓

DECLARATION: You, or someone on your behalf, must sign below.

I, ... DANIEL BROOKSHAW ....declare that the
(Full name of signatory in BLOCK LETTERS)

information given above is true and complete.

Signature .... Date 15 APRIL 19 98

A false declaration can result in prosecution.

L

0038584

VAT 100 (Half)   PCU (June 1996)

VAT ERRORS AND DEFAULTS

net errors of £2,000 or less

Net errors made in previous VAT periods of £2,000 or less can be adjusted in later VAT returns through the VAT Control Account (as we have just seen in the Case Study). 'Net error' is the difference between the total of errors in output tax and the total of the errors in input tax. In the majority of cases, hopefully, there will only be one error, and this will be the 'net error'. Typical errors are failure to charge output tax on chargeable supplies, charging at the wrong rate, or arithmetical errors in the accounts.

net errors over £2,000 – voluntary disclosure

If there should be a net error of more than £2,000 this should be advised to the local VAT Office on Form VAT 652 or in a letter as a *voluntary disclosure*. The details that will need to be disclosed are:

• the amount(s)
• the VAT period in which the error occurred
• whether the errors involved input or output tax (or both)
• whether the error was in favour of the business or Customs & Excise

Failure to disclose errors, however innocent they may be, can have serious consequences. A Customs & Excise investigation could result in a *misdeclaration penalty*, which could mean a 15% charge on unpaid VAT. No misdeclaration penalty can be charged if a voluntary disclosure is made.

defaults

If a trader fails to return the VAT 100 and any due payment within the set time limit (normally a month after the end of the VAT period), the trader is *in default* and a *surcharge liability notice* will be issued fixing a 12 month surcharge period. If there is a *further* default during this period, a *default surcharge* will be levied. This surcharge, subject to certain minimum limits, is calculated as a percentage of the VAT amount owing and can increase from 2% to 15% during the surcharge period.

SPECIAL SCHEMES

The illustration of the VAT Control Account on page 287 included entries for *special schemes*. These vary the way in which VAT is collected. They are designed to help businesses which may be put at a disadvantage if VAT is collected in the normal way.

annual accounting scheme

This scheme enables businesses to make VAT Returns *annually* rather than quarterly. This is a great advantage to the small trader for whom time is valuable; the only downside being that the accounts must be kept very accurately over the year – errors tend to compound themselves over time!

To qualify for this scheme a business must:

- have an annual taxable turnover of less than £600,000 at the time the scheme starts

- pay 90% of an estimate made of the likely annual VAT payment by nine equal monthly direct debit instalments starting in the fourth month of the VAT year

- pay the balance due with the annual VAT Return, due *two* months after the end of the VAT year

- have a taxable turnover of less than £750,000 by the end of the VAT year (if turnover exceeds this amount the business will have to leave the scheme)

Full details of this scheme are contained in the 'Annual Accounting' pamphlet published by HM Customs & Excise. Details are also available on the website: www.HMCE.co.uk

cash accounting scheme

This scheme allows businesses to account for VAT on the basis of the date of *payments* received and made rather than on the tax point on *invoices* received and issued. In other words a business under this scheme does not have to account for output tax on the date of the supply, but only when (and if!) payment is received, which could be many months later.

This is an enormous help to traders who have to pay their suppliers promptly but may have to wait a long time before receiving payment. It also provides automatic relief for VAT on bad debts: if the buyer does not pay up, no output VAT is declarable (as it would be if VAT was assessable on invoices rather than payments).

To qualify for this scheme a business must:

- anticipate annual taxable turnover of not more than £600,000

- have a 'clean' VAT record – ie all VAT Returns made on time, no assessments for VAT evasion or convictions for VAT fraud

- have a taxable turnover of less than £750,000 by the end of the VAT year (if turnover exceeds this amount the business will have to leave the scheme)

When registered under this scheme a supplier will continue to issue VAT invoices but will need to keep accounting records in a specific way:

- the tax point for payments in cash, by cheque, credit card, bank transfer is always the transaction date (eg the date on the credit card voucher)
- a cash book (or similar record) must be maintained summarising all payments made and received, with *a separate column for VAT*, suitable for providing the data for the VAT Return
- invoices issued or received for any payments made *in cash* must be receipted and dated

Full details of this scheme are contained in the 'Cash Accounting' pamphlet published by HM Customs & Excise.

bad debt relief

A *bad debt* is an amount owing which a supplier writes off in the books because he/she is unlikely ever to be paid – the buyer may have 'gone bust' for example. The cash accounting scheme explained above automatically protects the small trader against *bad debts*: if an invoice is not paid, no output VAT will have to be declared because no payment will be received.

This clearly does not apply to businesses not on the cash accounting scheme; what happens if output VAT paid over to Customs & Excise on the VAT Return is not received six or more months later by the supplier because the debt goes bad? HM Customs & Excise allows a refund to all suppliers through the VAT Return – this is known as *bad debt relief*.

Bad debt relief is available:

- for debts which are more than six months overdue (six months from the due date of the payment, or six months after the date of supply if it was later than the due payment date)
- when the output VAT has already been paid to HM Customs & Excise
- when the debt has been written off in the supplier's accounts and transferred to a separate bad debt account

The supplier must have a copy of the unpaid VAT invoice(s) and send a notice of the claim for bad debt relief to the 'bad' customer.

Bad debt relief is accounted for on the VAT Return by adding it to the Box 4 total (VAT reclaimed on purchases). As noted above, this figure must have been processed through a separate bad debt account. It will appear in the VAT control account on the left-hand side, as an addition to input tax.

Full details of this scheme are contained in the 'Relief from VAT on bad debts' pamphlet published by HM Customs & Excise.

retail schemes

VAT accounting for shops who may make a mixture of standard-rated, zero-rated and exempt supplies is potentially very complex. HM Customs & Excise has introduced a series of *retail schemes* to help retail suppliers. You will have seen the box on the VAT 100 form for completion by suppliers operating these schemes. There are five schemes for businesses with taxable turnover up to £10m. Larger businesses will have 'tailor-made' *bespoke* retail schemes arranged by HM Customs & Excise.

You do not at this stage in your studies need to know all the 'ins and outs' of retail schemes but you should note that the five standard schemes fall into three categories:

* *point of sale scheme*

    This is used when the VAT rate can be identified when the goods are sold at the till – the till will record the rate for each transaction.

* *apportionment schemes*

    These schemes apply when a retailer cannot realistically separate zero-rated and standard-rated goods at the till (eg buying food [zero-rated] and video tapes [standard-rated] at the corner shop). These schemes relate:

    – the proportion of VAT rates on outputs (sales at the tills) to the proportion of rates on inputs (what the retailer pays the wholesaler)
      or
    – an estimate is made of the expected selling price of goods at different rates and an appropriate percentage applied to the total takings

* *direct calculation schemes*

    The takings for the goods at the VAT rate which provides the smallest proportion of overall takings is calculated and deducted from the total takings on a daily basis.

DEALING WITH HM CUSTOMS & EXCISE

The normal point of contact with HM Customs & Excise is the local VAT office (look under Customs & Excise in the 'phone book). The staff are willing to help suppliers with advice and as regulatory bodies they are also likely to want to make sure that a supplier keeps accurate VAT records.

From time-to-time a supplier may receive an inspection visit from VAT officers who will go through the records with the proverbial 'toothcomb' to ensure that all the necessary documentation and accounting records are in order, VAT Returns are being submitted on time and VAT is not being underpaid or overpaid. If the officer(s) consider that VAT has been underpaid, HM Customs & Excise can raise an *assessment* demanding the VAT that they consider to be due. There are channels for formal appeals and tribunals to deal with disputes, should they occur.

In your studies it is stressed that guidance should be sought from the VAT office 'in a professional manner'. This means that any queries or problems should be referred to the local office through the appropriate channels. If your firm's accounts office is involved, this means an authorised official (supervisor or section head) should telephone or write to the VAT office. If the business is run by a sole trader, the enquiry will come from the owner.

Typical queries might include:

"Are these goods standard-rated or zero-rated"

"The business is being wound down and will close next year. Do we have to de-register for VAT?"

"We have discovered that we have underpaid output VAT by £3,000 on the last VAT Return. What should we do?"

"My acquisitions from Italy are invoiced in Italian Lira. What sterling figures should I use in the VAT records?"

The rule is: if in doubt, ask; but in a professional manner

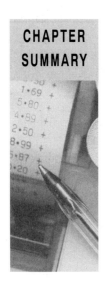

CHAPTER SUMMARY

• It is important that an organisation maintains accurate and comprehensive accounting records, keeping the records for at least six years. They may be needed for inspection by the Inland Revenue, by the Department of Social Security, by auditors and (for VAT registered businesses) by HM Customs & Excise.

• VAT records that must be kept include

  - copies of sales invoices

  - originals of purchase invoices

  - credit notes and debit notes issued and received

  - VAT control account

  - other associated records.

• VAT-registered businesses may use manual or computerised accounting systems. The normal sources of accounting data for the completion of the VAT Return are:

- sales and purchases day books (for credit items)

- cash book and petty cash book (for non-credit items)

• This data is compiled in a VAT control account which is structured as follows:

VAT control account – summary of entries

VAT deductible (input tax)	VAT payable (output tax)
Purchases Day Book VAT total, *less* any credit notes received/ debit notes issued	Sales Day Book VAT total, *less* any credit notes issued/debit notes received
Cash Book – items not in Purchases Day Book	Cash Book – items not in Sales Day Book
Petty Cash Book – VAT on small expenses	
Acquisitions from EU states	Acquisitions from EU states
Corrections of errors from previous periods (not exceeding £2,000 net)	Corrections of errors from previous periods (not exceeding £2,000 net)
Bad debt relief	
= TOTAL TAX DEDUCTIBLE	= TOTAL TAX PAYABLE
	less TOTAL TAX DEDUCTIBLE
	equals TAX PAYABLE ON VAT RETURN

• In addition the VAT control account will record VAT owing and paid to HM Customs & Excise (or VAT owed and paid by HM Customs & Excise) – but payments are not entered on the VAT Return.

• Computer accounting systems will normally keep a running VAT account to which all transactions involving VAT are posted. Some programs will additionally produce a VAT return printout.

• The VAT Return and payment (if required) should be completed and despatched within the timescale allowed (normally a month from the end of the VAT period); the VAT 100 should be signed by an authorised person.

• Net VAT errors of £2,000 or less can be corrected on a subsequent VAT Return. Errors over £2,000 should be disclosed as a 'voluntary disclosure' to HM Customs & Excise in a letter or Form VAT 652.

• If a VAT Return is not returned within the stipulated timescale, HM Customs & Excise will issue a twelve month surcharge liability notice; a further default within the twelve months may result in a default surcharge

- To help businesses which may be put at a disadvatage by the standard VAT Return system HM Customs & Excise has introduced a number of special schemes to help businesses: annual accounting, cash accounting, bad debt relief and retail schemes.

- Suppliers dealing with HM Customs & Excise should do so professionally; to do so will give HM Customs & Excise confidence in those suppliers.

**KEY
TERMS**

VAT inspection	a visit by VAT officers to ensure that adequate VAT records are being maintained and that the correct amount of VAT is being collected and reclaimed
VAT Control Account	an essential account which collects all the accounting data needed for the VAT Return; it may be maintained manually or by a computer accounting system
VAT Return	Form VAT 100 is completed by VAT-registered suppliers at the end of each VAT period in order to calculate the amount of VAT due to HM Customs & Excise or reclaimable from them; it also records statistical data about EU acquisitions
voluntary disclosure	disclosure of a net error over £2,000 in VAT calculations to HM Customs & Excise by a registered supplier
misdeclaration penalty	a penalty imposed on a VAT-registered supplier who is found by HM Customs & Excise to have errors and irregularities in the VAT records
surcharge liability notice	a notice issued by HM Customs & Excise to a VAT-registered supplier who has failed to make a VAT Return within the stipulated period – it lasts for 12 months
default surcharge	a percentage charge on an amount of unpaid VAT
annual accounting scheme	a scheme which enables businesses (with annual taxable turnover of £300,000 or less) to make VAT returns annually rather than quarterly – VAT owing is paid in regular instalments and the VAT 100 is due two months after the end of the VAT period

cash accounting scheme	a scheme which allows businesses (with annual taxable turnover of £350,000 or less) to account for VAT on the basis of payments received and made rather than the tax point on invoices received and issued; it provides automatic relief for VAT on bad debts
bad debt relief	a scheme available for any registered supplier whereby output VAT paid over to HM Customs & Excise on a debt which has subsequently (over 6 months after the due date) gone bad is reclaimable through the VAT 100
retail schemes	a variety of schemes for businesses in the retail trade where it is difficult to account to different rates of VAT at the point of sale; there are three main types of scheme: point of sale, apportionment and direct calculation

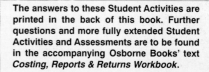

STUDENT ACTIVITIES

The answers to these Student Activities are printed in the back of this book. Further questions and more fully extended Student Activities and Assessments are to be found in the accompanying Osborne Books' text *Costing, Reports & Returns Workbook*.

15.1   Make a checklist of

(a)   the basic records that must be maintained by a business in order to account for VAT

(b)   additional accounting records which should be maintained to support the records mentioned in (a) above

15.2   What would be the problem as far as VAT is concerned if a VAT-registered business had not kept

(a)   copies of sales invoices issued

(b)   originals of purchase invoices received

15.3   In a manual accounting system what is the danger, as far as VAT calculation is concerned, in extracting VAT entries from the Sales Day Book and also from the Cash Book?

15.4   Construct VAT control accounts from the VAT figures shown on the next page. The figures have been extracted from the accounting records of four different businesses; in each case ensure that you calculate the VAT due or reclaimable for the VAT period. Note: any VAT payable or reclaimable for the previous period is to be ignored.

VAT FIGURES	Business A £	Business B £	Business C £	Business D £
Purchases Day Book	2,720.00	3,239.50	5,726.05	3,923.50
Sales Day Book	5,961.70	5,906.33	9,176.23	521.30
Credit notes received	326.50	107.60	195.50	170.90
Credit notes issued	501.29	321.90	391.80	81.25
Cash book purchases (non-credit)	275.60	179.29	173.76	1,256.81
Cash book sales (non-credit)	329.73	260.75	356.25	723.80
Petty cash book purchases	13.85	nil	18.92	41.20
EU Acquisitions	796.30	78.00	1,523.90	nil
VAT overpaid previous period	nil	nil	271.20	17.50
VAT underpaid previous period	nil	32.65	86.30	nil
Bad debt relief	nil	85.50	89.23	29.50

The format shown below can be used to set up the VAT Control Account. You will need to calculate the final amount of VAT due or reclaimable. If the final total is reclaimable it should be shown in brackets.

VAT deductible (input tax)	VAT payable (output tax)
Purchases Day Book VAT total, *less* any credit notes received/ debit notes issued	Sales Day Book VAT total, *less* any credit notes issued/debit notes received
Cash Book – items not in Purchases Day Book	Cash Book – items not in Sales Day Book
Petty Cash Book – VAT on small expenses	
Acquisitions from EU states	Acquisitions from EU states
Corrections of errors from previous periods (not exceeding £2,000 net)	Corrections of errors from previous periods (not exceeding £2,000 net)
Bad debt relief	
= TOTAL TAX DEDUCTIBLE	= TOTAL TAX PAYABLE
	less TOTAL TAX DEDUCTIBLE
	equals TAX PAYABLE/(RECLAIMABLE)

15.5 You work as an assistant in a firm of accountants and have been asked to draw up VAT Returns for four clients. You have extracted the relevant data from their accounting records and have set it out on a spreadsheet shown below.

You are to calculate the totals for all nine boxes of the four VAT Returns ready for checking. If you wish, you can use the table set out on the next page for entering the figures.

	Business 1 £	Business 2 £	Business 3 £	Business 4 £
VAT FIGURES EXTRACTED				
Sales day book	11,099.17	17,180.86	3,196.37	3,436.25
Credit notes issued	213.12	693.89	54.63	98.34
Cash sales	1,388.10	304.29	686.93	302.15
Purchases day book	6,297.83	10,806.39	1,104.75	10,166.32
Credit notes received	152.37	368.87	28.50	188.44
Cash purchases	321.81	1,014.70	52.50	nil
Petty cash expenses	nil	91.17	33.41	48.26
Bad debt relief	639.80	850.00	nil	250.00
Overpayment (previous period)	nil	258.92	nil	365.12
Underpayment (previous period)	nil	nil	95.20	109.90
EU acquisitions	nil	3,281.28	216.31	8,791.96
NET SALES AND RECEIPTS				
Zero-rated sales	126.75	8,326.18	1,507.29	75,800.00
Standard-rated sales	63,423.86	98,176.35	18,265.00	19,635.75
Credit notes issued	1,217.85	3,965.10	312.18	561.95
Cash sales (standard-rated)	7,932.01	1,738.81	3,925.37	1,726.58
Zero-rated purchases	1,290.00	3,706.70	295.80	2,560.22
Standard-rated credit purchases	35,987.60	61,750.80	6,312.87	58,093.30
Credit notes received	870.72	2,107.83	162.91	1,076.84
Cash payments (standard-rated)	1,838.96	5,798.32	300.00	nil
Petty cash expenses	nil	521.00	190.95	275.81
EU acquisitions	nil	18,750.21	1,236.09	50,239.80

Suggested answer layout for 15.5:

VAT 100 Box No.	Business 1	Business 2	Business 3	Business 4
1				
2				
3				
4				
5				
6				
7				
8				
9				

15.6   You are working in an accountant's office and receive a number of VAT enquiries from clients. What would your advice be in each case?

(a)   Oriental Supplies Limited overcharged VAT on an invoice during the previous VAT quarter and the VAT 100 has already been sent off. The amount involved is £350.00.

(b)   Olly Moore is a VAT-registered freelance computer consultant. Six months ago he started selling space on his Web site to advertisers. This has been very successful and sales during the first VAT quarter were higher than expected. Unfortunately in the rush to get this side of his business going, he omitted to charge VAT on the first batch of sales invoices. He reckons that during the first quarter he has failed to charge £4,200 of VAT. The relevant VAT 100 was sent off over two months ago.

(c)   Helen Underhill telephones to say that she has just realised that the book-keeper she hired last VAT quarter has failed to send off the VAT 100 in time. It has been incorrectly filed in the pending tray and is now over a month overdue. She has fired her book-keeper but is concerned about the late submission of the form which she hopes to get into the post this week.

15.7   What special VAT schemes would you recommend to VAT-registered businesses in the following circumstances? State in each case:

•   how the scheme differs from the normal arrangements

•   `the advantages of the scheme to the business

•   the practical accounting requirements of the scheme

(a)   Gilbert Gumbert is a busy sole trader, who has been registered for VAT for two years. He has an annual taxable turnover of £250,000. He also has a 'clean' VAT record with no records of default. He has problems however:

•   the time it takes him to fill in his VAT returns

•   the strain on cash flow of having to make quarterly VAT payments with his VAT 100

(b)   Fiona Strong is a successful 'trouble-shooting' management consultant with an annual taxable turnover of £150,000. She also has a 'clean' VAT record with no records of default. She has a wide range of clients but is constantly running into cash flow problems, largely because some of her clients are financially insecure:

•   her clients often demand long credit terms

•   her clients do not pay up on time

•   some of her clients do not pay up at all

•   she has to pay most of her expenses and overheads straightaway or within 30 days

15.8   Seamus O'Deah, a VAT-registered trader, has just been informed that a customer with six overdue invoices outstanding has been made bankrupt. Seamus wants to know:

(a)   which of the invoices listed below is eligible for bad debt relief (and why)

(b)   how any claim will be adjusted in his accounts and on the VAT 100 (state any VAT amount involved in the process)

The VAT invoices in question date over two years: 1998 and 1999. It is currently 30 June in the year 1999. Seamus' financial year-end of 30 June is also the end of his VAT quarter.

Invoice 7773, due for payment 30 March 1999, goods supplied 14 February 1999, VAT £45.00

Invoice 7645, due for payment 20 February 1999, goods supplied 21 January 1999, VAT £21.00

Invoice 7578, due for payment 28 December 1998, goods supplied 4 January 1999, VAT £34.40

Invoice 7510, due for payment 20 December 1998, goods supplied 20 November 1998, VAT £35.00

Invoice 7415, due for payment 30 November 1998, goods supplied 30 October 1998, VAT £45.20

Invoice 7200, due for payment 20 August 1998, goods supplied 22 July 1998, VAT £56.40

answers to student activities

CHAPTER 1: AN INTRODUCTION TO COST ACCOUNTING

1.1 (a) • The principle behind this Student Activity is the identification of relevant costs
   • Whilst the type of organisation selected may well not fit with the exact layout for a manufacturing business, as shown on page 7, the Activity should generate thought and discussion of costs involved
   • As an example, an outline of the costs incurred by a school or college is as follows:

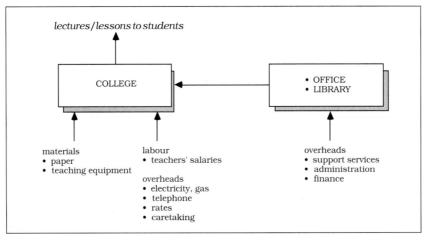

(b) • What are the units of output of the organisation to which costs can be charged?
   • The main sections of the organisation should be identified. Does the costing system in use charge costs to these sections, whether or not they are formally called cost centres?
   • In the school/college described above, the example cost unit is student hours, and cost centres examples are teaching departments, learning resources, administration.

1.2 Suggestions to include:

	COST UNIT	COST CENTRE
college of further education	student hour	teaching department learning resources administration
mixed farm	kilo of wheat head of cattle	field cattle shed

1.3 (a) See text, pages 10 and 11
   (b) • raw materials: variable
      • factory rent: fixed
      • telephone: semi-fixed
      • direct labour: variable
      • indirect labour: fixed
      • commission to sales staff: variable
   Classifying costs by nature identifies them as being fixed, or semi-fixed, or variable. This helps with decision making – the business might be able to alter the balance between fixed and variable costs in order to increase profits.For example, a furniture manufacturing business will have to make decisions on whether to use direct labour (variable cost) or machinery (fixed cost) for many of the production processes. The decision will be based very much on the expected level of sales, ie for

lower sales it is likely to make greater use of direct labour, while for higher sales a more machine-intensive method of production might be used.

1.4

tubular steel	direct materials
factory supervisor's salary	indirect labour
wages of employee operating moulding machine	direct labour
works canteen assistant's wages	indirect labour
rates of factory	indirect expenses
power to operate machines	indirect expenses*
factory heating and lighting	indirect expenses
plastic for making chair seats	direct materials
hire of special machinery for one particular order	direct expenses
cost of grease for the moulding machine	indirect materials
depreciation of factory machinery	indirect expenses
depreciation of office equipment	indirect expenses

* Note: the cost of power to operate machines has been classified above as an indirect expense. This is often the case because it is not worthwhile analysing the cost of power for each unit of production. An industry that uses a lot of power will often have meters fitted to each machine so that costs may be identified and allocated to production as a direct expense. Other, lesser users of power, are unlikely to calculate the separate cost and will consider power to be an indirect expense.

1.5

Cost item	Total cost £	Prime cost £	Production overheads £	Admin costs £	Selling and distribution costs £
Wages of employees working on the bottling line	6,025	6,025			
Wages of employees in the stores department	2,750		2,750		
Cost of bottles	4,050	4,050			
Safety goggles for bottling line employees	240		240		
Advertisement for new employees	125			125	
Depreciation of bottling machinery	500		500		
Depreciation of sales staff's cars	1,000				1,000
Royalty paid to local farmer	750	750			
Cost of trade exhibition	1,500				1,500
Computer stationery	210			210	
Sales staff salaries	4,095				4,095
TOTALS	21,245	10,825	3,490	335	6,595

1.6 (a)

Hughes Limited
Total cost statement for the year ended 31 December 1998

	£	£
Direct materials		118,830
Direct labour*		117,315
PRIME COST		236,145
Production overheads		
rent and rates	16,460	
factory power	3,825	
factory heat and light	1,185	
factory expenses and maintenance	4,095	
depreciation of factory plant and machinery	3,725	
		29,290
PRODUCTION COST		265,435
Non-production overheads		
Selling and distribution costs:		
advertising		11,085
Administration costs:		
office salaries and wages	69,350	
office expenses	3,930	
		73,280
TOTAL COST		349,800

*   *Note:* It has been assumed in the cost statement that all of the factory wages are
direct labour. With additional information, it would be possible to split the cost
between direct and indirect labour.

(b)

Hughes Limited
Profit statement for the year ended 31 December 1998

	£
Sales	426,350
less Total cost	349,800
PROFIT	76,550

CHAPTER 2: MATERIALS COSTS

2.1   ***Stock item D***
- maximum space = 350 units; maximum usage = 95 days x 3 units per day = 285 units; therefore maximum stock is 285 units
- minimum stock = 10 days x 3 units per day = 30 units
- re-order level = 30 units + (7 days x 3 units per day) = 51 units
- re-order quantity = 285 units − 30 units = 255 units

Stock item E
- maximum space = 350 units; maximum usage = 95 days x 4 units per day = 380; therefore maximum stock is 350 units
- minimum stock = 10 days x 4 units per day = 40 units
- re-order level = 40 units + (7 days x 4 units per day) = 68 units
- re-order quantity = 350 units − 40 units = 310 units

2.2

<table>
<tr><td colspan="6" align="center">**STOCK RECORD CARD**</td></tr>
<tr><td>Stock Description</td><td colspan="2">*A4 yellow card*</td><td></td><td></td><td></td></tr>
<tr><td>Stock units</td><td colspan="2">*reams*</td><td>Minimum</td><td colspan="2">*36 reams*</td></tr>
<tr><td>Stock Ref. No.</td><td colspan="2">*A4/Y3*</td><td>Maximum</td><td colspan="2">*105 reams*</td></tr>
<tr><td>Location</td><td colspan="2">*row7, bin5*</td><td>Re-order level</td><td colspan="2">*66 reams*</td></tr>
<tr><td></td><td></td><td></td><td>Re-order quantity</td><td colspan="2">*69 reams*</td></tr>
</table>

DATE	GOODS RECEIVED		GOODS ISSUED		BALANCE
	Reference	Quantity	Reference	Quantity	
1999					
1 May					*84*
4 May			*MR184*	*18*	*66*
6 May			*MR187*	*20*	*46*
10 May			*MR188*	*10*	*36*
14 May	*GRN4507*	*69*			*105*
17 May			*MR394*	*20*	*85*
20 May			*MR401*	*11*	*74*
26 May			*MR422*	*6*	*68*

2.3   (a)   stock record card
(b)   stock list
(c)   stock reconciliation
(d)   cost and net realisable value

2.4

FIFO

STORES LEDGER RECORD

Date	Receipts			Issues			Balance		
1999	Quantity	Price	Value	Quantity	Price	Value	Quantity	Price	Value
		£	£		£	£		£	£
January	20	3.00	60.00				20	3.00	60.00
February	10	3.50	35.00				20	3.00	60.00
							10	3.50	35.00
							30		95.00
March				8	3.00	24.00	12	3.00	36.00
							10	3.50	35.00
							22		71.00
April	10	4.00	40.00				12	3.00	36.00
							10	3.50	35.00
							10	4.00	40.00
							32		111.00
May				12	3.00	36.00			
				4	3.50	14.00	6	3.50	21.00
							10	4.00	40.00
							16		61.00

LIFO

STORES LEDGER RECORD

Date	Receipts			Issues			Balance		
1999	Quantity	Price	Value	Quantity	Price	Value	Quantity	Price	Value
		£	£		£	£		£	£
January	20	3.00	60.00				20	3.00	60.00
February	10	3.50	35.00				20	3.00	60.00
							10	3.50	35.00
							30		95.00
March				8	3.50	28.00	20	3.00	60.00
							2	3.50	7.00
							22		67.00
April	10	4.00	40.00				20	3.00	60.00
							2	3.50	7.00
							10	4.00	40.00
							32		107.00
May				10	4.00	40.00			
				2	3.50	7.00			
				4	3.00	12.00	16	3.00	48.00

AVCO

STORES LEDGER RECORD

Date	Receipts			Issues			Balance		
1999	Quantity	Price	Value	Quantity	Price	Value	Quantity	Price	Value
		£	£		£	£		£	£
January	20	3.00	60.00				20	3.00	60.00
February	10	3.50	35.00				20	3.00	60.00
							10	3.50	35.00
							30	3.17	95.00
March				8	3.17	25.33	22	3.17	69.67
April	10	4.00	40.00				22	3.17	69.67
							10	4.00	40.00
							32	3.43	109.67
May				16	3.43	54.84	16	3.43	54.83

Note: some figures have been rounded to the nearest penny

2.5

FIFO

STORES LEDGER RECORD: TYPE X

Date	Receipts			Issues			Balance		
1999	Quantity	Price	Value	Quantity	Price	Value	Quantity	Price	Value
		£	£		£	£		£	£
January	100	4.00	400.00				100	4.00	400.00
February				80	4.00	320.00	20	4.00	80.00
March	140	4.20	588.00				20	4.00	80.00
							140	4.20	588.00
							160		668.00
April	100	3.80	380.00				20	4.00	80.00
							140	4.20	588.00
							100	3.80	380.00
							260		1,048.00
May				20	4.00	80.00			
				120	4.20	504.00	20	4.20	84.00
							100	3.80	380.00
							120		464.00
June	80	4.50	360.00				20	4.20	84.00
							100	3.80	380.00
							80	4.50	360.00
							200		824.00

LIFO

STORES LEDGER RECORD: TYPE X

Date	Receipts			Issues			Balance		
1999	Quantity	Price	Value	Quantity	Price	Value	Quantity	Price	Value
		£	£		£	£		£	£
January	100	4.00	400.00				100	4.00	400.00
February				80	4.00	320.00	20	4.00	80.00
March	140	4.20	588.00				20	4.00	80.00
							140	4.20	588.00
							160		668.00
April	100	3.80	380.00				20	4.00	80.00
							140	4.20	588.00
							100	3.80	380.00
							260		1,048.00
May				100	3.80	380.00	20	4.00	80.00
				40	4.20	168.00	100	4.20	420.00
							120		500.00
June	80	4.50	360.00				20	4.00	80.00
							100	4.20	420.00
							80	4.50	360.00
							200		860.00

AVCO

STORES LEDGER RECORD: TYPE X

Date	Receipts			Issues			Balance		
1999	Quantity	Price	Value	Quantity	Price	Value	Quantity	Price	Value
		£	£		£	£		£	£
January	100	4.00	400.00				100	4.00	400.00
February				80	4.00	320.00	20	4.00	80.00
March	140	4.20	588.00				20	4.00	80.00
							140	4.20	588.00
							160	4.17	668.00
April	100	3.80	380.00				160	4.17	668.00
							100	3.80	380.00
							260	4.03	1,048.00
May				140	4.03	564.20	120	4.03	483.80
June	80	4.50	360.00				120	4.03	483.80
							80	4.50	360.00
							200	4.22	843.80

Note: some figures have been rounded to the nearest penny

FIFO

STORES LEDGER RECORD: TYPE Y

Date	Receipts			Issues			Balance		
1999	Quantity	Price	Value	Quantity	Price	Value	Quantity	Price	Value
		£	£		£	£		£	£
January	200	10.00	2,000.00				200	10.00	2,000.00
February	100	9.50	950.00				200	10.00	2,000.00
							100	9.50	950.00
							300		2,950.00
March				200	10.00	2,000.00			
				40	9.50	380.00	60	9.50	570.00
April	100	10.50	1,050.00				60	9.50	570.00
							100	10.50	1,050.00
							160		1,620.00
May	140	10.00	1,400.00				60	9.50	570.00
							100	10.50	1,050.00
							140	10.00	1,400.00
							300		3,020.00
June				60	9.50	570.00			
				40	10.50	420.00	60	10.50	630.00
							140	10.00	1,400.00
							200		2,030.00

LIFO

STORES LEDGER RECORD: TYPE Y

Date	Receipts			Issues			Balance		
1999	Quantity	Price	Value	Quantity	Price	Value	Quantity	Price	Value
		£	£		£	£		£	£
January	200	10.00	2,000.00				200	10.00	2,000.00
February	100	9.50	950.00				200	10.00	2,000.00
							100	9.50	950.00
							300		2,950.00
March				100	9.50	950.00			
				140	10.00	1,400.00	60	10.00	600.00
April	100	10.50	1,050.00				60	10.00	600.00
							100	10.50	1,050.00
							160		1,650.00
May	140	10.00	1,400.00				60	10.00	600.00
							100	10.50	1,050.00
							140	10.00	1,400.00
							300		3,050.00
June				100	10.00	1,000.00	60	10.00	600.00
							100	10.50	1,050.00
							40	10.00	400.00
							200		2,050.00

AVCO

STORES LEDGER RECORD: TYPE Y

Date	Receipts			Issues			Balance		
1999	Quantity	Price	Value	Quantity	Price	Value	Quantity	Price	Value
		£	£		£	£		£	£
January	200	10.00	2,000.00				200	10.00	2,000.00
February	100	9.50	950.00				200	10.00	2,000.00
							100	9.50	950.00
							300	9.83	2,950.00
March				240	9.83	2,360.00	60	9.83	590.00
April	100	10.50	1,050.00				60	9.83	590.00
							100	10.50	1,050.00
							160	10.25	1,640.00
May	140	10.00	1,400.00				160	10.25	1,640.00
							140	10.00	1,400.00
							300	10.13	3,040.00
June				100	10.13	1,013.00	200	10.13	2,027.00

Note: some figures have been rounded to the nearest penny

Balance sheet valuation at 30 June 1999:

	£	
Type X	824.00	(cost price, using FIFO)
Type Y	1,950.00	(net realisable value)
	2,774.00	

CHAPTER 3: LABOUR COSTS

3.1 N Ball: 35 hours x £8.00 per hour = £280.00 (no bonus)

T Smith: 37 hours x £9.00 per hour = £333.00 + bonus £9.00 = £342.00

L Lewis: 40 hours x £10.00 per hour = £400.00 + bonus £13.75 = £413.75

M Wilson: 38 hours x £7.00 per hour = £266.00 + bonus £4.08 = £270.08

3.2

MEMORANDUM

To: Office Manager

From: Accounting Technician

Date:

SUBJECT: REMUNERATION OF PRODUCTION-LINE WORKERS

I have been asked to produce a report on remuneration methods for production-line workers.

At present the company pays these workers on a time-rate basis. The main advantages of such a system from the viewpoint of both employer and employees are as follows:

- it is easy to calculate and understand
- there is no requirement to establish time allowances and piecework rates
- employees receive a regular wage, which is unaffected by fluctuations in output
- the system can be applied to all direct labour employees
- the quality of finished output does not suffer as a result of hurried work

The disadvantages of time rate are that:

- all production-line employees are paid the same, whether they work efficiently or inefficiently
- no incentive is given to employees to work harder
- the company needs to employ supervisors to ensure that output is maintained
- slow working by employees does not affect the basic wage, but could lead to the company having to pay overtime rates to ensure that output is completed.

Employee representatives have approached the company management with a request that other remuneration methods be considered. In particular piecework systems, or a time rate with a production bonus system have been suggested.

A *piecework system* is where payment is based on the quantity of output.

The main advantages of this are that:

- payment of wages is linked directly to output
- more efficient workers earn more than those who are less efficient
- work is done quicker and less time is wasted

The main disadvantages are that:

- the system is not suitable for all direct labour employees
- there may be difficulty in agreeing piecework rates between employer and employees
- the quality of the finished product may be low and more inspectors may be needed
- control system will be needed to check the amount produced by each worker
- from the employer's point of view, the quality of the finished product may be low
- pay calculations will be more complex

Employees need to be aware that pay is reduced if there are production problems, eg machine breakdown, or shortage of materials. A way around this is to use a piecework system with a guaranteed time rate. A further disadvantage is that there may be difficulties in agreeing piecework rates.

A time rate with a production bonus is a system used to encourage employees to be more efficient where work is not so repetitive. There are a number of variations of bonus including increased bonuses for higher levels of output, and group bonuses paid to groups of employees.

The main advantages of bonus systems are that:

- wages are linked to output, but a minimum wage – the time rate – is guaranteed each week
- work is done quicker and less time is wasted
- the more efficient workers earn more
- a bonus system can often be applied to the entire workforce

The disadvantages are that:

- from the employee's point of view, the bonus is not paid if circumstances such as machine breakdown, or shortage of materials occur
- from the employer's point of view, the quality of the finished product may be low and more inspectors will be needed
- there may be difficulty in agreeing bonus rates with employees
- control procedures are needed, and pay calculations will be more complex

Conclusion

Each of the three main methods of remuneration has advantages and disadvantages. In selecting a suitable system both employer and employee must consider that:

- reward should be related to effort and fair to all staff
- the system should be easy to manage and administer, and be cheap and efficient to run
- it should be easy for employees to understand how pay is calculated
- payment should be made at regular intervals and soon after the event
- the principles of the scheme should remain constant, but there should be flexibility to deal with changes in production techniques

3.3 (a) • L Fry: £400.00 (time rate)
  • R Williams: £315.00 (piecework rate)
  • P Grant: £362.50 (piecework rate)

(b) • not suitable for all direct labour employees
  • employees' pay is reduced if there are production problems
  • quality of the finished product may be low
  • more inspectors may be needed
  • control systems needed to check the amount produced by each worker
  • more complex pay calculations
  • may be difficulty in agreeing piecework rates with employees

3.4 Gross wages

		£
• Steve Kurtin:	35 hours at £5.50 per hour =	192.50
	4 hours overtime at £7.333 per hour =	29.33
	production bonus 45 x 25p =	11.25
		233.08

- Pete Singh: 35 hours at £6.50 per hour =   227.50
                        3 hours overtime at £8.667 per hour =   26.00
                        4 hours overtime at £9.75 per hour =   39.00
                        production bonus 57 x 25p =   14.25
                                                                                             306.75

Piecework rate for Steve Kurtin
£233.08 ÷ 45 = £5.18 per 1,000 copies printed

3.5   MOULDING   FINISHING

- Standard hours saved   –   500
- Bonus (£)   –   2,025*
- Total labour cost (£)   31,160   38,475

   * £36,450 ÷ 4,500 hours = £8.10 x 500 hours = £4,050 ÷ 2 = £2,025

3.6   - *work-in-progress £2,100*: the cost of direct labour incurred by the company for the work on manufacturing the product

   - *production overheads £900:* the cost of indirect labour incurred by the company for the week

   - *non-production overheads £700:* the administration labour costs for the week

   - *total payroll for the week £3,700:* the total of net wages paid to employees, income tax and National Insurance Contributions, and pension contributions

CHAPTER 4: EXPENSES

4.1   (a)   *Capital expenditure:* expenditure incurred on the purchase, alteration or improvement of fixed assets. Examples: purchase of premises, vehicles, machinery; legal costs of buying property; installation and setting up of a machine.

   (b)   *Revenue expenditure:* expenditure incurred on running costs. Examples: fuel for vehicles; repairs to premises; labour costs of running the business.

4.2   (a)   *Direct expenses:* those expenses that are attributable to particular units of output. Examples: royalties payable to the designer of a product; special items bought in for a particular product or job; power costs metered to output; depreciation methods linked directly to output (such as units of output or service method).

   (b)   *Indirect expenses:* those expenses that are not attributable directly to particular units of output. Examples: rent and rates, heating and lighting, depreciation methods not linked directly to output (such as straight-line and reducing balance methods).

4.3   Fred Jarvis' wages will be shown in wages control account as:

   –   *debit* cash/bank, income tax and NIC, and pension contributions

   –   *credit* property account

   Thus the cost of his labour is debited to the fixed asset account of property (rather than work-in-progress, as would be the usual case for production-line employees). As he is building an extension to the warehouse, his wages (and also the cost of the materials he uses) are treated as capital expenditure because he is adding to the value of a fixed asset.

4.4   **Graph A**

•   shows a *fixed cost,* which remains constant over a range of output levels

•   as output increases, the *cost per unit* falls

•   at an output beyond the limit of the graph, the fixed cost will increase as another factory needs to be rented; the nature of such a cost is known as a *stepped fixed cost.*

Graph B

•   shows a *variable cost,* which alters directly with changes in output levels

•   as output increases then the cost increases, ie the cost per unit remains the same

4.5

		capital expenditure	revenue expenditure
(a)	purchase of motor vehicles	✓	
(b)	depreciation of motor vehicles		✓
(c)	payment of office rent		✓
(d)	salaries of office staff		✓
(e)	legal fees relating to the purchase of property	✓	
(f)	re-decoration of office		✓
(g)	installation of air-conditioning in office	✓	
(h)	wages of own employees used to build extension to the stockroom	✓	
(i)	installation and setting up of a new machine	✓	

4.6

		direct expenses	indirect expenses	either*
(a)	hire of machinery for a particular job	✓		
(b)	office rent		✓	
(c)	cleaning materials		✓	
(d)	power costs			✓
(e)	royalty paid to designer for each unit of output	✓		
(f)	sales staff car expenses		✓	
(g)	depreciation of production machinery			✓
(h)	consultant's fees relating to a particular job	✓		
(i)	heating and lighting		✓	

(d) Power costs are direct expenses where machinery is separately metered and used for a particular product or job; otherwise, they are indirect expenses.

(g) Depreciation of production machinery is a direct expense when the depreciation method is linked directly to output (such as units of output or service method; it is an indirect expense when the depreciation method is not linked directly to output (such as straight-line and reducing balance methods).

4.7

		fixed	semi-fixed	variable
(a)	rates of business premises	✓		
(b)	royalty paid to designer for each unit of output			✓
(c)	car hire with fixed rental and charge per mile		✓	
(d)	employees paid on piecework basis			✓
(e)	straight-line depreciation	✓		
(f)	units of service depreciation			✓
(g)	direct materials			✓
(h)	telephone bill with fixed rental and charge per unit		✓	
(i)	office salaries	✓		

4.8

(a) cleaning materials for the machines: indirect materials
(b) wages of factory supervisor: indirect labour
(c) clay from which pots are made: direct materials
(d) royalty paid to designer: direct expenses
(e) salary of office clerk: indirect expenses*
(f) electricity used to heat the kilns: indirect expense (or possibly a direct expense – see note to question 4.6(d) above)
(g) rates of factory: indirect expense
(h) depreciation of office equipment: indirect expense
(i) wages of production line workers: direct labour
(j) salesperson's salary: indirect expenses*
(k) interest charged on bank overdraft: indirect expenses

* Note: Both the salary of the office clerk and the salesperson's salary have been classified as indirect expenses, rather than indirect labour. This is because neither of them work in the factory and so the cost cannot be attributed directly to production. By contrast, the wages of the factory supervisor are classified as indirect labour – here the employee does work in the factory, and the cost is more closely linked to production.
- *production overheads:* (a), (b), (f), (g)
- *selling and distribution overheads:* (j)
- *administration overheads:* (e), (h)
- *finance overheads:* (k)

4.9 •

	high output	15,000 units	£65,000
less	low output	10,000 units	£50,000
equals	difference	5,000 units	£15,000

• amount of variable cost per unit:

$$\frac{£15,000}{5,000} = £3 \text{ variable cost per unit}$$

• at 10,000 units of output the cost structure is:

	total cost	£50,000
less	variable costs (10,000 units x £3 per unit)	£30,000
equals	fixed costs	£20,000

• check at 15,000 units of output when the cost structure is:

	variable costs (15,000 units x £3 per unit)	£45,000
add	fixed costs (as above)	£20,000
equals	total costs	£65,000

• therefore fixed costs, at these levels of output, are £20,000

4.10

1999	**BUDGETED PRODUCTION COSTS**		
Units	250,000	300,000	350,000
Costs	£	£	£
Variable costs:			
Materials	400,000	480,000	560,000
Labour	325,000	390,000	455,000
Expenses	100,000	120,000	140,000
	825,000	990,000	1,155,000
Fixed costs:			
Labour	96,500	96,500	96,500
Overheads	107,500	107,500	107,500
	204,000	204,000	204,000
TOTAL PRODUCTION COST	1,029,000	1,194,000	1,359,000
COST PER UNIT	£4.12	£3.98	£3.88

- Variable costs per unit are:
  - materials, £1.60 (ie £400,000 ÷ 250,000 units)
  - labour, £1.30
  - expenses, £0.40
- Fixed costs remain fixed at the higher levels of output
- The costs at higher levels of output are on the basis that
  - there is a linear relationship for variable costs
  - there are no stepped fixed costs
- The fall in cost per unit as output increases occurs because the fixed costs are being spread over a greater number of units, ie the fixed cost per unit falls

CHAPTER 5: OVERHEADS

5.1
- allocation of overheads – the charging to a cost centre of those overheads that have been directly incurred by that cost centre
- apportionment of overheads – the charging to a cost centre of a proportion of overheads

5.2 (a)

OVERHEAD ANALYSIS SHEET		
	MOULDING	FINISHING
Budgeted total overheads (£)	9,338	3,298
Budgeted machine hours	1,450	680
Budgeted overhead absorption rate (£)	6.44*	4.85**

*   £9,338 ÷ 1,450 hours

**   £3,298 ÷ 680 hours

(b)

JOB OVERHEAD ANALYSIS SHEET		
	MOULDING	FINISHING
Job machine hours	412	154
Budgeted overhead absorption rate (£)	6.44	4.85
Overhead absorbed by job (£)	2,653.28*	746.90**

*   412 hours x £6.44 per hour

**   154 hours x £4.85 per hour

(c) **Units of output**
- Using this method, production overhead is absorbed on the basis of each unit of output.
- This would be appropriate where units of output are identical and where each spend the

same amount of time in the departments.
- It does not seem appropriate for use by Wyvern Fabrication as the company appears to have different types and sizes of jobs passing through its two departments – to use units of output, each job would be charged the same rate.

Direct labour hour
- With this method, production overhead is absorbed on the basis of the number of direct labour hours worked.
- While this is a commonly-used method, it is inappropriate where some output is worked on by hand while other output passes quickly through a machinery process and requires little direct labour time.
- This method may be appropriate for Wyvern Fabrication; however, much depends on the balance between direct labour hours and machine hours in the two production departments.

5.3 (a)

cost	basis of apportionment	total	dept A	dept B	dept C
		£	£	£	£
Rent and rates	Floor area	7,210	3,090	1,545	2,575
Depn. of machinery	Value of machinery	10,800	5,400	3,240	2,160
Supervisor's salary	Production-line employees	12,750	6,800	3,400	2,550
Machinery insurance	Value of machinery	750	375	225	150
		31,510	15,665	8,410	7,435

(b)   37 hours x 48 weeks = 1,776 direct labour hours per employee
Dept A: 8 employees = 14,208 hours = £1.10 per direct labour hour
Dept B: 4 employees = 7,104 hours = £1.18 per direct labour hour
Dept C: 3 employees = 5,328 hours = £1.40 per direct labour hour

5.4 (a) and (b)

cost	basis of apportionment	total	machining	finishing	maintenance
		£	£	£	£
Rent and rates	Floor area	5,520	2,760	1,840	920
Buildings insurance	Floor area	1,320	660	440	220
Machinery insurance	Value of machinery	1,650	1,200	450	–
Lighting and heating	Floor area	3,720	1,860	1,240	620
Depn of machinery	Value of machinery	11,000	8,000	3,000	–
Supervisory salaries	No. of employees	30,000	18,000	9,000	3,000
Maintenance dept salary	Allocation	16,000	–	–	16,000
Factory cleaning	Floor area	4,800	2,400	1,600	800
		74,010	34,880	17,570	21,560
Re-apportionment of maintenance dept	Value of machinery	–	15,680	5,880	(21,560)
		74,010	50,560	23,450	–

(c)   35 hours x 47 weeks = 1,645 direct labour hours per employee
Machining Dept: 6 employees = 9,870 hours = £5.12 per direct labour hour
Finishing Dept: 3 employees = 4,935 hours = £4.75 per direct labour hour

(d)   Depending on the method and type of production, the company could use overhead
absorption rates based on:
- units of output
- direct labour hour
- machine hour

These are discussed in the text (pages 90 to 92); in addition, the company could consider the
use of activity based costing (pages 94 to 99). Alternative methods could be based on a
percentage of certain costs, eg direct materials, direct labour, prime cost.

5.5

	total	business studies	general studies	administration	technical support
		£	£	£	£
Overheads	81,600	40,000	20,000	9,600	12,000
Technical support	–	6,000	3,000	3,000	(12,000)
				12,600	–
Administration	–	8,400	4,200	(12,600)	–
	81,600	54,400	27,200	–	–

5.6   Reciprocal method – manual calculation

	total	Triple X	Scrumpy	stores	maintenance
		£	£	£	£
Overheads	41,000	20,000	10,000	5,000	6,000
Stores	–	3,000	1,000	(5,000)	1,000
				–	7,000
Maintenance	–	3,500	2,800	700	(7,000)
Stores	–	420	140	(700)	140
Maintenance	–	70	56	14	(140)
Stores	–	10	4	(14)	–
	41,000	27,000	14,000	–	–

Reciprocal method – using formulas
- Triple X: £20,000 + 0.6 stores + 0.5 maintenance
  Scrumpy: £10,000 + 0.2 stores + 0.4 maintenance
  Stores service department: £5,000 + 0.10 maintenance
  Maintenance service department: £6,000 + 0.2 stores

- Amount of stores overheads:

  £5,000 + 0.10 (£6,000 + 0.2 stores) = £5,000 + £600 + 0.02 stores

  Therefore 0.98 stores = £5,600

  So stores = £5,714 (ie £5,600 ÷ 0.98)

- Maintenance overheads is calculated as:

  £6,000 + 0.2 stores = £6,000 + (0.2 x £5,714) = £6,000 + £1,143 = £7,143

- Amounts of overhead charged to the production departments are:

  Triple X: £20,000 + (0.6 x £5,714) + (0.5 x £7,143)

                   = £20,000 + £3,428 + £3,572 = £27,000

  Scrumpy: £10,000 + (0.2 x £5,715) + (0.4 x £7,143)

                   = £10,000 + £1,143 + £2,857 = £14,000

5.7 (a) $\dfrac{\text{total overheads}}{\text{total hours}}$ = $\dfrac{£59,900}{3,290}$ =   £18.21 per partner hour

      (b) $\dfrac{£59,900 + £60,000}{3,290}$ =   £36.44 per partner hour

      (c) 2 hours x 47 weeks x £18.21   =   £1,711.74 per partner (ie £3,423.48 in total)

5.8 (a) Units of output: 80 + 40 = 120 units per month = £8.33 per unit.

          Direct labour hour: (3 hours x 80 seats) + (3.5 hours x 40 seats)
= 380 direct labour hours per month = £2.63 per hour.

          Machine hour: (1 hour x 80 seats) + (2.5 hours x 40 seats)
= 180 machine hours per month = £5.56 per hour.

          Alternative methods could be based on a percentage of certain costs, eg direct labour.

      (b) *Units of output*

'Standard'	£36.50 + £8.33	=	£44.83
'De Luxe'	£55.00 + £8.33	=	£63.33

          Direct labour hour

'Standard'	£36.50 + £7.89	=	£44.39
'De Luxe'	£55.00 + £9.21	=	£64.21

          Machine hour

'Standard'	£36.50 + £5.56	=	£42.06
'De Luxe'	£55.00 + £13.89	=	£68.89

          Note: some figures have been rounded to the nearest penny

(c) See text. Units of output method charges same amount to different models; machine hour rate charges most to 'de luxe' model. On balance, direct labour hours may be the best method to use because the products are more labour-intensive than machine-intensive.

5.9 (a) Cost pools – collections of costs linked to particular activities. Examples: materials procurement (purchasing), materials handling, setting up of machines.

(b) Cost drivers – activities which cause costs to be incurred. Examples: cost per purchase order, cost per materials movement, cost per setting up.

5.10 (a) *calculation of weekly overheads for set ups and quality inspections*

			£	£
set ups:	produce Exe	5 x £250	1,250	
	produce Wye	50 x £250	12,500	
				13,750
quality inspection:	product Exe	5 x £150	750	
	product Wye	50 x £150	7,500	
				8,250
TOTAL				22,000

At present the weekly overheads are charged on the basis of labour hours:

	£
product Exe (500 hours)	11,000
product Wye (500 hours)	11,000
TOTAL	22,000

(b) *activity based costing*

	£	£
product Exe		
5 set ups at £250	1,250	
5 quality inspections £150	750	
		2,000
product Wye		
50 set ups at £250	12,500	
50 quality inspections £150	7,500	
		20,000
TOTAL		22,000

(c)

MEMORANDUM

To:

From:

Date:

Subject: Absorption of overheads

- At present, the company charges the overheads of set ups and quality inspections to output on the basis of direct labour hours. Thus the total overheads of £22,000 are split £11,000 equally to the two products.
- By using the activity based costing system, there is a more accurate reflection of the cost of demand on the support functions of set up and quality inspection.
- The cost of 50,000 units of product Exe is reduced by £9,000 (ie £11,000 – £2,000), while the cost of 50,000 units of product Wye is increased by £9,000 (ie from £11,000 to £20,000).
- This may well have implications for the viability of product Wye and for the selling prices of both products.

CHAPTER 6: METHODS OF COSTING

6.1 The method of costing for each business should be justified; however, the following are the most likely methods:
- *accountant* – job costing, because each job will take a different length of time and is likely to involve a number of staff, each with different skill levels
- *bus company* – service costing, where the object is to find the cost per unit of service, eg passenger mile; job costing used for 'one-offs', eg quoting for the transport for a trip to the seaside for an old people's home
- *baker* – batch costing, where identical units are produced in batches, eg loaves; job costing could be used for 'one-off' items, eg a wedding cake
- *sports centre* – service costing, or job costing for 'one-off', eg hire of the main sports hall for an exhibition
- *hotel* – different methods of costing are likely to be used, eg service costing for the rooms, batch costing in the restaurant, and job costing for special events
- *construction company* – contract costing for large, complex projects which last for a long period of time; job costing for smaller, more routine work

6.2

			£	£
Direct materials:	100m x £7.50		750.00	
	75m x £4.00		300.00	
				1,050.00
Direct labour:	35 hours x £6.00			210.00
Overheads:	35 hours x £8.50			297.50
(a)	TOTAL COST			1,557.50
	Profit (20% of total cost)			311.50
(b)	SELLING PRICE			1,869.00

6.3 (a)

```
JOB COST SHEET
Replacement Cylinder Head
```

		£
Direct Materials		
100 kg of high-strength steel at £10 per kg		1,000.00
Direct Labour		
Foundry:	10 hours at £10.00 per hour	100.00
Finishing:	15 hours at £12.00 per hour	180.00
Overheads		
Foundry:	80% of direct labour cost	80.00
Finishing:	12 machine hours x £20 per hour	240.00
TOTAL COST		1,600.00
Profit (25% of total cost)		400.00
SELLING PRICE		2,000.00

(b) and (c)

```
JOB COST SHEET
Replacement Cylinder Head
```

		ESTIMATE £	ACTUAL £	VARIANCE £
Direct Materials				
Actual 100 kg X £11		1,000.00	1,100.00	100 ADV
Direct Labour				
Foundry:	actual 12 hours at £10.00 per hour	100.00	120.00	20 ADV
Finishing:	actual 14 hours at £12.50 per hour	180.00	175.00	5 FAV
Overheads				
Foundry:	80% of direct labour cost	80.00	96.00	16 ADV
Finishing:	11 machine hours x £20 per hour	240.00	220.00	20 FAV
TOTAL COST		1,600.00	1,711.00	111 ADV
Profit (25% of total cost)		400.00	289.00	111 ADV
SELLING PRICE		2,000.00	2,000.00	–

6.4   *Total costs:*

	£
Depreciation of diesel trains £30,000* x 6 trains	180,000
Leasing charges for track	500,000
Maintenance charges for trains	455,000
Fuel for trains	105,000
Wages of drivers and conductors	240,000
Administration	260,000
	1,740,000

* (£650,000 – £50,000) ÷ 20 years = £30,000 per train per year

Cost per passenger mile:

$$\frac{£1,740,000}{2.5m\ journeys\ x\ 5\ miles} = £0.1392\ per\ passenger\ mile$$

6.5

Cost element	Costs	Completed Units	Work-in-progress			Total	Cost per Unit	WIP valuation
			Units	% complete	Equivalent Units	Equivalent Units		
	A	B	C	D	E	F	G	H
					C x D	B + E	A ÷ F	E x G
	£						£	£
Direct materials	11,500	20,000	5,000	100	5,000	25,000	0.46	2,300
Direct labour	9,000	20,000	5,000	50	2,500	22,500	0.40	1,000
Production overheads	18,000	20,000	5,000	50	2,500	22,500	0.80	2,000
Total	38,500						1.66	5,300

(a)   Cost per toy is £1.66 each

(b)   Work-in-progress valuation is £5,300:

	£
20,000 completed units at £1.66 each	33,200
work-in-progress valuation	5,300
total costs for month	38,500

CHAPTER 7: STANDARD COSTING

7.1   STANDARD COST OF PRODUCING 1,000 CASTINGS

	£	£
Materials		
5,500 kg of ordinary steel at £3.50 per kg	19,250.00	
2,000 kg of high tensile steel at £10.00 per kg	20,000.00	
		39,250.00
Labour		
1,000 hours of foundry workers' wages at £10.50 per hour	10,500.00	
1,500 hours in machine shop at £12.75 per hour	19,125.00	
		29,625.00
Overheads		
fixed production overheads at £5.00 per casting	5,000.00	
variable production overheads at £4.50 per casting	4,500.00	
		9,500.00
STANDARD COST		78,375.00

7.2

STANDARD COST REPORT

product   cardboard boxes,
             size 750 mm x 400 mm x 300 mm

budgeted output   5,000 boxes   **date**

actual output   4,500 boxes   **period**   week 3
                                    October 1999

	standard cost			actual cost	variance
	cost per unit £	output	total cost £	£	£
materials	0.06	4,500	270.00	280.00	10.00 ADV
labour	0.10	4,500	450.00	425.00	25.00 FAV
overheads:					
fixed	0.03	4,500	135.00	150.00	15.00 ADV
variable	0.02	4,500	90.00	85.00	5.00 FAV
TOTAL	0.21	4,500	945.00	940.00	5.00 FAV

(a) *Factors which may have caused the variances:*

- materials
  - the cost may be higher or lower than standard
  - the use of materials may be higher or lower than standard
- labour
  - wage rates may be higher or lower than standard
  - the workforce may be more efficient or less efficient than standard
- overheads
  - fixed overheads may be more or less than standard
  - variable overheads may be more or less than standard

(b) *Further analysis:*

- variances and sub-variances should be calculated
- for materials, the sub-variances are price and usage
- for labour, the sub-variances are rate and efficiency
- sub-variances can also be calculated for overheads
- the managers responsible for each section of the business will be asked to explain the reasons for any significant variances and sub-variances of their section
- corrective action will be taken where appropriate

7.3 (a) *The sub-variances:*

(see text, pages 130 and 132, for the methods of calculating the sub-variances)

Materials price variance

(75p – 80p) x 800 kg	=	£40	ADV

Materials usage variance

(900 kg – 800 kg) x 75p per kg	=	£75	FAV
TOTAL MATERIALS VARIANCE	=	£35	FAV

Labour rate variance

(£5.00 – £5.50 x 140 hours	=	£70	ADV

Labour efficiency variance

(150 hours – 140 hours) x £5.00 per hour	=	£50	FAV
TOTAL LABOUR VARIANCE	=	£20	ADV

(b) *Using the variances and sub-variances:*

- the managers responsible for each section of the business will be asked to explain the reason for any significant variances and sub-variances of their section

- the buying department should explain the 5p per kilo adverse variance in the cost of materials

- the production department should explain the favourable variance in materials usage – perhaps better quality materials have been used with less wastage

- the human resources, or personnel, department will need to explain the 50p per hour higher labour rate – perhaps there has been a pay rise; alternatively, overtime rates may have had to be paid, which the production department will be asked to explain

- the production department should be asked to explain the favourable variance in labour efficiency – perhaps more use has been made of machines

- it may be that sub-variances are linked, eg more expensive materials have less wastage; skilled employees (on higher pay rates) work more efficiently

- the managers responsible for the fixed and variable overheads will need to explain the variances in these items

- corrective action may need to be taken in some areas despite the overall favourable variance in total cost

7.4

	Material A £ p	Material B £ p	Material C £ p	Material D £ p
(a) materials price variance	120.00 FAV	200.00 ADV	500.00 FAV	250.00 ADV
(b) materials usage variance	100.00 ADV	400.00 FAV	1,000.00 FAV	100.00 FAV
(c) total materials variance	20.00 FAV	200.00 FAV	1,500.00 FAV	150.00 ADV

7.5

	Product 1 £ p	Product 2 £ p	Product 3 £ p	Product 4 £ p
(a) labour rate variance	3.50 ADV	2.00 ADV	7.50 FAV	7.50 ADV
(b) labour efficiency variance	5.00 FAV	4.50 ADV	36.00 ADV	24.00 ADV
(c) total labour variance	1.50 FAV	6.50 ADV	28.50 ADV	31.50 ADV

7.6   (a)   labour rate variance:

(£6.50 – £6.75) x 65 hours   =   £16.25 ADV

(b)   idle time variance:

6 hours x £6.50   =   £39.00 ADV

(c)   labour efficiency variance:

(60 hours – 59 hours*) x £6.50   =   £ 6.50 FAV

* actual hours 65, less idle time 6 hours

(d)   total labour variance:

(60 hours x £6.50 per hour) – (65 hours x £6.75 per hour)   =

£390   –   £438.75   =   £48.75 ADV

7.7 (a) Materials price variance

(£0.80 – £0.84*) x 6,500 kg   =   £260.00 ADV

* £5,460 ÷ 6,500 kgs

Materials usage variance

(6,000 kgs – 6,500 kgs) x £0.80   =   £400.00 ADV

TOTAL MATERIALS VARIANCE**   =   £660.00 ADV

** (6,000 kgs x £0.80) – (6,500 kgs x £0.84)   =

£4,800   –   £5,460   =   £660.00 ADV

(b)   *Possible reasons:*
   • The price of chocolate has risen by 4p per kilo, which is 5 per cent. This price rise could be as a
     result of general inflation or by a worldwide rise in the cost of raw materials, or could be as a result
     of buying a better quality of chocolate.
   • The usage of chocolate has risen by 500 kgs in the month, which is an increase of more than 8
     per cent. This could be caused by inefficient production processes, or with a change in the quality
     of chocolate used.

7.8 (a) Labour rate variance

(£5.00 – £5.20*) x 840 hours   =   £168.00 ADV

* £4,368 ÷ 840 hours

Labour efficiency variance

(850 hours – 840 hours) x £5.00   =   £ 50.00 FAV

TOTAL LABOUR VARIANCE**   =   £118.00 ADV

** (850 hours x £5.00) – (840 hours x £5.20)   =

£4,250   –   £4,368   =   £118.00 ADV

(b) **Possible reasons:**

- The labour rate has increased by 20p per hour, which is 4 per cent. This could be as a result of a general pay rise, or could be caused by employing a better grade of labour, resulting in more efficient production.

- The efficiency variance shows that production has taken 10 fewer hours than budgeted. This could be caused by the use of more efficient production techniques or as a result of using more skilled labour.

7.9 (a) Based on the actual output of 600 pots, the extract from the standard cost report is as follows:

	standard cost			actual cost	variance
	cost per unit £	output	total cost £	£	£
overheads:					
fixed	0.50	600	300.00	308.00	8.00 ADV
variable	0.25	600	150.00	126.00	24.00 FAV
					16.00 FAV

(b) FIXED PRODUCTION OVERHEADS

- *fixed production overhead total variance*

(150 hours* x £2.00)   –   (140 hours x £2.20)   =

£300   –   £308   =   £ 8 ADV

* 170 hours x (600 pots ÷ 680 pots)

- *fixed production overhead expenditure variance*

(170 hours x £2.00)   –   (140 hours x £2.20)   =

£340   –   £308   =   £32 FAV

- *fixed production overhead volume variance*

(170 hours x £2.00)   –   (150 hours x £2.00)   =

£340   –   £300   =   £40 ADV

FIXED PRODUCTION OVERHEAD TOTAL VARIANCE   =   £ 8 ADV

The volume variance is further analysed into:

- *fixed production overhead capacity variance*

(170 hours – 140 hours) x £2.00   =   £60 ADV

- *fixed production overhead efficiency variance*

(150 hours – 140 hours) x £2.00	= £20 FAV
FIXED PRODUCTION OVERHEAD TOTAL VARIANCE	= £40 ADV

VARIABLE PRODUCTION OVERHEADS

- *variable production overhead total variance*

(150 hours x £1.00)	–	(140 hours x £0.90)	=	
£150	–	£126	=	£24 FAV

- *variable production overhead expenditure variance*

(140 hours x £1.00)	–	(140 hours x £0.90)	=	
£140	–	£126	=	£14 FAV

- *variable production overhead efficiency variance*

(150 hours – 140 hours) x £1.00	= £10 FAV
VARIABLE PRODUCTION OVERHEAD TOTAL VARIANCE	= £24 FAV

(c) FIXED PRODUCTION OVERHEADS

- The total variance is adverse by £8, ie the actual cost is greater than the standard cost.
- The actual expenditure on fixed overheads is favourable by £32, but the volume variance is adverse by £40 because actual output is less than budgeted output.
- The volume variance is further analysed to show an adverse capacity variance of £60, ie a shortfall in capacity of 30 hours, and a favourable efficiency variance of £20, ie 140 hours were taken to do 150 hours of work.

VARIABLE PRODUCTION OVERHEADS

- The total variance is favourable by £24, ie the actual cost is less than the standard cost.
- The expenditure variance is favourable by £14 (because overhead has been under-absorbed).
- The efficiency variance is favourable by £10 because 140 hours were taken to do 150 hours of work.

7.10 (a) **Materials price variance**

(£2.00 – £2.10*) x 61,000 kgs	=£6,100.00 ADV
* £128,100 ÷ 61,000 kgs	

Materials usage variance

(60,000 kgs – 61,000 kgs) x £2.00	=£2,000.00 ADV
TOTAL MATERIALS VARIANCE**	=£8,100.00 ADV

** (60,000 kgs x £2.00)	– (61,000 kgs x £2.10)	=	
£120,000	– £128,100	=	£8,100.00 ADV

Labour rate variance

(£5.00 – £5.20*) x 11,850 hours   =   £2,370.00 ADV

* £61,620 ÷ 11,850 hours)

Labour efficiency variance

(12,000 hours – 11,850 hours) x £5   =   £ 750.00 FAV

TOTAL LABOUR VARIANCE**   =   £1,620.00 ADV

** (12,000 hours x £5.00)   – (11,850 hours x £5.20)   =

    £60,000   –   £61,620   =   £1,620.00 ADV

(b)

VARIANCE SCHEDULE			
PRODUCT: 6,000 bags of 'Zeta'		**Period:** June 1999	
		£	£
Materials variances			
Price			6,100 ADV
Usage			2,000 ADV
			8,100 ADV
Labour variances			
Rate			2,370 ADV
Efficiency			750 FAV
			1,620 ADV
TOTAL PRIME COST VARIANCE			9,720 ADV

REPORT

- Both the total materials and total labour variances are adverse. In particular, the reasons for the materials variance needs urgent investigation.
- Significant sub-variances of £2,000 or more are:
  - materials price   £6,100 ADV
  - materials usage   £2,000 ADV
  - labour rate   £2,370 ADV
- Both the cost of materials and their usage have increased. The price rise could be as a result of general inflation or a worldwide rise in the cost of raw materials to make Zeta, or could be as a result of buying better quality raw materials. The increase in usage of raw materials could be caused by inefficient production processes, or with a change in the quality of materials used.
- Whilst the labour rate has increased, efficiency has improved. These two could well be inter-linked: it may be that a higher grade of labour has been used, which is more efficient in working practices. However, the increased labour cost outweighs by a long way the improvement in efficiency. It might be that a pay rise has been awarded to the workforce; at the same time employees have become more efficient in the production processes.

7.11 (a) **Materials price variance**

(£3.00 – £3.10) x 4,800 kgs	=	£480.00 ADV

Materials usage variance

(4,750 kgs* – 4,800 kgs) x £3.00	=	£150.00 ADV
* 9,500 square metres x 0.5 kg		
TOTAL MATERIALS VARIANCE**	=	£630.00 ADV

** (4,750 kgs x £3.00) – (4,800 kgs x £3.10)	=	
£14,250 – £14,880	=	£630.00 ADV

Labour rate variance

(£5.00 – £5.20) x 4,700 hours	=	£940.00 ADV

Labour efficiency variance

(4,750 hours* – 4,700 hours) x £5.00	=	£250.00 FAV
* 9,500 square metres x 0.5 hours		
TOTAL LABOUR VARIANCE**	=	£690.00 ADV

** (4,750 hours x £5.00) – (4,700 hours x £5.20)	=	
£23,750 – £24,440	=	£690.00 ADV

(b)

VARIANCE SCHEDULE				
PRODUCT: 9,500 square metres of 'Aztec' carpet		**Period:** February 1999		
		£		£
Materials variances				
Price				480 ADV
Usage				150 ADV
				630 ADV
Labour variances				
Rate				940 ADV
Efficiency				250 FAV
				690 ADV
Fixed overhead variances				
Expenditure				2,270 FAV
	Capacity	1,800 ADV		
	Efficiency	300 FAV		
Volume				1,500 ADV
				770 FAV
TOTAL VARIANCE				550 ADV

REPORT

- Both the total materials and total labour variances are adverse.
- The total fixed overhead variance is favourable.
- Significant sub-variances of £500 or more are:
  - labour rate   £940 ADV
  - fixed overhead expenditure   £2,270 FAV
  - fixed overhead capacity   £1,800 ADV
- Both the cost of materials and their usage have increased. The price rise could be as a result of general inflation or a worldwide rise in the cost of raw materials, or could be as a result of buying better quality raw materials. The increase in usage of raw materials could be caused by inefficient production processes, or with a change in the quality of materials used.
- Whilst the labour rate has increased, efficiency has improved. These two could well be inter-linked: higher grade labourmay have been used, which is more efficient in working practices. However, the increased labour cost outweighs by a long way the improvement in efficiency. It might be that a pay rise has been awarded to the workforce; at the same time employees have become more efficient in the production processes.
- The favourable fixed overhead variance means that fixed overheads were over-absorbed by £770. The main reason for this is the favourable expenditure variance of £2,270, indicating that actual overheads were less than those budgeted. The adverse capacity variance of £1,800 is caused by a lower level of production than that budgeted; however, the effect of this is reduced by a favourable efficiency variance of £300, giving a total volume variance of £1,500 adverse.

7.12 (a) efficiency ratio $=$ $\dfrac{(1,890 \text{ units} \times 0.5 \text{ hours})}{1,050 \text{ hours}}$ $\times$ $\dfrac{100}{1}$ $=$ 90%

(b) capacity ratio $=$ $\dfrac{1,050 \text{ hours}}{1,000 \text{ hours}}$ $\times$ $\dfrac{100}{1}$ $=$ 105%

(c) activity ratio $=$ $\dfrac{(1,890 \text{ units} \times 0.5 \text{ hours})}{1,000 \text{ hours}}$ $\times$ $\dfrac{100}{1}$ $=$ 94.5%

MEMORANDUM

To:

From:

Date: June 1999

Subject: Control ratios

- The efficiency ratio of 90% shows that there is scope for raising the output of the business and the efficiency of the workforce.
- The capacity ratio of 105% shows that more hours were worked than were planned during May.
- The activity ratio of 84.5% shows the overall performance of the business for the month.
- Comparisons need to be made with the control ratios for previous months to see if a trend can be established.

CHAPTER 8: BOOK-KEEPING FOR COSTING

8.1   (c)

8.2   (d)

8.3   (a)   factory rent – manufacturing account

(b)   production supervisors' wages – manufacturing account

(c)   insurance of factory buildings – manufacturing account

(d)   depreciation of office equipment – profit and loss account

(e)   sales commission – profit and loss account

(f)   raw materials purchased – manufacturing account

(g)   advertising – profit and loss account

8.4

CROWN HEATH MANUFACTURING COMPANY
MANUFACTURING AND PROFIT AND LOSS ACCOUNT
for the year ended 31 December 1998

	£	£
Opening stock of raw materials		10,500
Add Purchases of raw materials		27,200
		37,700
Less Closing stock of raw materials		10,200
COST OF RAW MATERIALS USED		27,500
Direct labour		12,600
PRIME COST		40,100
Add Production overheads:		
Indirect labour	3,900	
Rent and rates	1,200	
Power	2,000	
Depreciation of factory machinery	900	
Repairs to factory buildings	300	
Sundry factory expenses	900	
		9,200
PRODUCTION COST OF GOODS COMPLETED		49,300
Sales		60,400
Opening stock of finished goods	4,300	
Production cost of goods completed	49,300	
	53,600	
Less Closing stock of finished goods	3,200	
COST OF SALES		50,400
Gross profit		10,000
Less Non-production overheads		6,500
Net profit		3,500

8.5

BARBARA FRANCIS

MANUFACTURING AND PROFIT AND LOSS ACCOUNT

for the year ended 31 December 1998

	£	£
Opening stock of raw materials		31,860
Add Purchases of raw materials		237,660
		269,520
Less Closing stock of raw materials		44,790
COST OF RAW MATERIALS USED		224,730
Direct labour		234,630
PRIME COST		459,360
Add Production overheads:		
Rent and rates	24,690	
Power	7,650	
Heat and light	2,370	
Sundry expenses and maintenance	8,190	
Depreciation of plant and machinery	7,450	
		50,350
PRODUCTION COST OF GOODS COMPLETED		509,710
Sales		796,950
Opening stock of finished goods	42,640	
Production cost of goods completed	509,710	
	552,350	
Less Closing stock of finished goods	96,510	
COST OF SALES		455,840
Gross profit		341,110
Less Non-production overheads:		
Rent and rates	8,230	
Salaries	138,700	
Advertising	22,170	
Office expenses	7,860	
		176,960
Net profit		164,150

8.6 *Note that transactions are recorded in the integrated book-keeping system in the order in which they took place.*

Dr		Capital Account		Cr
	£			£
Balance c/d	67,000	Bank		50,000
		Profit and loss		17,000
	67,000			67,000
		Balance b/d		67,000

Dr		Bank Account		Cr
	£			£
Capital	50,000	Machinery		20,000
Debtors	25,000	Labour		10,000
		Production overheads		5,000
		Non-production overheads		4,000
		Creditors		7,000
		Balance c/d		29,000
	75,000			75,000
Balance b/d	29,000			

Dr		Machinery Account		Cr
	£			£
Bank	20,000			

Dr		Materials Account		Cr
	£			£
Creditors	7,500	Work-in-progress		6,000
		Balance c/d		1,500
	7,500			7,500
Balance b/d	1,500			

Dr		Creditors' Account		Cr
	£			£
Bank	7,000	Materials		7,500
Balance c/d	500			
	7,500			7,500
		Balance b/d		500

Dr	Labour Costs Account		Cr
	£		£
Bank	10,000	Work-in-progress	10,000

Dr	Production Overheads Account		Cr
	£		£
Bank	5,000	Work-in-progress	5,000

Dr	Non-Production Overheads Account		Cr
	£		£
Bank	4,000	Profit and loss	4,000

Dr	Sales Account		Cr
	£		£
Profit and loss	37,000	Debtors	37,000

Dr	Debtors' Account		Cr
	£		£
Sales	37,000	Bank	25,000
		Balance c/d	12,000
	37,000		37,000
Balance b/d	12,000		

Dr	Work-in-Progress Account		Cr
	£		£
Direct materials	6,000	Finished goods	19,000
Direct labour	10,000	Balance c/d	2,000
Production overheads	5,000		
	21,000		21,000
Balance b/d	2,000		

Dr	Finished Goods Account		Cr
	£		£
Work-in-progress	19,000	Cost of sales	16,000
		Balance c/d	3,000
	19,000		19,000
Balance b/d	3,000		

Dr	**Cost of Sales Account**		Cr
	£		£
Finished goods	16,000	Profit and loss	16,000

Dr	**Profit and Loss Account**		Cr
	£		£
Non-production overheads	4,000	Sales	37,000
Cost of sales	16,000		
Net profit (to Capital account)	17,000		
	37,000		37,000

Trial balance at 31 July 1999

	Dr	Cr
	£	£
Capital		67,000
Bank	29,000	
Machinery	20,000	
Materials	1,500	
Creditors		500
Debtors	12,000	
Work-in-progress	2,000	
Finished goods	3,000	
	67,500	67,500

8.7 • work-in-progress account £16,500: the cost of direct labour incurred by the company for the week on manufacturing the product

   • production overheads accounts £5,900: the cost of indirect labour incurred by the company for the week

8.8 • Debit: profit and loss account £125

   • Credit: production overheads account £125

   The amount of under-absorbed overhead is debited to profit and loss account where it adds to the total costs of the business, and so reduces profit.

8.9 • Debit: production overheads account (finishing department)

   • Credit: profit and loss account

   The amount of over-absorbed overhead is credited to profit and loss account where it increases profit.

8.10 **Department A**

- overhead absorbed by cost units £3.00 x 1,240 hours   =   £3,720
- actual cost of production overhead   =   £3,800
- under-absorption of overhead   =   £ 80

Department B

- overhead absorbed by cost units £6.00 x 1,660 hours   =   £9,960
- actual cost of production overhead   =   £9,040
- over-absorption of overhead   =   £ 920

Dr	**Production Overheads Account: Department A**		Cr
	£		£
Bank	3,800	Work-in-progress	3,720
		Profit and loss (under-absorption)	80
	3,800		3,800

Dr	**Production Overheads Account: Department B**		Cr
	£		£
Bank	9,040	Work-in-progress	9,960
Profit and loss (over-absorption)	920		
	9,960		9,960

8.11 (d)

8.12

Dr	**Materials Account**		Cr
	£		£
Variance account (materials price variance)	95		

Dr	**Labour Costs Account**		Cr
	£		£
		Variance account (labour rate variance)	102

Dr		Production Overheads Account		Cr
	£			£
		Variance account (variable prod o/h expenditure variance)		35

Dr		Work-in-Progress Account		Cr
	£			£
Variance account (labour efficiency variance)	55	Variance account (materials usage variance)		40
Variance account (variable prod o/h efficiency variance)	47			

Dr		Variance Account		Cr
	£			£
Materials usage variance	40	Materials price variance		95
Labour rate variance	102	Labour efficiency variance		55
Variable prod o/h expenditure variance	35	Variable prod o/h efficiency variance		47
Profit and loss account	20			
	197			197

Note: As an alternative, separate variance accounts for each variance can be used; each variance – favourable or adverse – is then transferred separately to profit and loss account.

CHAPTER 9: REPORTING INFORMATION

9.1   See pages 182 and 183.

9.2   Costs and revenue.

9.3   False. See page 184.

9.4   See pages 185 and 186.

9.5   (a)   revenue, running costs, number of beds, number of employees, number of out-patients, number of in-patients

(b)   revenue, running costs, number of employees, number of clients, number of hours worked, types of jobs carried out

(c)   revenue, cost of production, overheads, units produced (by product), employees, hours worked

(d)   figures for *each site*: revenue, costs, number of employees, opening hours, floor area, number of clients signed up, number of clients using facilities

CHAPTER 10: MEASURING PERFORMANCE

10.1

	(a) units	(b) %
January	120	96
February	109	87
March	131	105
April	136	109
May	110	88
June	123	98
July	178	142
August	135	108
September	93	74
October	150	120
November	134	107
December	112	90
Total	1,531	1,224

(c)   128 and 102% respectively.

Comments:

•   There are seasonal fluctuations, eg more policies than average in July, ready for the summer registrations.

•   Average productivity is 128 units (target 125), reflected in efficiency of 102%.

10.2 (a)

	cost (£)
January	200
February	192
March	200
April	183
May	175
June	186
July	200
August	200
September	188
October	179
November	187
December	192
Total	58,200

(b)   £58,200/308 units = £189

Comments:

• Seasonal fluctuations (more installed just before holiday period and just before Christmas).

• Costs are lower when larger numbers of units are sold – economies of scale.

10.3 (a)

		daily utilisation %
Monday	56/56	100
Tuesday	50/56	89
Wednesday	28/56	50
Thursday	56/56	100
Friday	48/56	86

(b)   Weekly hours available = 8 x 7 x 5 =   280
Hours worked during the week =   238
Labour utilisation for week 238/280 x 100 =   85%

Because the business is highly dependent on computers, idle time is likely to be the result of computer breakdown, or power cut, or even poor time recording (less likely). Idle time is high on Wednesday, which suggests that the management has not utilised the staff time efficiently – the staff could have used the time for administrative tasks, or contacting existing or prospective customers. Friday, is of course, Friday – there may have been an extended lunchtime for some form of celebration.

10.4

		Week 1	Week 2	Week 3	Week 4
(a)	labour productivity	£60	£64	£68	£70
(b)	capital productivity	16p	20p	22p	24p
(c)	efficiency %	103%	105%	110%	114%
(d)	cost per unit	£7.50	£7.50	£8.64	£8.75

Comments:

• the level of production is rising over the period to meet demand
• productivity is rising over the period
• capital productivity and efficiency are also increasing, reflecting the same trend
• cost per unit is rising sharply – reflecting the overtime worked and rising material costs
• this rise in costs is not a cause for immediate concern as the extra sales more than compensate; in the long term the company will need to look at its working practices and supplier situation

10.5

	Jan-March	April-June	July-Sept	Oct-Dec	Total
Sales (£)	280,000	350,000	375,000	210,000	1,215,000
Cost of sales (£)	168,000	217,000	221,250	128,100	734,350
Gross profit (£)	112,000	133,000	153,750	81,900	480,650
Gross profit %	40%	38%	41%	39%	40%
Overheads (£)	70,000	77,000	80,000	65,000	292,000
Net profit (£)	42,000	56,000	73,750	16,900	188,650
Net profit %	15%	16%	20%	8%	16%
ROCE %	-	-	-	-	15%

Comments:

• sales are very seasonal – as one would expect in the agricultural industry
• gross profit remains steady, reflecting a stable gross profit margin – a healthy sign
• net profit varies with the seasonal fluctuation in sales – the main reason being overheads staying at more or less the same level, but sales being variable

10.6

	January	Feb	March	April	May	June
	£	£	£	£	£	£
Raw materials	40,000	42,000	45,000	46,500	52,100	53,950
Direct costs	15,000	16,500	17,554	18,100	19,925	18,200
Production overheads	5,000	5,000	5,300	7,450	8,300	8,350
Production cost	60,000	63,500	67,854	72,050	80,325	80,500
plus 20% profit	12,000	12,700	13,571	14,410	16,065	16,100
Transfer cost	72,000	76,200	81,425	86,460	96,390	96,600
Costs per unit to Sprint	60.00	60.96	63.12	66.00	71.40	69.00
Units sold (number)	1,200	1,250	1,290	1,310	1,350	1,400
Cost per unit (£)	50.00	50.80	52.60	55.00	59.50	57.50

10.7 (a) At £47.50 the price of the imported frame is below Wyvale's *production* cost. This is a serious problem because Wyvale might consider importing frames rather than making them. Sprint Cycles would be unhappy about the transfer cost and would undoubtedly ask for a reduction. The ultimate decision is a group one – depending on the cost of halting production and laying off the workforce.

(b) Wyvale's cost of frame production is lower than the imported frame's price, so it is worth continuing making the frames. Wyvale may, however, have to reduce the transfer price.

CHAPTER 11: REPORT WRITING

Tutors may wish to adopt the short formal report with headings, or the more simple report without headings. We would recommend the former, as it brings the concept of structure more forcibly to mind.

11.1 See chapter for headings and answer to 10.4 for points to be raised.

11.2 See next page.

	performance indicator	Kidderport	Stourminster	Persham	Total
(a)	labour productivity:				
	units/employees	480	475	367	433
	sales/hours	£27	£26	£22	£25
(b)	sales/£1 capital employed	80p	79p	81p	80p
(c)	cost per unit	43.75	44.21	49.09	45.69
(d)	sales per m^2	£240.00	£211.11	£176.00	£206.35
(e)	gross profit %	46%	42%	35%	41%
(f)	net profit %	13%	12%	2%	9%
(g)	return on capital employed	10%	9%	1%	7%

The report should *assess* the performance indicators (not just say figure A is bigger than figure B etc). In particular the poor performance of Persham and its effect on the group performance should be highlighted. Students should note:

productivity

Labour productivity is about 20% - 25% lower at Persham than at the other shops; this is not too serious; in fact capital productivity is highest at Persham at 82p. These indicators result from the fact that sales are buoyant at Persham – 2,200 units sold (more than Stourminster). The problems seem to lie elsewhere.

cost per unit

Persham has the highest cost per unt (£49.09). This again points to the root problem.

resource utilisation

Persham has the lowest sales per m^2 of floorspace. Better use could perhaps be made of merchandising.

profitability

Gross profit percentage is lowest at Persham. One possible reason is that they are not getting the best terms from suppliers; alternatively they could be giving greater discounts to stimulate sales.

Net profit percentage and ROCE are poor at Persham (only 1%). Overhead costs are clearly too high here and should be investigated.

CHAPTER 12: USING TABLES AND DIAGRAMS

12.1   Errors:

- no heading to table
- there are two years 3 – year 4 in extreme right-hand column
- £ labels missing
- gross profit Year 3 should be £650
- Year 1 total £150, year 2 £250, Year 3 £270

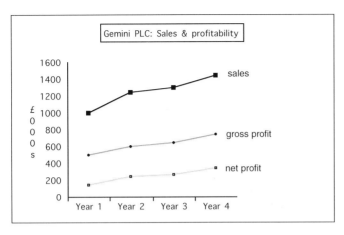

12.2 (a)

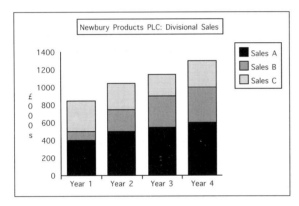

This chart shows clearly the upward trend in sales, but is less helpful in showing the *comparative* sales trends. A component bar chart or line graph will do this more clearly (see [b]).

(b)

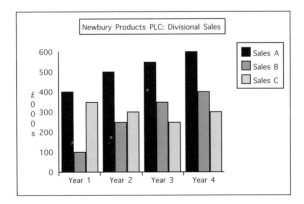

This chart makes it easy to see the divisional sales trends, but less easy to see any group sales trend (for which the compound bar chart is more suitable)

(c)

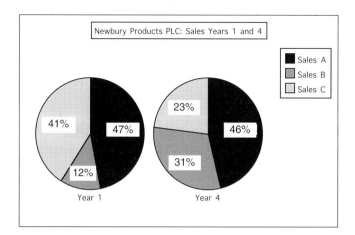

Pie charts are excellent for showing proportions of a whole – and they are widely used for this – but they do not show relative quantities. They are therefore not very helpful in this context as they are clumsy in illustrating year-to-year trends: the eye cannot easily trace changes in sectors.

12.3
- mean   £10.20
- median   £5.90
- mode   £10.00

The mean is the most arithmetically reliable as it takes all values into consideration.

12.4   Moving average data starting from day 4: 6, 6.5, 7.5, 8, 8.75, 9.25, 10, 10.5, 10.75, 11, 11.25, 12.25

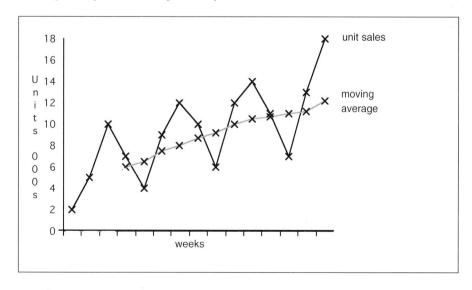

The trend is clearly upwards. The moving average evens out the fluctuations. It would be possible to extrapolate a projection line for the short term.

12.5 (a) Cumulative frequency: 4, 16, 37, 49, 52

(b) Graph drawn from this data (see page 232 for the format).

(c) The graph is steepest between cumulative frequencies of 110 and 120. This indicates that the most common frequencies are in the range 110 to 120.

12.6 (a) - (d)

month	sales (£M) year 1	sales (£M) year 2	cumulative sales (£M) year 2	moving half-year total (£M)
January	6	8	8	55
February	7	9	17	57
March	9	10	27	58
April	10	12	39	60
May	11	12	51	61
June	10	11	62	62
TOTAL	53	62		

(e)

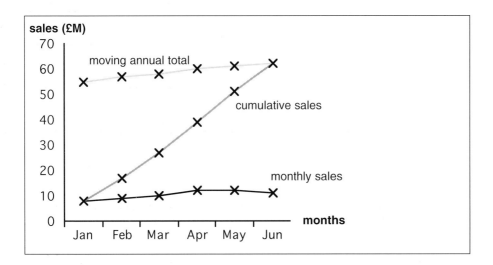

The chart shows that sales (Year 2) level off in May and fall in June (lower trend line). This appears to be a seasonal trend because the same happened in Year 1 (see table).

The moving half-year total line (top line) shows a consistently healthy upwards slope, indicating an increase on the previous year for each of the first six months of Year 2.

The cumulative total (middle line) shows a steady rise, which is consistent with a steady sales pattern.

12.7 (a)

	Year 1	Year 2	Year 3	Year 4	Year 5
Sales	100	101	104	109	111
Net profit	100	102	107	108	109

Both sales and profits are increasing each year in line with each other, steadily rather than rapidly.

(b)

	Year 1	Year 2	Year 3	Year 4	Year 5
Sales (£)	350,000	337,577	334,763	334,659	319,841
Net profit (£)	45,000	43,742	44,024	42,713	40,185

When adjusted for the RPI, both sales and profits are declining significantly in real terms.

CHAPTER 13: REPORTS FOR OUTSIDE AGENCIES

13.1

CUTE IDEAS	Trading Report		Quarter ended .....31./03..../.year		
	£		£	£ variance	% variance
Sales A (actual)	13,500	Sales Target A	15,000	1,500	10
Sales B (actual)	18,000	Sales Target B	21,000	3,000	14
Total Sales (actual)	31,500	Total Sales Target	36,000	4,500	13

10% Commission on sales £3,150   (cheque enclosed)

Comments
Points to include: acknowledgment of fall in sales (mentioning variance) and attributing the factors mentioned in the question; future performance could be estimated in general terms.

signature   *R Smith*   **date** (in first week of April + year)

13.2 (a)   Total trade debtors £29,216 (split into 3 time periods) + stock £8,760 + bank £5,631 + VAT due £890 = £44,497 current assets.

Trade creditors £15,489 (split into 2 time periods) + PAYE due £1,720 + corporation tax due £8,920 = £26,129 current liabilities.

(b)   The bank should be happy with her figures: current assets comfortably exceed current liabilities (by £18,368, ie the working capital of the company).

CHAPTER 14: THE PRINCIPLES OF VAT

14.1 Sales of chargeable supplies and imports – sales of business goods and services by VAT registered persons.

14.2 Three from EC Directives, VAT Act, Finance Acts, VAT Guide, HM Customs & Excise, SSAP 5.

14.3 A person registered for VAT, eg sole trader, partnership, limited company, club, charity.

14.4 Input tax is a tax on purchases and expenses and may normally be reclaimed by the supplier; output tax is tax charged on chargeable supplies and is due to HM Customs & Excise. Normally the arithmetic difference between the two is payable to HM Customs & Excise on the VAT Return.

14.5 A supplier may reclaim VAT if the amount of input tax in any VAT period exceeds the amount of output VAT. VAT is also reclaimable in the case of bad debt relief (covered in Chapter 15).

14.6 The VAT is paid to the supplier, who is accountable, together with other businesses involved in the production process, to HM Customs & Excise for the VAT (see diagram on page 263).

14.7 In July 1998: standard 17.5%, reduced 5%, zero 0%.

14.8 Zero-rated VAT is VAT at 0% charged on taxable supplies. Exempt supplies are supplies which are not taxable. See page 264 or the 'VAT Guide' for examples.

14.9 When the annual VAT threshold has been reached. When the annual VAT threshold is likely to be reached within the next 30 days.

14.10 (b) (c) (d) (e).

14.11 (a) £17.06

14.12 (a), (d) in respect of the proportion of the bill which relates to business expense

14.13 VAT registration number missing, invoice number missing, issue date missing, VAT amount has been rounded up (should be £36.67). Wrong cast in total: £36.68 taken as £63.68.

14.14 (a)   the date of issue of the tax invoice

(b)   the payment for the goods (the pro-forma invoice is not a tax invoice)

(c)   the date of issue of the tax invoice (the 14 day rule)

(d)   the date of the invoice (as this is a regular practice); strictly speaking this should be approved by the local VAT office

14.15 (a)   the invoices are valid VAT invoices as they are all under £100 and fall into the 'less detailed' category which can quote VAT-inclusive totals

(b)   using the VAT fraction of $7/47$, the net and VAT amounts are:

£74.47 + £13.03 VAT = £87.50

£35.00 + £6.12 VAT = £41.12

£40.00 + £7.00 VAT = £47.00

£47.45 + £8.30 VAT = £55.75

£84.30 + £14.75 VAT = £99.05

14.16 There is no problem with this request. He can use a 'modified invoice' which totals rather than itemises VAT

14.17 (a)   VAT @ 17.5% on £250 should be £43.75 (invoice total £293.75),ie £2.50 overcharge

VAT @ 17.5% on £400 should be £70 (invoice total £470.00), ie £10 undercharge.

(b)   *Overcharge:* either issue a credit note or accept a debit note from the customer for £2.50, or if this is not done, account to HM Customs & Excise as excess output tax. The former is preferable.

Undercharge: either ABC Wholesalers should issue an adjusting invoice or pay the £10 due to HM Customs & Excise themselves.

(c)   The letter in the first case should contain an apology and possibly enclose a credit note.

In the second case either a letter of apology should be sent to the customer (together with an adjusting invoice), or if the supplier is going to stand the loss, an appropriate memo should be sent to the Accounts Manager, explaining the circumstances and stating the importance of maintaining good customer relations.

14.18 (a)   The goods are zero-rated on despatch and VAT is collected from the German buyer by the German tax authorities at the prevailing German rate.

(b)   The buyer's valid VAT registration number must be quoted on the VAT invoice (this number will be prefixed GE). The goods are sent to Germany and documentary evidence of despatch must be obtained by the supplier within 3 months of despatch.

(c)   The earlier of the date on the VAT invoice, or the 15th of the month following the month of supply. The first is the most likely of these.

(d)   VAT will have to be charged on the goods by the supplier at the appropriate rate in Germany.

14.19 (a)   No   (b) No

14.20 (a)   Form VAT101.

(b)   Appropriate boxes on the VAT 100 (all suppliers), and Supplementary Declaration forms if the annual Instrastat threshold is reached.

CHAPTER 15: VAT RECORDS AND THE VAT RETURN

15.1 See text; (a) page 285 (b) page 286

15.2 (a) there is no evidence (as required by HM Customs & Excise) for collection of output VAT

(b) there is no evidence (as required by HM Customs & Excise) for claiming back of input VAT

15.3 Danger of double counting of output VAT – both in the Sales Day Book and also in the Cash Book when the money is received from the customer. VAT collected from the Cash Book VAT column should be for supplies *not* sold on credit.

15.4

VAT control account – Business A			
VAT deductible: input tax	£	**VAT payable: output tax**	£
Purchases Day Book £2,720.00		Sales Day Book £5,961.70	
less credit notes £326.50	2,393.50	*less* credit notes £501.29	5,460.41
Cash Book	275.60	Cash Book	329.73
Petty Cash Book	13.85		
EU Acquisitions	796.30	EU Acquisitions	796.30
TOTAL INPUT TAX	3,479.25	TOTAL OUTPUT TAX	6,586.44
		less TOTAL INPUT TAX	3,479.25
		equals VAT DUE	3,107.19

VAT control account – Business B			
VAT deductible: input tax	£	**VAT payable: output tax**	£
Purchases Day Book £3,239.50		Sales Day Book £5,906.33	
less credit notes £107.60	3,131.90	*less* credit notes £321.90	5,584.43
Cash Book	179.29	Cash Book	260.75
EU Acquisitions	78.00	EU Acquisitions	78.00
Bad debt relief	85.50	Undercharge (previous period)	32.65
TOTAL INPUT TAX	3,474.69	TOTAL OUTPUT TAX	5,955.83
		less TOTAL INPUT TAX	3,474.69
		equals VAT DUE	2,481.14

VAT control account – Business C

VAT deductible: input tax	£	VAT payable: output tax	£

Purchases Day Book £5,726.05
  less credit notes £195.50
	5,530.55	Sales Day Book £9,176.23
		  less credit notes £391.80
			8,784.43

Cash Book	173.76	Cash Book	356.25
Petty cash book purchases	18.92		
EU Acquisitions	1,523.90	EU Acquisitions	1,523.90
Bad debt relief	89.23		
Net overpayment (previous period)	184.90		
TOTAL INPUT TAX	7,521.26	TOTAL OUTPUT TAX	10,664.58
		less TOTAL INPUT TAX	7,521.26
		equals VAT DUE	3,143.32

VAT control account – Business D

VAT deductible: input tax	£	VAT payable: output tax	£

Purchases Day Book £3,923.50
  less credit notes £170.90
	3,752.60	Sales Day Book £521.30
		  less credit notes £81.25
			440.05

Cash Book	1,256.81	Cash Book	723.80
Petty cash book purchases	41.20		
Bad debt relief	29.50		
Overpayment (previous period)	17.50		
TOTAL INPUT TAX	5,097.61	TOTAL OUTPUT TAX	1,163.85
		less TOTAL INPUT TAX	5,097.61
		equals VAT RECLAIMABLE	(3,933.76)

15.5

VAT 100 Box No.	Business 1	Business 2	Business 3	Business 4
1	12,274.15	16,791.26	3,923.87	3,640.06
2	none	3,281.28	216.31	8,791.96
3	12,274.15	20,072.54	4,140.18	12,432.02
4	7,107.07	15,933.59	1,378.47	19,323.32
5	5,167.08	4,138.95	2,761.71	(6,891.30)
6	70,264	104,276	23,385	96,600
7	38,245	88,419	8,172	110,092
8	none	none	none	none
9	none	18,750	1,236	50,239

15.6   (a)   The overcharge being under £2,000, and there being no other similar errors, can be adjusted in the next VAT Return by adding the £350 to the input side of the VAT Control Account. The £350 will have to be credited to the customer on a credit note (unless the customer has already issued a debit note).

       (b)   This undercharge is over the £2,000 limit and so Olly will have to make a voluntary disclosure by letter or on Form VAT 652 to the local VAT office. This will avoid the possibility of a later misdeclaration penalty.

       (c)   Any VAT 100 which is submitted late will be subject to a 12 month surcharge liability notice for the fiirst default and to a default surcharge if there is a further default during that period. Further details can be found in the Customs & Excise booklet 'Default Surcharge'.

15.7   (a)   The annual accounting scheme (see page 297)

       (b)   The cash accounting scheme (see pages 297-298)

15.8   (a)   Invoices 7773, 7645 outside time period. Invoice 7578 not eligible (date of supply within 6 months).

           Invoices 7510, 7415 and 7200 eligible (due date and date of supply over 6 months)

           Total bad debt relief reclaimable £136.60

       (b)   The total bad debt (net sales figure) must be entered in a bad debts account and written out of the sales ledger.

           The VAT element must be entered in the VAT Control Account (inputs side) and then, when the VAT Return is processed, be added to the VAT 100 Box 4 total (VAT reclaimed on purchases). The VAT due or reclaimable will thus be adjusted for the VAT which was not paid to the supplier by the bankrupt customer.

appendix 1

photocopiable documents

STOCK RECORD CARD

Stock description ....

Stock units ....

Stock ref. No. ....

Location ....

Minimum ....

Maximum ....

Re-order level ....

Re-order quantity ....

DATE	GOODS RECEIVED		GOODS ISSUED		BALANCE
	Reference	Quantity	Reference	Quantity	

STOCK RECORD CARD

Stock description ....

Stock units ....

Stock ref. No. ....

Location ....

Minimum ....

Maximum ....

Re-order level ....

Re-order quantity ....

DATE	GOODS RECEIVED		GOODS ISSUED		BALANCE
	Reference	Quantity	Reference	Quantity	

STORES LEDGER RECORD

Date	Receipts			Issues			Balance		
	Quantity	Price	Value	Quantity	Price	Value	Quantity	Price	Value
		£	£		£	£		£	£

VARIANCE SCHEDULE			
PRODUCT:		**Period:**	
		£	£
Materials variances			
Price			
Usage			
Labour variances			
Rate			
Efficiency			
Variable overhead variances			
Expenditure			
Efficiency			
Fixed overhead variances			
Expenditure			
	Capacity		
	Efficiency		
Volume			
TOTAL VARIANCE			

REPORT

INDEX

UPDATING NOTE

This note has been compiled following guidance to Centres from the AAT Chief Assessor for Unit 6.

The context is the calculation of materials variances in the chapter on Standard Costing (page 131).

when are materials price variances calculated?

Many businesses which use standard costing systems identify and calculate the materials price variance at the time an invoice is received. In this way, any price variance is reported in the accounting period in which it is incurred (which may not be the same as the period in which the materials are issued or used).

For example, the standard cost of an item is £2.00 per unit; 1,000 units are purchased today at a price of £2.20 each. The materials price variance is £200 adverse, ie (£2.00 – £2.20) x 1,000 units. This amount is debited to the variance account – see pages 169/170 – at the time of purchase, whether or not the units have been issued or used. (Note that a favourable variance will be credited to the variance account.)